OPEN FOR BUSINESS

OPEN FOR BUSINESS
Building the New Cuban Economy

Richard E. Feinberg

Brookings Institution Press
Washington, D.C.

The Brookings Institution is a private nonprofit organization devoted to research,
education, and publication on important issues of domestic and foreign policy. Its
principal purpose is to bring the highest quality independent research and analysis
to bear on current and emerging policy problems. Interpretations or conclusions in
Brookings publications should be understood to be solely those of the authors.

Library of Congress Cataloging-in-Publication data are available.
ISBN 978-0-8157-2767-5 (cloth)
ISBN 978-0-8157-2768-2 (epub)
ISBN 978-0-8157-2769-9 (pdf)

9 8 7 6 5 4 3 2 1

Photos by Richard E. Feinberg

Typeset in Minion and Helvetica Neue Condensed

Composition by Cynthia Stock
Silver Spring, Maryland

Contents

Morro Castle and Lighthouse, first built in 1589 to stand guard over the entrance to Havana Harbor

Cuba Opens a Door
to the World
The United States Engages

On the morning of December 17, 2014, I was walking casually down a placid side street in Havana, making my way toward a gray, concrete building where a conference on relations between the United States and Cuba was entering its third and final day. I was one of a dozen or so U.S. scholars gathering in a large auditorium full of some 200 Cuban diplomats, scholars, and graduate students. As I approached the entrance way, I could sense a heightened energy in the air, a buzz of expectation."What's up?" I inquired.

"We're expecting a big announcement later this morning."

"No doubt something about Alan Gross [the United States Agency for International Development (USAID) contract worker being held by the Cubans allegedly for spying]," I ventured.

"Yes, maybe coupled with the release of the remaining Cuban Five [formerly five, now three Cubans convicted of spying on anti-Castro Cubans in Miami and being held in U.S. jails]. Won't that be wonderful?" exclaimed a random Cuban standing outside the building entrance.

Then the stranger added, "We've been told that around 11 a.m. they will put up big screens and show 'live' the speeches of Obama and Raúl."

That really caught my attention: jointly orchestrated presidential statements of this sort are very rare in international diplomacy. They were totally unprecedented in what for decades had been hostile relations between Washington and Havana. Maybe it's something more than just a spy swap, I conjectured.

1

I had been arguing for several months that "the stars may finally be aligned," that after so many disappointments and delays the Obama White House might now be well positioned to move forward decisively on U.S.-Cuban relations. "Raúl Castro Ruz, facing a weak economy, appeared genuinely interested in better relations," I had told the *Financial Times* two weeks earlier.[1]

But Obama and Castro would go even further than I had anticipated.

In the Havana auditorium, the Cubans naturally gave their own president first billing. While the presidential speeches were delivered simultaneously, first we watched Raúl, followed by the U.S. leader.

The image of the Cuban commander-in-chief sitting at an unadorned table was stark, spectacularly outdated in terms of visual media aesthetics. Eighty-three-year-old Raúl Castro, who had served as head of the Cuban armed forces his entire adult life, was wearing his light olive military uniform, with four visible stars on each epaulet. Hanging behind him were modest-sized pictures of Cuba's national heroes, most notably Jose Martí. Castro chose to read his speech from pieces of paper that he held at an angle, apparently to facilitate his vision. He held a prepared text, making it clear to all Cubans that the speech he was about to read was official policy, approved by himself and the senior leadership, the all-powerful political bureau of the Communist Party of Cuba, which Raúl chaired as first secretary of the party's Central Committee. He fully expected all Cubans to fall into line behind his authoritative pronouncement.

Raúl began cautiously, his demeanor sober. "Throughout these 56 years of Revolution, we have kept our unswerving loyalty to those who died in defense of our principles since the beginning of our independence wars in 1868. . . ."[2]

Then the Cuban president switched gears, relaying details of the phone conversation he had had the day before with President Obama, in which they made headway on "some topics of mutual interest for both nations."

The first bombshell: "As Fidel promised on June 2001, when he said 'They shall return!' Gerardo, Ramon, and Antonio have arrived today to our homeland." The Cubans in the audience screamed loudly. For years, the country had been plastered with posters of the "Five Heroes," the five Cuban men being held in U.S. prisons for spying.

Raúl continued, "For humanitarian reasons, today we have also sent the American citizen Alan Gross back to his country . . . and [released] those persons whom the Government of the United States had conveyed their interest in," referring to 53 political prisoners who were being released over a series of weeks.

And then, quickly, the central message: "We have also agreed to renew diplomatic relations . . . We propose . . . mutual steps to improve the bilateral atmosphere and advance towards normalization of relations, based on the principles of international law." A second, much louder scream emerged from the stunned audience.

Their president continued, "We acknowledge our profound differences, particularly on issues related to national sovereignty, democracy, human rights, and foreign policy. I reaffirm our willingness to dialogue on all these issues . . . We must learn the art of coexisting with our differences in a civilized manner."

The remarks were as brief as they were laden with historic impact. In unison, the ecstatic audience jumped to its feet and spontaneously sang the Cuban national anthem. Friends embraced, wet tears streamed down the cheeks of many. One Cuban colleague turned to me and whispered, "I feel such a relief, as though a huge burden has been lifted from my shoulders." Another Cuban woman added, "I too feel as though a dark cloud has dissipated, for the first time in my life I can glimpse the sunlight."

The remarks of President Obama were then broadcast. Again, the Cubans were very happy, but it was their own president who had marked the definitive break with the past. It seemed to be the dawning of a new era in Cuba's relations with its mighty northern neighbor—and for many Cubans, the dawning of hopes for a brighter future. On the streets of Havana, groups of students could be seen marching behind the national flag, cheering and singing.

Cubans were so taken aback by the news that many thought it miraculous. Indeed, the date of the announcement was none other than the celebrated day of Saint Lázaro, the patron saint of cures and miracles, who is melded with the Afro-Yoruban-derived deity Babalú Ayé.

Henceforth in Cuba, this memorable day, a dramatic turning point in Cuban history, would be referred to as "17D" (*diez y siete diciembre*).

Other diplomatic missions in Havana were knocked off balance. So long as Americans had stood on the sidelines, other nationalities—Europeans, Brazilians, Canadians—had seized center stage in Havana's diplomatic theatre. Suddenly, the 800-pound gorilla had stormed into the room, and other nations feared that their glory days were behind them.

Ambassadors from the European Union complained to me that the White House had not had the courtesy to at least inform them of the big announcement ahead of time (although the State Department had begun informing European capitals the previous evening). Some predicted that European investors would now rush in, before the big U.S. corporations arrived in force.

Later that week, a senior Chinese diplomat remarked to me with a smile, "Now we know why the Cuban government is projecting a high growth figure for 2015! They are anticipating a rush of U.S. tourists."

The question remained, however: Why, after so many decades of mutual antagonism, had Washington and Havana suddenly decided to smoke the pipe of peace?

Why Now?

In the case of major diplomatic initiatives, especially ones that mark a sharp break with the past, there is often more than one explanation behind White House decisions. In this case, motivating factors included 1) international diplomacy, 2) changes under way within Cuba (and U.S. perceptions thereof), and 3) shifts in U.S. domestic politics. All of these elements had to come together, pushing in the same direction, to account for the dramatic policy shift.

A Latin American Ultimatum

At the 2012 Summit of the Americas in Cartagena, Colombia (best remembered for the misconduct of U.S. Secret Service agents), the Latin Americans ganged up on President Obama, demanding that Cuba be invited to the next summit or they would not attend—not that most Latin American leaders cared for Cuban communism, but most Latin Americans harbored a visceral dislike for the harsh U.S. commercial embargo against Cuba. Many diplomats felt that decades of implacable U.S. hostility had served only to hand the Castro government an excuse for internal repression; in their view, a policy of engagement would be more likely to produce positive change on the island. The Latin Americans wanted to fully reincorporate Cuba into inter-American institutions, and the periodic Summit of the Americas meetings were among the dwindling number of institutions from which Cuba was still excluded.

Initially, U.S. diplomats discounted the Latin American threat not to attend the next summit, scheduled for Panama City in April 2015. Just bluster for public consumption, they maintained. But as the date for the Panama meeting approached, the Latin Americans repeated their ultimatum: No Cuba, no summit.

President Bill Clinton had initiated the Summit of the Americas in Miami in December 1994. Although the conclaves of 34 heads of state and government moved around the capitals of the Western Hemisphere, the United States still played a leadership role at most meetings. In recent years, as Latin American governments formed various inter-American groupings that purposefully excluded the United States (and Canada), the Summit of the Americas meetings took on an even greater salience for U.S. diplomacy in the region.

So the White House was boxed in. To preserve the summits, it would have to accept Cuba at the table. But it did not want to risk a tense atmosphere where the president of the United States appeared to be sitting uncomfortably near a bitter antagonist, at the insistence of other (smaller and weaker) nations. There was a real danger that the other Latin American leaders would roundly applaud the Cuban representative, to the embarrassment of the U.S. delegation.

How to fix the entire setting? The answer: advance U.S. interests and follow through on a policy change President Obama had wanted to make for years by altering the very nature of the U.S.-Cuban relationship. Transform it from one of antagonism to one of, if not friendship, at least normality. Be courageous and extend an olive branch of peace and friendship. The Latin Americans would love it. Indeed they did. And Raúl Castro delivered in spades.

Once in Panama, Raúl took his turn to speak at the plenary session of leaders. He opened with a long list of traditional grievances against the United States. Listening live to his remarks in the Panama Convention Center, I was worried. "No, it's not possible that Raúl is going to mess this up," I said to myself. Just as my mood was turning to despair, Raúl paused and turned toward Obama, who was seated just a few yards away: "President Obama, I do not blame you. As you have said, you weren't even born yet." A nice gesture, I thought. Castro continued, rising to the dramatic moment: "I have read your books, Mr. President." Castro smiled, "Not every word. . . ." And then the clincher: "But I have concluded that you are an honest man, a man true to his humble origins. . . . I admire him."

It was a remarkable tribute from a proud communist revolutionary to the leader of the free world, and a far cry from the more traditional Marxist analysis, so frequently uttered by Fidel Castro, that all U.S. presidents, regardless of their initial intentions, were or inevitably became tools of American capitalism and imperialism and hence hostile to Cuban socialism and independence.

For the rest of the summit, Barack Obama was a widely respected figure—and he will likely remain so throughout Latin America and the Caribbean for the remainder of his presidency. He will be seen as the courageous man who had stood down the powerful lobby of right-wing Cuban Americans, the brave, open-hearted U.S. leader who was willing to accept political diversity in the hemisphere, even at the doorstep of the United States. The smarter minds in Latin America well understood that the United States was acting out of strength and self-assurance. They knew that over time, the United States would change its Cuba policy, but it was Cuba itself—its internal affairs—that would eventually undergo the most profound change.

New Cuban Rhythms

When Fidel Castro fell seriously ill in 2006, his younger brother, Raúl, stepped into the breach as acting president, formally becoming president in his own right in 2008. In comparison to Fidel, who displayed unshakeable ideological affinity for socialist planning and visceral antagonism to the United States and international business, Raúl showed himself to be a cautious pragmatist. He allowed a small-business private sector to emerge, permitted markets in residential real estate and cars, allowed most Cubans to travel abroad without special exit permits, and began to make noises about seeking more foreign investment. Cuban cities started to buzz with new businesses, and citizens no longer feared voicing their criticisms of the regime's poor economic performance.

The U.S. Interests Section (a diplomatic representation short of an embassy) was slow to report on these departures. It housed little expertise in economics, instead maintaining a standard focus on human rights abuses. It reminded me of the U.S. compound in the Soviet Union during the mid-1980s, when most residents, whether diplomats or journalists, discounted the changes being engineered by Mikhail Gorbachev: "We've seen these piecemeal reforms before, they are superficial and easily reversed," was a common refrain.

So I had taken it on myself to investigate the economic reforms under way in Cuba, and to explain them in three separate monographs, published by the Brookings Institution during 2011–13 and widely disseminated in Washington policy circles.[3] I gave one of them to the lead policy adviser for Latin American affairs at the National Security Council (a position I had held during the administration of Bill Clinton). He called a few days later and asked that a half-dozen copies be delivered to the White House, so that he could distribute them around to his colleagues.

When a country begins the transition from an authoritarian top-down economic model toward a more market-driven system, U.S. diplomats reflexively seek to assist the pro-reform factions and to bolster incipient private enterprise. Once the U.S. government began to see such an opportunity emerging in Cuba, the forward-leaning officials naturally wanted to engage. The White House began to consider the obstacles—in U.S. politics and in U.S.-Cuba relations—that stood in the way of initiating a new era of positive engagement. But to shift its policy on Cuba, the White House first had to remove the political obstacles strewn throughout the complex, contentious U.S political system.

The handoff from Fidel to Raúl—brothers with remarkably different personalities—was another critical factor in creating an opening for a U.S. policy shift. Fidel Castro had proven repeatedly that he relished an antagonistic relationship with the United States. When Bill Clinton began to ease restrictions in February 1996, Castro ordered the shoot-down of two small civilian planes piloted by Brothers to the Rescue, a provocative exile group based in Miami. The Cubans had repeatedly urged the U.S. government to halt the flights, warning of consequences. Nevertheless, the Cubans had other options, such as buzzing the unarmed aircraft or forcing them to alter their flight path. Surely, Fidel, who served as his own well-informed desk officer for U.S. politics, appreciated that a deadly shoot-down would stop Clinton in his tracks and sour bilateral relations. Fidel had met with senior aides shortly before the shoot-down and had asked: "Who here thinks we are prepared for good relations with the United States?" Not sure what the correct answer was, the aides remained silent, until one responded, "No, comandante, we are not." "Correct!" proclaimed Fidel. The shoot-down decision also coincided with a domestic crackdown on political opponents.

Despite a reputation for being tough, even ruthless at times, Raúl seemed less likely than his older brother to indulge in histrionics and sudden reversals. Raúl promised to be a more reliable interlocutor. And for several years Raúl had been making noises about wanting a more normal relationship with the United States. Furthermore, Raúl had very good, hard reasons for seeking better relations across the Florida Straits. As will be explained shortly, Cuba's international economic strategies had reached a dead end, and the island economy was very badly in need of more foreign exchange. A surge of tourists from the United States—even better if combined with a loosening of restrictions on monetary remittances by Cuban Americans—would carry with it a quick injection of hard currency into the anemic Cuban economy.

We do not have access to the conversations within the political bureau of the Cuban Communist Party (Partido Comunista de Cuba, PCC), the country's true decisionmaking body. But one can easily imagine Raúl Castro relaying his decision to establish diplomatic relations with the United States in order to breathe life into the Cuban economy and make Cuban socialism more sustainable. He would have to assure the PCC that he would not sacrifice the gains of the revolution and would proceed cautiously and slowly. Nor would he compromise Cuba's political system or national sovereignty. Who among the PCC top leadership, close colleagues for many decades, would challenge Raúl's authority or doubt his reliability?

Miami and Washington

In the 1950s Cuba was a popular playground for American tourists seeking escape from the northern winters. Overnight railroad sleeping cars combined with steamships crossing the Florida Straits—and increasingly, regular airplane service—brought Havana nightlife and Varadero beaches easily within reach. The island was all the more comfortable for the presence of many brand-name U.S. corporations that supplied the nation's electricity and banking services and owned much of the industry and agriculture. Many leading hotels were also familiar to U.S. visitors; some of the hotel owners were infamous mafia capos such as Myer Lansky and Santo Trafficante Jr. (the *The Godfather* movie famously fictionalized a mob conclave in Havana on the eve of the 1959 revolution.) Celebrities of the day, such as swimmer Esther Williams and Senator John F. Kennedy, and a regular stream of performing artists, including Ginger Rogers,

Eartha Kitt, and Frank Sinatra, filled in the scene. A resident on the island, Ernest Hemingway immortalized the nobility of Cuban fishermen in *The Old Man and the Sea* (1952).

These intimate connections made it all the harder to comprehend—or accept—that a regime in Cuba would suddenly oust American businesses and diplomats. Even more frightening was that at the height of the Cold War, it would declare itself an ally of the Soviet Union. More shocking still, Cuba would become the staging ground for Russian nuclear-armed missiles, threatening America's strategic superiority and sense of invulnerability. The Cuban missile crisis (October 1962) is remembered as the most dangerous moment in the Cold War.

At first, the United States was captivated by the saga of the bearded young fighters descending from the Sierra Maestra mountains to defeat the evil, blood-drenched dictator Fulgencio Batista (who famously fled Havana on New Year's Eve 1958). But soon Americans were shocked and outraged at the anti-American, left-wing rhetoric of Fidel Castro. In a quick succession of escalating actions and reactions, Castro expropriated U.S. properties and dismissed U.S. diplomats, the United States slashed commercial ties, and the Kennedy administration launched the ill-fated Bay of Pigs invasion. Few imagined that U.S. economic sanctions against Cuba would become the most comprehensive and long-lasting in the history of U.S. international relations and endure for more than 50 years. The U.S. economic embargo (which the Cubans label "the blockade") has prohibited nearly all forms of trade and investment. Congress later codified the embargo in the 1996 Cuban Liberty and Democracy Solidarity Act, better known as the Helms-Burton legislation.

At the outset, heated U.S. opposition to the government of Fidel Castro was grounded in Cold War logic. But as hundreds of thousands of Cuban emigrants settled in south Florida, increasingly Cuba policy became a matter of domestic politics.

By the 1990s, Florida had become a crucial swing state in presidential campaigns. In the 1992 contest, Bill Clinton narrowly lost the state to George H. W. Bush, but he did carry counties in south Florida with heavy Cuban American populations, including Miami-Dade County. During his first term, Clinton worked hard to turn around Florida politics, and his Cuba policy was very sensitive to Cuban American opinion. Hillary Clinton's sister-in-law, a conservative Cuban American, regularly directed materials on Cuba policy into the White House fax machine, and some of those made their way onto the president's desk. (As Clinton's national security adviser on Latin America, it was my duty to respond to some of those contentious faxes.) Clinton regularly consulted with Cuban Americans in the Florida Democratic Party, and politics influenced his decision to host the first Summit of the Americas in Miami. When the shoot-down occurred in early 1996, Clinton was furious and promptly huddled with his Cuban American allies to consider how to best mitigate the political damage. In the landslide 1996 elections, Clinton easily carried Florida. But in 2000 Al Gore's presidential hopes were undone in the Florida recount, and Cuba policy had played a role: the decision by the U.S. Department of Justice to return young Elián González to his father in Cuba, following his mother's drowning during their treacherous passage from the island to the United States, had been extremely unpopular in south Florida.

By the time of the 2008 presidential campaign, Barack Obama's team sensed that opinions on Cuba policy were shifting in south Florida. Many of the original hard-line refugees were passing away. More recent arrivals were less concerned with combatting communism and more interested in maintaining ties with their relatives and friends on the island. While making clear his distaste for Castro's communism, Obama pledged to relax restrictions on travel and on family remittances by Cuban Americans. In a foreshadowing of future events, Obama asserted in one of the Democratic primary debates that he would not shy away from meeting with America's foes, including Castro. Early in his presidency, at the 2009 Summit of the Americas in Port of Spain, Trinidad and Tobago, Obama went further, promising a "new beginning" and a "new direction" in U.S.-Cuban relations and asserting: "I'm prepared to have my administration engage with the Cuban government on a wide range of issues—from drugs, migration, and economic issues, to human rights, free speech, and democratic reform."[4]

Obama moved cautiously during his first term. As promised, his administration eased restrictions on travel and the sending of remittances by Cuban Americans (a return to policies of the Clinton administration, revoked during the Bush years). The president lowered the anti-Castro rhetoric. But Obama did not seek to dismantle the long-standing economic sanctions that prohibited most trade and investment between the United States and Cuba. The White House waited to see what impact its mild measures would have on Cuban American politics. Obama carried Florida, albeit narrowly, in his 2012 reelection bid and did reasonably well among Cuban Americans; according to exit polls, he split their votes with Mitt

Romney, including in Miami-Dade County. The White House concluded that Obama could move forward on Cuba policy without incurring political damage and that a more relaxed policy could even be a political winner.

An opinion poll of Cuban American voters in Miami-Dade County taken in early 2014 provided further evidence that a forward-leaning Cuba policy could sustain political support. An overwhelming 71 percent of respondents supported Obama's relaxation of travel restrictions. Of particular interest, 68 percent favored the establishment of diplomatic relations with Cuba. Further, a majority approved of a policy that would lend support to independent business owners in Cuba, with approval especially strong among younger voters and recent arrivals.[5] A nationwide poll revealed similar trends, with 56 percent of respondents indicating support for normalizing relations or engaging more directly with Cuba.[6] After the breakthrough of 17D, pollsters continued to find that more positive engagement with Cuba had traction within the Cuban American community and nationwide.[7] Indicative of the power of the presidency in setting a foreign policy agenda, by July 2015 nearly three-quarters of Americans— and 83 percent of Democrats—said they approved of the United States reestablishing diplomatic relations with Cuba, up 10 percentage points since January. A similar majority favored ending the U.S. trade embargo.[8]

In Obama's second term, Cuba fit squarely within a broader theme of his foreign policy: engagement with unfriendly regimes in the hopes of negotiating mutually beneficial gains. By lessening tensions, the thinking went, engagement might also nudge those nations' internal politics toward more openness—and more positive opinions of the United States. The 2015 nonproliferation accord with Iran—the most important foreign policy achievement of the Obama administration—fit this narrative. Cuba and Iran became legacy issues for the Obama presidency.

In moving forward to normalize diplomatic relations and relax some travel and other economic restrictions, Obama departed from the traditional foreign policy approach of tit-for-tat bargaining, of requiring that the other party make reciprocal "concessions" before moving forward. The problem with this historical, step-by-step approach is that it effectively placed Havana in the driver's seat: if Cuba did not want to move forward, it could counter U.S. offers with impossible demands, or even take steps to undermine Washington, as Fidel Castro had done with the 1996 shoot-down. Instead, by choosing to move forward unilaterally, Obama reserved the strategic initiative for himself. The president felt confident that he was acting from strength: for the United States, Cuba was a small island no longer posing a strategic threat, so he could afford to risk new approaches. Obama also felt that in the long run, a more open U.S. posture would be likely to help Cuba move toward a more open economy and, quite possibly, more pluralistic politics.Nevertheless, there was some risk that the Cuban government could reverse the forward course of its internal reforms, making Obama look naïve and weak. Fidel Castro had engineered such backsliding during the late 1990s, once he felt more securely in power following the shock of the collapse of the Soviet Union. Now, while a resurgence of the hard-liners in Havana could not be ruled out, a full-fledged reversal seemed unlikely. Raúl Castro was personally identified with the reform process. The rest of the world—including socialist nations such as China and Vietnam—had moved even further in their economic reform programs and with obvious success. Indeed, crushing the hopes of millions of Cubans would be the more dangerous path: history suggests that popular revolts occur precisely when hopes have been raised and then suddenly dashed.

New U.S. Rules Governing Travel and Commerce

Following the announcement of the decision to normalize diplomatic relations, Secretary of State John Kerry traveled to Havana, and on August 14, 2015, formally raised the American flag in front of the reopened U.S. embassy. A similar ceremony had occurred at the reopening of the Cuban embassy on 16th Street in Washington, D.C., earlier that summer. During 2015 the executive branch issued a string of new regulations governing travel and commerce with Cuba, revising the long-standing Cuban Assets Control Regulations (CACR) and Export Administration Regulations (EAR).[9] Previously, the administration had authorized travel under 12 categories, but most travel still required specific licenses issued by the U.S. Treasury's Office of Foreign Assets Control. Now, individuals who fell within the 12 categories would no longer need to apply for a license to travel. They would only need to check a box on a simple form and self-validate the category under which they would travel, promising not to waste their time in purely touristic activities, which remain prohibited by U.S. law. The 12 authorized categories covered a wide range of possible activities:
  • Family visits,
  • Official business of the U.S. government, foreign governments, and certain intergovernmental organizations,

- Journalistic activity,
- Professional research and professional meetings,
- Educational activities,
- Religious activities,
- Public performances, clinics, workshops, athletic and other competitions, and exhibitions,
  - Support for the Cuban people,
  - Humanitarian projects,
  - Activities of private foundations or research or educational institutes,
  - Exportation, importation, or transmission of information or information materials, and
  - Certain authorized export transactions.

The new regulations sought to make travel easier by authorizing regular commercial airlines (as opposed to special—and expensive—charter flights), as well as cruise ships, ferries, and yachts, to travel to Cuba. The administration also authorized the use of U.S. credit and debit cards in Cuba.

Remaining caps on remittances to Cuban nationals (excluding Cuban government or Cuban Communist Party officials) were lifted. U.S. citizens traveling to Cuba could carry any amount of cash for donations to Cubans. Remittances were allowed not only for family members but also for humanitarian projects or to spur the development of private businesses, which is how some Cubans had been using them for years.

In a potentially significant innovation, U.S. citizens were now authorized to engage in commerce—exporting and importing—with independent Cuban entrepreneurs, authorized as self-employed persons (*cuentapropistas*) by the Cuban government or otherwise documented. In addition to trade, U.S. citizens could assist such entrepreneurs by establishing programs of microfinance and business training. U.S. citizens engaging in authorized activities were allowed to establish a physical presence in Cuba, such as an office, retail outlet, or warehouse, in order (for example) to sell materials for the construction of privately owned buildings or private agricultural activities.

On humanitarian grounds, the U.S. Congress had previously relaxed restrictions on U.S. sales of certain agricultural goods and medicines. Otherwise, commerce with state-owned enterprises, which still dominate the Cuban economic landscape, remained prohibited with one big exception: telecommunications, which was controlled by the state monopoly, Empresa de Telecomunicaciones de Cuba S. A. (ETECSA). U.S. firms were now authorized to sell an array of telecommunications services, including hardware and software and consumer devices.

As a result of this multipronged easing of U.S. economic sanctions, U.S. travel to Cuba surged in 2015, and the Cuban government reported a doubling of its GDP growth rate to 4 percent. For U.S. policy, the increase in travel allowed for more people-to-people contact between Americans and Cubans. And the purchase of products and services from the emerging Cuban private sector—including private restaurants, bed and breakfasts, and artistic creations—helped to sow the seeds of a more market-oriented, pluralistic economy.

But the Cuban government was slow to respond to the more innovative segments of the U.S. offer. At the end of 2015, it had not yet established efficient facilities to permit sales with the private sector—whether by omission or design—but was instead allowing bureaucratic obstacles to maintain the trade embargo. ETECSA had not seized on the offer for telecommunications equipment and services; reportedly, it had turned down a proposal by Google to facilitate Internet connections throughout the island. Why the Cuban foot-dragging? The state trading companies that monopolized international trade were not accustomed to dealing with the emerging private sector. Their only experience with the U.S. market was in agriculture and some medicines; U.S. exporters had been supplying the Cuban market since 2000, when the U.S. Congress carved out an exception from the general embargo. The Cuban trade sector would need to innovate, yet the lumbering public sector was slow in adapting to new opportunities.Further, some in the Cuban government objected to a trading scheme that would, in effect, privilege the Cuban private sector over state-owned enterprises. Ricardo Cabrisas, vice president of the Council of Ministers and the senior official in charge of international economics, lectured a visiting U.S. secretary of commerce, Penny Pritzker: Cuba would "forever" remain a state-directed socialist economy; the market would be allowed only a secondary role. Meanwhile, rather than focus on taking advantage of the Obama offers and building on them, the Cuban government preferred, in its public rhetoric, to continue to rail against the U.S. economic embargo, as if little had changed. Indeed, U.S. sanctions still prohibited investment and most commerce.

From their October visit, Pritzker and her technical team returned with a deeper awareness of the many roadblocks—bureaucratic, ideological, and legal—to economic change facing Cuba and U.S.-Cuban relations. Rodrigo

Malmierca, the Cuban minister of foreign trade and investment who is generally labeled a leader of the pro-reform thinkers within the Cuban elite, suggested to Pritzker's delegation that he was not opposed to sales to private entrepreneurs, but that U.S. products would have to pass through Cuban state trading firms. The U.S. delegation wondered how the U.S. export and import firms could verify that the end-users were indeed legitimately in the nonstate sector. U.S. companies wanted the U.S. government to issue further regulations clarifying such procedures. Another serious lacuna in the U.S. regulations was finance and banking. U.S. financial intermediaries continued to ask for further clarifications as to what transactions they were permitted to support with commercial credits. International trade typically moves on credit, and the cash-strapped Cuban economy was especially in need of payments assistance. Cuba had been diverting its purchases of agricultural imports from U.S. farmers, affirming that other nations were offering credit to finance their sales of foodstuffs.

Some U.S. firms in the information sector were able to enter the Cuban market. With their lighter footprint, they gained Cuban government consent without having to pass through the multilayered approval process that awaits more traditional foreign investors. Airbnb, the online lodging rental service, added Cuba to its website and rapidly signed up some 2,000 preexisting B&B businesses for inclusion in its list of local hosts. U.S. telecommunications carriers, including Verizon and Sprint, have offered long-distance calling, albeit at high roaming rates. Sony Music inked a deal giving it rights to distribute certain Cuban recordings. A group of U.S. investors gained programming rights to rebroadcast Cuban television and other media via a new channel, CubaNetwork. Nevertheless, the weight of the U.S. embargo on economic exchange remained in place: most potential U.S. trade and investment with Cuba was still off-limits. The Cuban position on U.S. equity investments, should U.S. regulations permit them, was offered by Minister Malmierca during a visit to France: "We won't keep out American business people, they are welcome, but we want to keep our relations diverse. We don't want to be tributary to anyone."[10]

As the first anniversary of 17D approached, senior U.S. government officials debated whether to risk another round of commercial liberalization measures. Those opposed to further significant steps argued that it made sense to wait until the Cuban government had reorganized its international trade bureaucracy to facilitate transactions and had resolved internal tensions between its orthodox and pro-reform tendencies. Others asserted that the Obama administration should double down: Obama had already taken the heat from Cuba policy hard-liners and Republicans, and public opinion polls showed strong and growing support for administration initiatives, so why not push forward? With some responsiveness in Havana, Obama's Cuba legacy would be more firmly embedded in history.

The double-down position largely prevailed, and on January 26, 2016, the Treasury and Commerce Departments announced further amendments easing sanctions.[11] Responding to business input, the new regulations freed U.S. banks to provide credit for authorized exports. Responding to Cuban government objections that previous U.S. regulations had favored the local private sector, the new rules permitted sales, on a case-by-case basis, to certain Cuban government agencies and state-owned enterprises for products that "meet the needs of the Cuban people," in the areas of agriculture, artistic endeavor, education, food processing, disaster preparedness, public health and sanitation, residential construction and renovation, public transportation, and the construction of infrastructure, including water supplies and energy. The new regulations also sought to remove remaining obstacles to commercial air service, and to facilitate the production in Cuba of U.S. media programming, including movies and television shows.

Obama in Havana

On the afternoon of March 20, 2016, Air Force One landed at José Martí International Airport in Havana, Cuba. For the first time ever, an American president had traveled to Cuba for the express purpose of an official state visit. (In 1928 Calvin Coolidge had only come for an inter-American conference in Havana.) Barack Obama was warmly embraced (outside of some official circles) by most Cubans—for his positive engagement and its promise of better economic relations, his intelligent discourse and elegant yet respectful composure, and for mirroring the multiracial Cuban population.

Just prior to the forty-eight-hour sojourn, the Obama administration had announced yet another round of initiatives eating away at the economic embargo. U.S. citizens were now permitted to travel independently, without a sponsoring organization, although still were required to engage in educational activities and meaningful interaction with the Cuban people. Direct mail service was re-established: after fifty-three years, on March 16, 2016, the first direct flight delivering mail from the United States arrived in Cuba. Cuban citizens, such as athletes, artists, and academics, were permitted to earn compensation while in the United States. Although the prohibition on importing most Cuban-made goods and services remained in place, a new exemption was allowed for Cuban-origin software.

To the relief of Cuba's increasingly strained hospitality industry, the U.S. and Cuban governments authorized Starwood Hotels and Resorts to refurbish and manage—but not purchase—two hotels in Havana, including the elegant Hotel Inglaterra (owned by the state tourism enterprise Gran Caribe), and possibly one more. Other U.S.-based hospitality chains seem likely to follow.

The president's schedule was designed to promote more fluid movements of peoples, goods, and ideas across the Florida Straits, and to nudge forward economic reforms on the island. Obama dined at a privately owned restaurant in downtown Havana, San Cristobal Paladar, and publicly praised the cuisine. He met with groups of private entrepreneurs and political dissidents. At his final and most public event, he engaged in sports diplomacy by attending, with a visibly chummy Raúl Castro, a friendly baseball game between the visiting Tampa Bay Rays and the Cuban national team (the U.S. squad won 4–1). The overflow crowd was festive, yet remarkably well-behaved.

At a special event arranged by the White House and meant to highlight enterprise and opportunity, Obama's remarks followed themes aligned closely with those developed throughout this book. And I was honored when White House speechwriters approached me to help craft those remarks. The president told his Cuban audience:

> To its credit, the Cuban government has adopted some reforms. Cuba is welcoming more foreign investment. Cubans can now buy and sell property, and today many Cubans own their own homes and apartments. It's easier for Cubans to travel, to buy a cellphone, for farmers to start cooperatives, and for a family to start their own business. . . . Cuba's economic future—its ability to create more jobs and a growing middle class, and meet the aspirations of the Cuban people—depends on growth in the private sector, as well as government action. . . . Entrepreneurs flourish when there's an environment that encourages their success. When professionals like architects and engineers and lawyers are allowed to start their own businesses, as well. When entrepreneurs can get loans from banks—capital to start and expand their businesses. And then we need wholesale markets

where you can buy supplies. When there's a single currency and modern infrastructure so you can get your goods to market and import supplies. . . . And I can tell you one of the reasons I'm so confident in the potential of the Cuban people is because you have some important advantages. Your commitment to education and very high literacy rates—that gives you an enormous advantage in the 21st century.

In his remarks, Obama singled out one of the millennials portrayed in chapter 7, Yon Gutiérrez, cofounder of AlaMesa, an app to connect Cubans to restaurants. Also at the event was Yamina Vicente, whose event planning business is described in chapter 6. That evening she confided to me at an after-party in Havana: "I cried during our meeting with Obama—and I rarely cry. Here was the leader of the most powerful nation on earth meeting with us, and listening to us with sophisticated understanding, when our own leaders never ever do."

Obama assured the Cubans he would continue to call on Congress to lift the remaining economic sanctions, but he added that the Cuban government could help—by allowing more U.S. firms to trade with the Cuban private sector and cooperatives—and could now permit transactions with

President Obama waves to a festive, capacity crowd at the exhibition game between the Tampa Bay Rays and the Cuban national team in Havana, March 22, 2016. Seated to his immediate left is President Raúl Castro.

some state-owned enterprises. So far, the Cuban government has permitted very few such transactions. Some U.S. firms—Verizon and Sprint; Airbnb; now Starwood Hotels and Resorts; and various U.S. commercial airlines, ferry services, and cruise lines—are signing deals. But most visiting U.S. business executives have departed empty-handed, discouraged either by the many Cuban government–imposed obstacles to commerce they encountered on the island, or by the remaining U.S. sanctions. One action that could help: Cuba's settlement of outstanding U.S. property claims arising from expropriations in the early years of the revolution. And the country could encourage a meaningful bilateral human rights dialogue. In effect, the U.S. president has tossed the ball into the court of the Cuban government.

A Road Map for *Open for Business: Building the New Cuban Economy*

Open for Business traces Cuba's efforts to rebuild its economy following the disappearance of its long-term patron, the Soviet Union. Chapter by chapter, the book explains how the resilient Cuban leadership established economic relations with the dynamic emerging market economies, at home authorized the launching of small-scale private businesses, and, more haltingly, opened a window to foreign investment—all this without yielding power over most economic resources and decisions. *Open for Business* explores success stories in this new local private sector and among foreign-owned firms, suggests new patterns for future expansion, reports on how Cuban millennials see the changes taking place in Cuba and on what they aspire to for themselves. Finally I speculate on how Cuba is likely to look in 2030.

The next chapter in this book reviews the past performance of the Cuban economy in international perspective. Compared to other nations, Cuba boasts good results in delivering social services but poor outcomes in producing individual consumption items. The chapter dissects Raúl Castro's 2011 blueprint for "perfecting socialism" for its critical revelations, bright spots, and internal contradictions. Among the most significant reforms-in-progress today are the growth of the small-business private sector, the promised opening to foreign investment, the emergence of markets for family residences and cars, and greater freedom for Cubans to travel abroad. These welcome innovations have raised hopes for a sunny future, one offering Cubans greater opportunities to develop their creative talents and the human capital accumulated in higher education. But many structural problems have not yet been adequately addressed, and despite an uptick in 2015 from the surge in U.S. visitors and remittances, economic growth has remained disappointingly sluggish. Industrial and agricultural production has continued to lag, and savings and investment remain well below the rates necessary to drive an economy forward. Merchandise exports are insufficient to relieve the foreign exchange tourniquet that continues to place severe downward pressure on economic activity; for 2016, Raúl Castro pointed to lower international commodity prices to warn of another disappointing year of low growth. Overall, economic performance is well below Cuba's capacity to produce goods and services and to raise the population's standard of living.

U.S. citizens and policymakers often think that they are the only sun in Cuba's universe. In fact, since the burnout of its long-term benefactor, the Soviet Union, Cuba has forged trading partnerships with many other nations. These partnerships, and in particular those formed over the last two decades with emerging market economies (notably China, Brazil, Mexico, and Venezuela) are the subject of chapter 3. Initially, Cuba reached out to Europe, Canada, and a widening array of friendly states in Latin America. Currently, Spanish firms manage many of the expanding number of hotels and all-inclusive resorts in Cuba, where tourists enjoy sun and surf, explore Cuba's protected coral reefs and hidden mangrove forests, or experience Havana's many cultural offerings. A Canadian company jointly owns mining operations in Cuba's Holguín Province, providing Cuba with valuable foreign exchange earnings. In joint ventures with Cuba's national petroleum company, large Chinese petrochemical firms extract oil from onshore wells. Most recently, a Brazilian construction firm is modernizing the Mariel Port so that it can accommodate very large container ships transiting the newly widened Panama Canal as well as host international investors in a highly touted special development zone.Initially the emerging market strategy bore fruit, as two-way merchandise trade soared from under $2 billion in 2003 to over $8 billion in 2008.[12] But rather than being the early take-off stage of a vibrant expansion in Cuban commerce, 2008 turned out to be a peak achievement, after which Cuba's emerging market trade fell backward. Cuba could not generate the exports required for balanced trading relationships, and its emerging market partners tired of extending credits that Cuba proved unable to repay. Nor were these partners able to develop sufficient on-island investments to generate the value-added exports that would anchor sustainable commerce. The lesson from the emerging market experiences: no set of geopolitical alliances will provide Cuba with the capital and technology it needs unless it creates a more welcoming investment climate and becomes a more efficient and reliable business partner. Today, the exhaustion of the emerging market strategy—not only the slump in Venezuela—explains in part why the leadership of the Cuban Communist Party elected to seek a rapprochement with the United States.

Chapters 4 and 5 offer a full analysis of Cuba's foreign investment regimes. Chapter 4 carefully examines the new foreign investment law and the promising Mariel Special Development Zone and describes the numerous barriers that prospective investors face in entering the Cuban market. Also assessed is the exciting portfolio of investment opportunities that Cuba is now advertising on the world stage. Chapter 5 offers a rare look inside existing joint ventures and drills down into seven case studies in mining, brand exports (Cuban *puros* cigars), hospitality, and consumer products. The case studies find that profitable joint ventures are already making valuable contributions to the Cuban economy. If Cuba improves its business climate, foreign investment could play a central role in increasing the productivity and competitiveness of the Cuban economy, creating new opportunities and higher wages for the Cuban workforce, and diffusing dynamism throughout the economy.

Within the Cuban state socialist system, there exists a dynamic independent private sector some two million strong, along with a middle class that may constitute a majority of the population—and these are rapidly emerging to define the new Cuba. As chapter 6 reveals, the growing private sector is sopping up some of the workers laid off from bloated state payrolls and providing the Cuban consumer and international tourist with a widening range of more attractive goods and services. A common imagery fixes Cuba as a poor society whose middle classes departed in the wake of the revolution; yet in Cuba today the middle class has been replenished (albeit with depressed levels of private consumption). But it remains to be seen whether the powerful Cuban state is prepared to allow private business and the overlapping middle classes to extend their wings and grow. In-depth conversations with two dozen pioneering entrepreneurs and informal conversations with many others around the island suggest the energy and dynamism of the emerging private sector, but also reveal people's chronic frustrations. Among the common complaints (some noted by Obama in his remarks to entrepreneurs in Havana): the inaccessible state banking system, scarcity of critical inputs and of commercial rental space, burdensome taxation, and more generally the uncertainty surrounding government regulations. These barriers must be lifted if private initiative is to thrive and the Cuban economy is to emerge from its prolonged stagnation.

The millennials (ages 20–35, also labeled Generation Y) will define the new Cuba, if not today certainly in a future that is rapidly approaching. In chapter 7, the rising stars of the next generation describe with remarkable frankness their dreams for themselves and their beloved country. In original interviews recently conducted in Cuba, a dozen charismatic millennials imagine the new Cuban economy and society they would like to build, and the obstacles that must be removed for their aspirations to be realized. The interviewees also comment on Cuba's new relationship with the United States and how they hope it will evolve over the next 10–15 years. The final chapter dares to peer out to 2030 and to imagine three distinct scenarios for Cuba's future: 1) stalled reform, where forces of inertia maintain their grip and many millennials exit; 2) decay, where an ugly botched transition descends into economic stagflation and an explosion of hellish vices; and 3) a sunny soft landing, where comprehensive economic reform yields higher per capita incomes and consumption, and the political outcome is wide open.

Cuba harbors ample assets—more than many other nations undergoing transitions from their authoritarian heritage. But Cuba is also saddled with destructive liabilities that Cubans would do well to recognize and exorcise. Cuba watchers can only hope that wise leadership emerges and that Cuba has its fair share of good luck. In that case, "Open for Business"—the banner on government brochures that today is an advertising slogan but still an aspiration—will become a vibrant reality.

The Old Cuban Economy and Raúl Castro's Efforts to Fix It

The tragedy of the Cuban Revolution is this: it endowed its citizens with abundant human capital, while it sadly left them bereft of the tools or incentives to gainfully employ their acquired talents. The underperforming Cuban economy is characterized by lagging industrial and agricultural production, insufficient savings and investment rates, sluggish exports and chronic deficits in merchandise trade, and repeated suspensions of service on external debts. The Cuban government has wisely recognized these debilities: in May 2011 it promulgated reform guidelines with 313 initiatives aimed at redressing these and other structural flaws. Alas, the guidelines were replete with internal contradictions and continued to render homage to central planning; nevertheless, the voices pushing for reform were strong enough to insert language that, if energetically and consistently acted upon, would transform Cuba's political economy and social ethics.

Distorted Economic Development and Gradual Reforms

In its early years, the Cuban Revolution made great strides toward providing universal access to high-quality health care and guaranteeing public education, at least through ninth grade, for all citizens. Although some of these gains have eroded, Cuba continues to score highly in global rankings of social indicators (box 2-1). Adult literacy is virtually universal and

23

Box 2-1. Human Development Index Ranking
of Selected Latin American Countries, 2014

Chile: 41	Panama: 65	Dominican Republic: 102
Cuba: 44	Costa Rica: 68	El Salvador: 115
Uruguay: 50	Jamaica: 96	Honduras: 129

Source: United Nations Development Program, *Human Development Report 2014* (New York, 2014).

the mean schooling is more than 10 years. Child mortality rates are a low 5 per 1,000 live births, and life expectancy at birth is 79 years—strong accomplishments on par with those of developed countries. As in some postindustrial societies, the well-educated population, at 11.2 million, is trending slightly downward; fertility rates among Cuban women are low (1.6 children per female).[1] Cuba achieved many of the United Nations' Millennium Development Goals decades ago.

In the social realm, Cuba compares very favorably with neighboring Dominican Republic, where despite a measurably higher per capita national income, child mortality is 27 per 1,000 live births, life expectancy is just 73 years, mean schooling is 7.5 years, and 10 percent of the population remains illiterate.[2] Cuba plays in the same premier league ("high human development," in the taxonomy of the United Nations Development Program, UNDP) as those Latin American nations well known for their social achievements: Chile, Uruguay, and Costa Rica.

The Revolution's Neglect

But social standards enjoyed by Cubans today are not sustainable without an increase in labor productivity, international competitiveness, and export capacity. Cuba must correct the extraordinary imbalance between its social progress and the low efficiency of its productive sectors. In many developing economies, the availability and distribution of social services lag behind productive investments in factories and farms. Cuba suffers from the opposite malady.

Predominantly set by government fiat and based on job categories rather than on labor productivity, wage scales are ludicrously low, and socialist ethics keeps the spread between the wages of senior management and lower-paid labor within an exceptionally narrow band (around 4:1). The median salary per month in government entities in 2014 was CUP 584 (that is, 584 Cuban pesos). At the official exchange rate of CUP 24 to US$1, that's $24.33 per month! It is no wonder there is a frantic search for jobs that offer privileged access to foreign currency. Hence the joke: "A Cuban neurosurgeon recounted a dream of working as a porter in an international hotel. His friend quipped: 'No way! You really are an optimist!'"

True, the state provides its citizens with many goods and services with zero or nominal charges, including education, health care, housing, transportation, and a rations booklet worth about two weeks of basic staples. But Cubans still spend about half of their monetary income on food, leaving very little disposable income for household and personal consumption.

An alternative for those with portable skills is emigration. A still youthful alumnus of Havana's prestigious Lenin High School—a man in his 20s—calculated that about half of his graduating class was living overseas. Now that the Cuban government has made it much easier for Cubans to travel abroad (no longer requiring a formal exit pass, simply a Cuban passport), emigration rates are rising. Some Cubans are able to obtain residency visas from foreign governments, while others abuse tourist visas and simply overstay their allotted time, carefully avoiding contact with the authorities. Still others obtain visas from Mexico or some other Latin American country and proceed to walk to the U.S. border, where U.S. immigration policy immediately affords them safe haven and a path to permanent residence. But all is not lost for the Cuban economy. Many of these émigrés send a portion of their wages back home to friends and relatives. In effect, Cuba is becoming an exporter of labor services.

When Raúl Castro formally took the reins of power in 2008, per capita GDP in Cuba had fallen well below levels attained elsewhere in the region. Today, official Cuban statistics place Cuban per capita national income at $7,200 (2014). Yet in socialist Cuba, government-fixed exchange rates and internal prices are so distorted, so far removed from reflecting either the true costs of production or some realistic supply-demand equation, that the per capita income measure could be only a rough estimate.[3] Even so, the official estimate for Cuba's per capita income falls well below the income levels achieved by other Latin American countries with similar social accomplishments: Costa Rica's per capita national income surpasses $10,000, and Chile's and Uruguay's are around $15,000. Cuba's per capita income also registers well below those of the two largest Latin American populations, Mexico ($9,900) and Brazil ($11,500).[4]

A stroll around Havana is more revealing than the uncertain Cuban government statistics. The housing stock is dreadfully dilapidated, and transportation systems are relics of the 1950s. For some tourists, this decay evokes romantic notions of faded glories, a nostalgic voyage to a bygone era frozen in time, while other visitors find it shocking and depressing. In the more densely populated urban neighborhoods, the assemblages of idle, underemployed youth resemble those all too common in U.S. inner cities—notwithstanding the official Cuban unemployment rate of 2.7 percent (2014).[5]

The Cuban Revolution allocated its resources to public goods such as schools and health clinics, and the education and health of the Cuban people benefited immensely. But the revolution neglected individual consumer goods, sometimes even denouncing those who indulged in them as egotistical and bourgeois. Consumer items produced by the domestic economy were often in short supply, of shoddy quality, and with outdated designs, while the scarcity of foreign exchange constrained imports. In most supermarkets and retail outlets, consumer choices were few and shelves were often bare, reminiscent of life in Eastern Europe and the Soviet Union during the Cold War era of central planning. For many Cubans, the best hope of obtaining new clothes or the latest in electronics is still from relatives traveling abroad to stuff their baggage with presents for the return home. Within most people's apartments, the few visible household durables, such as televisions and blenders, are often badly in need of repairs. And this is in the relatively well-heeled capital. The eastern provinces—the cradle of the Cuban Revolution—are poorer still.

Painful Post-Soviet Adjustments

Through the 1980s, the pervasive inefficiencies in Cuba's productive apparatus were masked by massive subsidies from the Soviet Union, estimated to have averaged more than $4 billion per year between 1986 and 1990—an enormous 15 percent of Cuba's GDP.[6] When the Soviet Union collapsed and the subsidies were suddenly withdrawn, the Cuban economy suffered a steep dive, national income tumbling by some 35 percent in the early 1990s. Suddenly, Cubans faced serious shortages of food for their families, gasoline for their buses and trucks, inputs for their Soviet-era factories, and other basic necessities of life.

In response to this massive external shock, in the 1990s the Cuban authorities instituted some partial reforms to the inherited Soviet system of central planning. In a sharp reversal of the revolution's earlier policies of across-the-board nationalizations, a more mature Cuba courted joint venture investments in hotels, mining, energy, and communications. Desperate for hard currency, Cuba welcomed international tourism, including visits by exiled Cuban Americans formerly branded as *gusanos* (worms). Other market-oriented reforms implemented in the 1990s included the following:[7]

• Self-employment and the hiring of relatives in select occupations, notably in small private restaurants and boutique hotels, were legalized. This opening helped to create jobs and absorb employees laid off from state enterprises that had been closed for lack of the inputs formerly imported from COMECON (Council for Mutual Economic Assistance) trading partners. Self-employment, which had accounted for only 1.6 percent of all workers in 1981, peaked at 4.1 percent in 1999 before it was repressed again for a decade or more.

• In the agricultural sector, Soviet-style state farms were converted into semiprivate cooperatives (although land ownership remained in state hands). Farmers were permitted to sell some of their production, after meeting their obligations to state wholesalers, in "farmers' markets" at decontrolled prices. The joke of earlier days ("We Cubans only have three problems: breakfast, lunch, and dinner") became less relevant as the availability of fresh fruits and vegetables increased.

• The possession and use of hard currency was decriminalized, as was the transfer of dollars from Cubans living abroad. Remittances from the Cuban diaspora rose from zero in 1989 to $700 million by 1999, surpassing revenues earned from traditional sugar exports.

These initial reforms succeeded in halting and partially reversing the post-Soviet downturn and dire austerity: the innovation was not enough to give Cuba a new economic model or to place it in a sustainable growth path, but was sufficient to allow the Cuban government to survive a treacherous political moment. Defying the predictions of many, including some in the U.S. intelligence community, the resilient Cuban regime escaped the fates of the communist parties of Eastern Europe.

Its overriding political objectives having been secured by the late 1990s, the Cuban government chose to halt and partially reverse the economic opening. Once again, Fidel Castro shifted the government's ideological posture, denouncing private enterprise and open markets as unacceptably petty bourgeois and prone toward corruption. The revolutionary leader characterized the emerging private sector as a source not of productivity and opportunity but of "parasites" breeding injustice and inequality. A series of onerous taxes and regulations choked the incipient microenterprise sector, decreasing the number of independent enterprises. The government recentralized the authorization of foreign exchange, requiring joint ventures to appeal to the authorities in the Central Bank and Ministry of Foreign Trade for approval of international transactions. Overall, the economy remained centralized and socialized, with the state employing most of the workforce (over 80 percent), owning most of the means of production, setting most prices, and authorizing most investment and production targets. Government functionaries and Communist Party officials had again asserted their domination over economic decision making.

As the 1990s wore on, attitudes toward foreign direct investment (FDI) also became more restrictive. Official statistics on foreign investment are incomplete and inconsistent; it is difficult to distinguish stocks from flows, or early announcements of intention from completed investments. But it appears clear that both new investments and the stock of total investments declined sharply after 2002.[8] The government chose to eliminate smaller firms to concentrate on larger, strategic joint ventures and, eventually, to focus more attention on state-to-state projects with Venezuela, China, and Brazil. There were also a pile of complaints from foreign investors touching on virtually every aspect of business operations, including low profit margins, rigid labor requirements, noncompliance with contracts, delayed access to foreign exchange, and arbitrary, unpredictable actions by government bureaucrats.[9] Intrusive vigilance by the state security apparatus irritated some expatriates unaccustomed to political oversight.

Raúl's Economic Reform Guidelines: From Distribution to Growth

Raúl Castro assumed presidential powers in the wake of the serious illness of his older brother Fidel in 2006 (initially on a temporary basis, permanently since 2008). Under Raúl's leadership, Cuba has resumed the truncated economic reform process begun during the 1990s. In April 2011, at its Sixth Party Congress, the Communist Party of Cuba (PCC) approved the "Guidelines for the Economic and Social Policies of the Party and the Revolution," a lengthy document containing 313 points on a broad range of topics.[10]

A product of an intense bureaucratic process that also entailed broad consultations with both academics and the general public, the Communist Party–approved guidelines are rife with internal contradictions. One can imagine the fierce internal debates between orthodox planners and reform advocates. Single paragraphs contain wording apparently designed to satisfy both parties. Many sectors of the economy are given "priority," and there is a marked absence of sequencing, timelines, or deadlines. The guidelines contain few numbers and no quantitative analyses and are more about goals than methods—that is, about the "what" rather than the "how." Certainly, the guidelines do not constitute a coherent national development model.

In some respects, the guidelines are reminiscent of the tepid reform documents commonly promulgated during the 1970s and 1980s in socialist Eastern Europe. Such documents suggest both the leadership's recognition that the system is not working and its failure to fully grasp why; nods in the direction of market mechanisms and nonstate management are repeatedly subsumed under genuflections to the hegemony of socialist planning.

Nevertheless, within the 313 points of the Cuban guidelines, reform-minded drafters were able to insert language that demands important shifts in thinking and that, if fully acted upon, would transform Cuban political culture and social ethics. The guidelines call for abandoning state paternalism in favor of individual responsibility, for shifting from a culture of socialist egalitarianism to "an equality of rights and opportunities," for replacing universal subsidies of goods (such as the ration card) with targeted subsidies to the most needy, for paying workers according to the quality of their labor, and for championing efficiency and growth. And while central planners are repeatedly given the final word, the guidelines decentralize power to municipalities (metropolitan areas) and to nonstate enterprises (self-employed workers, private farmers, franchises, cooperatives of various forms), while granting state-owned firms greater managerial autonomy.

Problems to Fix

The guidelines recognize many of the economy's glaring shortcomings and in particular suggest reforms for the balance of payments, domestic agricultural production, the external debt, national savings, state-owned enterprises, and the educational system.

The balance of payments. The constraint on the balance of payments must be alleviated and exports made more competitive on international markets. (The guidelines discard Fidel's characteristic antiglobalization rhetoric.) The guidelines remark that tourism could offer a range of niche options, including golf courses, boat marinas, and cruise ships, as well as ecotourism and health tourism. (Some of these options presciently assume a large influx of tourists from the United States.) Other promising export sectors cited include biotechnology and pharmaceuticals, nickel and other minerals, professional services (especially medical but also in sports and culture), revived citrus and sugar industries, and also free trade zones ("special development zones"). However, no major changes are proposed in the treatment of foreign investment. These will come later.

Domestic agricultural production. Through further distributing idle state lands and granting management independence to the various forms of cooperatives, domestic agricultural production should increase and act as a substitute for food imports. Pricing policies should favor production while taking into account the needs of consumers and international prices.

The external debt. The situation related to external debt must be normalized to regain access to new financing, and new commitments should be "strictly complied with." Firms should also comply with the financial terms of domestic contracts.

National savings. National savings must be increased. Subsidies to individuals (for example, the rations booklet, free meals at the workplace) and to money-losing state-owned firms should be slashed. The tax system should be overhauled.

State-owned enterprises. Greater autonomy in labor, investment, and pricing policies should be granted to state-owned enterprises. As a rule, state subsidies to firms should be cut, and those firms facing repeated losses should be liquidated. (In 2010, state transfers to firms and cooperatives had cost 11.2 percent of GDP.)[11]

The educational system. Education should be geared to better meet the needs of the economy and updated to yield more graduates in science and technology. Primary education should be rationalized to reflect demographic trends (lower birth rates). Higher education must be made more rigorous; in a retreat from Fidel's policies of university education for all, enrollments should be sharply reduced. (Indeed, by 2014 university enrollment was slashed by 63 percent.)[12]

A Work in Progress

However, the precise mechanisms whereby these generally laudable goals were to be achieved was often left unclear. There was no coherent set of incentives to augment export competitiveness, such as by establishing competitive exchange rates, offering assistance to exporters through affordable trade credits and international marketing networks, enabling competitive cost structures, and more generally creating a favorable investment climate for export-oriented firms. Similarly, the aspirations for normalizing external debts were not accompanied by a debt management strategy that would ensure sufficient hard currency and international reserves. Exhortations for agricultural self-sufficiency did not adequately address such key issues as property rights and pricing mechanisms; instead, state-run distributors were assured a continuing role in regulating prices.[13] Whether the state was to actually refuse credits to money-losing but politically well-connected state-owned firms—that is, impose a hard budget constraint—remained to be tested; precedents from the now defunct socialist regimes of Eastern Europe were not encouraging.

The guidelines deferred other key issues for further study, including the eventual abolition of the dual monetary and exchange-rate systems. The power relations among state, provincial, and municipal authorities remained to be defined. And many reforms were to be implemented "gradually," a concept invoked repeatedly throughout the guidelines.

The Cuban reform process is a work in progress. Since 2011 the government has implemented pieces of the guidelines in fits and starts.[14] At times the reform momentum has appeared to pick up steam, giving hope to those who anticipate a self-reinforcing cascade of changes. At other times the reform process has stalled, orthodox tendencies apparently having regained the upper hand. No one has been completely happy. Those fearing reform decry what they perceive as rising social inequality and petty corruption, which they attribute—falsely in many respects—to the incipient reforms. Those Cubans desiring more rapid change are frustrated by the cautious gradualism of Raúl Castro and his aging senior associates.

Overall, by 2015 some important changes were visible. More Cubans had shifted into the nonstate sector of small-scale enterprise (as described in greater detail in chapter 6); the Cuban version of homesteaders had reclaimed some abandoned farmlands; cooperatives had gone from being a rarity to an increasingly commonplace presence in the Cuban landscape; and markets were thriving in residential real estate and used cars. New laws were on the books regulating foreign investment and state-owned enterprises.

Some of the most significant changes under way were these:[15]

Self-employment licenses. In September 2013 the government allowed for the private exercise of 201 occupations, up from 181. Other reforms allowed small private firms to hire employees, not just family members, as previously had been the case. Commercial districts in Havana were increasingly dotted with new restaurants and small retail outlets, often located within owners' homes. Licenses were issued for private taxis, barbershops, and beauty salons, even as many middle-class professions (lawyers, engineers, architects) were still excluded from private practice. By 2014 over 18,000 rooms in family homes and apartments were being offered as bed and breakfast–style rentals, constituting up to 30 percent of the supply of lodging available for international tourism; and more than 1,700 private restaurants were improving the island's culinary offerings, especially for tourists.[16] All told, as of end-2015, the government had issued 496,400 self-employment licenses, up from 330,000 four years earlier.[17] Many of these businesses had existed previously in informal black markets; once legalized, the firms became a source of fiscal revenues.[18]

Foreign investment. In early 2014 the legislature passed an updated foreign investment law as well as regulations governing the new development zone of Mariel. The 2011 guidelines had treated foreign investment cautiously, relegating it to a subsidiary role in national development. In contrast, the texts of the new laws and regulations gave FDI more prominence in development strategy, and Rodrigo Malmierca, the minister of international commerce and investment, emphasized it in his public statements. Nevertheless, the bureaucratic approval process remained time-consuming and opaque, and new investment approvals were sporadic at best, leaving the impression that the orthodox tendencies in the government were prevailing in this critical area, especially outside of tourism (chapters 4 and 5 treat FDI in greater detail).

Idle state farmlands. These farmlands were distributed to homesteaders. By end-2012, 1.5 million hectares of idle state land (of a total of 1.9 million hectares) had been distributed to 174,271 individuals, although not all had yet initiated production.[19] The distributed lands were held in "usufruct," a form of leasing by the government, under 10-year renewable contracts, with limitations on the hiring of contract labor and compulsory sale at state-fixed prices of about 70 percent of production. Farmers were permitted to build homes and barns on their plots, practices that had been prohibited in the past. Government statistics on agricultural production did not show a corresponding surge, but they might not have fully captured foodstuffs sold on private markets.

Cooperatives. Because the government viewed cooperatives as a form of nonstate business that was less individualistic, less "petty bourgeois," than purely individual enterprise, it decreed favorable tax treatment and other advantages for cooperative ventures. However, whereas municipal authorities could quickly authorize individual self-employed businesses, cooperatives required approval at the exalted level of Council of Ministers! By May 2014, 498 nonagricultural cooperatives had been approved, 329 of which were operating by mid-2015.[20] Of those approved, most (384) had been spun off from the state sector and leased their outlets from the state. The majority of co-ops were restaurants, fruit and vegetable venders, and construction firms and were located in Havana. Preliminary results indicated that co-ops offered better services to customers and higher profits and wages to co-op members (after reducing the workforce). As the government spins off more restaurants, cafeterias, beauty salons, and barbershops, some 9,000 new cooperatives may be constituted by 2017.

Enterprise autonomy. No issue is more neuralgic for a socialist system than the relations between state and enterprise. Cuban ministries were accustomed to controlling the major decisions governing firm behavior. Beginning in 2014–15 (under Decree 323), state firms, which account for the lion's share of national output, were granted authority to decide how to best allocate up to 50 percent of after-tax profits, once commitments to the annual plan have been carried out. State-owned enterprises could earmark these resources for working capital or long-term investment, for research and training, or for workers' salaries (to bring them in line with productivity gains). Output that exceeded quotas set by the planning agency could be sold at market prices. Firms suffering losses for two years or more would have to turn a profit or be downsized, merged, or shut down. At the same time, the government created holding companies, *Organizaciones Superiores de Dirección Empresarial* (literally "superior organizations of enterprise direction"), which raised questions about how much freedom would be granted to individual firms. It is too soon to judge whether the reforms will improve the autonomy and efficiency of the state sector. One leading analyst has expressed skepticism, labeling the reforms as "timid."[21]

Home ownership. Many Cubans own their own residences, and some have a second vacation home, but until recently they were not allowed to sell them. Now, Cuban citizens and foreign permanent residents can buy and sell homes at prices freely arrived at by seller and buyer. Suddenly Cubans who had had virtually no accumulated wealth were sitting on financial assets of considerable value. "Housing capital, which had been frozen for 50 years, can now be sold to change residence, invest in microbusiness, buy a cheaper dwelling and use the remaining funds to improve life, or get a small capital to settle abroad."[22] The profession of real estate broker was made legal, and websites began to advertise properties for sale. Nonresident foreigners were still forbidden from home ownership, although some foreigners, including Cuban Americans, risked buying homes and placing their titles in the name of a Cuban relative or friend. Cuban state-owned banks were not prepared to finance housing mortgages, so transactions were cash-only. Given all the uncertainties facing the Cuban economy, price appraisal was challenging.

Subsidies and budget. Some state subsidies were cut and the fiscal budget deficit was reduced, falling from 4.9 percent of GDP in 2009 to 1.3 percent in 2013 (although the deficit was allowed to inch up in 2014–15 to provide some stimulus to the slow-growth economy). Items were deleted from the monthly rations booklets. Wage protection for the unemployed became less generous, and the retirement age was extended by four years (to 65 for men, 60 for women). According to some reports, as many as 500,000 employees were dismissed from the government payroll, even as the threat once uttered by Raúl Castro to dismiss 1 million state employees (20 percent of the national workforce) stalled, due to opposition from unions, public attachment to a paternalistic state, and the shortage of alternative employment opportunities.

Cumulatively, these reforms are potentially significant. Whether they will affect the daily lives of most Cubans depends upon the all-important implementation, and on whether future amendments move in the direction of further liberalization or tougher restrictions. Will incipient markets, for small-scale business and real estate, be given access to critical inputs, including credit and imported goods, and will foreigners—as traders and buyers—be allowed to participate? Will wholesale markets be allowed to supply private firms, and will the categories of authorized private activities

---

Box 2-2. Habana Vieja: Mission to Accomplish

The massive, inspiring Habana Vieja (Old Havana) was once upon a time the architectural jewel of the Spanish Empire in the Americas. Having fallen into deep decay in recent decades, it has been undergoing a carefully considered but painfully slow renovation. The renovations of its sister colonial old towns—Cartagena, Colombia; San Juan, Puerto Rico; and Panama City, Panama—are admittedly smaller in scope but have proceeded much more rapidly. Eventually, Habana Vieja will return to its former glory, not as an entrepôt for the transshipment of precious metals and African slaves, but reborn as a cultural-historical destination for tourists from around the world. As a rush of visitors descends upon Cuba over the coming decade, Habana Vieja should be ready to profit from the influx.

To accelerate the respectful renovation of Habana Vieja, and to better match the ambitious aspirations of the city's smart planners with financial resources, Cuban authorities need to reconsider their attitudes toward private investment from both international and Cuban sources. Of course, building permits should conform to renovation plans that preserve the city's historical legacy.

Here are some acceleration measures, most of which are aligned with the 2011 economic guidelines, for Cuban authorities to consider:

• Extend a warmer welcome to international investment in hotels and allow foreign firms to hold equity shares as wholly owned as well as joint venture enterprises.

• Encourage more hotels and other enterprises, whether government owned or private, to contract services from the small-scale private firms (ranging from IT professionals to construction teams) flowering under the 2011 economic guidelines.

• In allocating retail space, give preference to local artisans and designers over international luxury brands, in order to build a tourism industry with backward linkages that generate employment throughout the Cuban economy.

• Revamp the regulations governing the performing arts—for example, allow higher ticket prices and facilitate payment of a living wage to actors and local musicians, rendering Havana a vibrant showcase city for Cuban artistic talent.

• Seek larger-scale international cooperation and invite foundations, multilateral agencies, and private donors to become important partners in creating an innovative, prosperous, and magnificent twenty-first-century Havana.

---

be expanded to encompass the white-collar professions? Will ministries truly decentralize decisionmaking to individual firms, and will firms eventually be given greater control over other critical matters such as product mix and prices? Will the Council of Ministers expand the categories for self-employment and speed the approval of cooperatives? Will the government design a favorable regulatory framework, which would, for example, facilitate the renovation of Old Havana (box 2-2)? Will the government truly open the economy to foreign investors and create a favorable business climate? The epic battle between champions of state control (planning agencies and ministries and many in the PCC) and its opponents (those pressing for more decentralized decisionmaking and market mechanisms) is ongoing and has the potential to persist over many years.

The Cuban Economy Today: Still Underperforming

President Raúl Castro's economic program had an immediate positive impact in some sectors, including tourism, mining, energy, and biotechnology. The growth of the small-business private sector, and the promised opening to foreign investment, gave many hope for a brighter future where Cubans could develop their creative talents and accumulated human capital. But many structural problems remain unaddressed, and despite an uptick in 2015 from the surge in U.S. visitors and remittances, growth has remained sluggish. Reflecting slumping commodity export prices, growth is projected to dip again to 2 percent in 2016.[23] Industrial and agricultural production has continued to lag, and savings and investment rates remain well below the rates necessary to drive an economy forward. Merchandise exports are insufficient to relieve the foreign exchange tourniquet that continues to place severe downward pressure on economic activity. Overall, economic performance is well below Cuba's capacity to produce goods and services and to gradually but persistently raise the population's standard of living.

Lagging Industrial and Agricultural Production

Cuba's Soviet-era industrial plant collapsed after the loss of Soviet supplies and markets (figure 2-1). Despite some recovery from a very deep trough, at end-2013 industrial output stood at only 55 percent of its 1989 levels. Food and beverages rebounded somewhat after 1989, but apparel and shoe production remained very depressed, and production of machinery and transportation practically vanished altogether.[24] At end-2013, production of construction materials was less than a third of its Soviet-era levels, a serious shortfall for an economy so badly in need of new residential housing and commercial space. Industrial employment fell proportionately, dropping to under 10 percent of today's workforce. (There is a silver lining here: Cuba has already absorbed some of the costs of adjustment inherent

Figure 2-1. Industrial Output, 1989–2013

Index (1989 = 100)

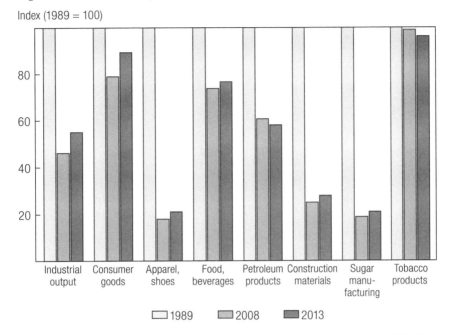

Source: Oficina Nacional de Estadística e Información (ONEI), *Anuario Estadístico de Cuba,* 2010, 2014, "Industria Manufacturera," tables 11.1, 11.2 (www.onei.cu/CatalogoPublicaciones.html).

in industrial restructuring, raising hopes that the transition to a more market-oriented system might not have to entail another sharp depression.)

In recent years, agricultural production has been especially disappointing. By 2010 agricultural output had recovered from mid-decade droughts and hurricanes but only to regain 2000 levels.[25] Distressed farmers complain about shortages of critical inputs (fertilizers, fuel, and machinery), lack of financial credits, and the repressed prices set by the government for their harvests. Despite government programs to distribute idle lands to farmers, much farmland still lies fallow, as any traveler in rural areas can see. As a result of shortfalls in domestic agricultural production, Cuba must allocate scarce foreign exchange to feed the population: in 2014 Cuba imported $1.9 billion in foodstuffs, including rice ($270 million), dried beans ($77 million), and other dietary staples such as wheat flour ($268 million), powdered milk ($253 million), chicken ($183 million), and fruits and vegetables ($123 million).[26] In response, the government has made increasing agricultural production for domestic consumption a priority goal.

Figure 2-2. The Rise of the Service Sector

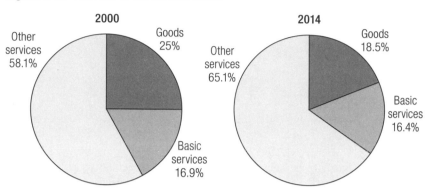

Source: ONEI, *Panorama Económico y Social,* 2010, 2014, "Producto Interno Bruto" (www.onei.cu/Catalogo Publicaciones.html).

With industry and agriculture lagging, the goods sector of the economy has shrunk from 25 percent to under 19 percent of total production during the last decade and a half (figure 2-2). In contrast, the service sector has expanded dramatically: basic services (utilities, transportation, communications) plus other services now account for 81.5 percent of national output. These lopsided proportions might be appropriate for an advanced economy with high productivity in the service sector. But for Cuba, they are another indicator of a distorted economic development.

Insufficient Investment Rates

Driving these disappointing production results are low national investment rates. The ratio of gross capital formation to GDP averaged about 12.5 percent from 1996 to 2008, startlingly low by international standards; in a survey of 157 countries, Cuba's investment rate has been consistently below the lowest 10th percentile during the period 1990–2008.[27] Especially disappointing is that rates of capital formation have declined even further, averaging just 8.5 percent in the four years 2011–14. (The government had routinely fallen short of its own investment targets, for example realizing only 76 percent of planned investments during 2007–09.)[28] Low investment rates are explained by equally low internal savings rates, the limited inflows of foreign capital, and the high cost of capital compared to the meager wages paid to labor.

Figure 2-3. Cuba Merchandise Trade Deficit, 2000–14

US$ billions

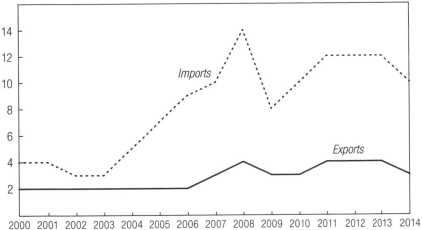

Source: ONEI, *Anuario Estadístico de Cuba,* 2014, "Sector Externo," table 8.3 (www.onei.cu/aec2014.htm).

The Balance of Payments Tourniquet

The severe shortage of foreign exchange presents a harsh binding constraint on the Cuban economy. Each time that export earnings dip, as has occurred in successive cycles, the government is compelled to contract imports, and economic activity suffers. In 2009 a biting foreign exchange constraint forced the government to radically squeeze imports, from $14.2 billion in 2008 down to $8.9 billion (figure 2-3). This harsh shock was engineered by slowing the entire economy: GDP growth during 2009–10 registered under 2 percent. The investment-to-GDP ratio fell to 9 percent in 2009, insufficient to sustain existing plant and equipment or to drive forward economic growth and create good jobs. Export earnings picked up in 2010–11, facilitating an expansion of imports of goods and services and a modest recovery of economic activity. But export growth slowed and then contracted in 2012–14, once again compelling the government to slice imports, and economic growth ground to a halt in 2014. Trapped in a vicious circle, underperforming merchandise exports and woefully slack investment rates are both a cause and result of this secular macroeconomic stagnation and painful, cyclical contractions.

Remarkably, Cuba exports only $5 billion to $6 billion per year in merchandise goods, just about 7 percent of its annual output.[29] If reported service exports are factored in—these include Venezuela's generous payments for Cuba's transfer of medical and other skilled personnel—Cuba's ratio of exports of goods and services to gross domestic product would be 24 percent. Even this export ratio is still unacceptably low for a small island economy, reflective of the low international competitiveness of much of Cuba's industrial and agricultural sectors. Compare this vital indicator of competitiveness to the exports-to-GDP performances of Chile (34 percent), Costa Rica (35 percent), or Barbados (37 percent), not to mention Vietnam (86 percent) or Malaysia (80 percent).[30]

Cuba's merchandise exports (by volume) have been stagnant since 2000. The monetary value of merchandise exports increased in 2007–11 when Cuba's terms of trade were favorable, but in 2012–14, when the prices of Cuba's commodity exports fell, Cuba's export earnings decreased as well. Too many state-owned firms in industry and agriculture lack the modern technology and marketing channels to succeed in international markets; the overvalued exchange rate discourages exports; and firm managers are not incentivized to explore new markets overseas. In its search for foreign exchange, Cuba has become increasingly dependent upon tourism receipts and remittances from Cubans living abroad. Indeed, some commentators suggest that the Cuban government is purposefully facilitating emigration as a form of service exports, so that Cubans working abroad can funnel a portion of their income back home and bolster the island's import capacity and living standards.[31] While tourism and remittances can be valuable components of a national income strategy, by themselves they cannot generate sufficient high-value-added employment to complement the talents of Cuba's highly developed human resources.

Cuba has managed to narrow its bulging foreign exchange shortfall thanks to the largesse of Venezuela, which during the rule of Hugo Chávez and his successor, Nicolás Maduro, bartered its oil for the services of Cuban medical personnel on terms highly favorable to Cuba. But this is a dangerous dependency on one generous external partner of increasingly uncertain durability.

External Debt Burdens: Cleansing the Record

Over the decades, Cuba accumulated large stocks of external debts—to the former Soviet Union, to official government creditors in Europe and elsewhere, and to private financial institutions. Arrears on scheduled payments were a long-standing feature of Cuba's poor external debt performance, resulting in a loss of creditworthiness and dependence on politically driven lines of credit from friendly governments. The 2011 economic reform guidelines proposed to normalize the nation's external debt profile and thereby regain access to global finance. Since then Cuban negotiators have successfully restructured debts owed to many official creditors, freeing some foreign entities to consider reopening their credit windows (to the extent that Cuba's still-poor credit rating allows). Debts owed to some commercial creditors remain to be rescheduled. For Cuba to fully regain access to international credit markets, official and commercial, its export performance would need to be more robust and promising, thereby demonstrating capacity to service future debt obligations.

Cuba publishes only very partial and delayed statistics on its external debts. According to Cuba's Central Bank, as of 2012 (the last year for which published data are available) the "active external debt" totaled $12.5 billion, of which $10.4 billion was medium and long term. In addition, the Central Bank recognized $15 billion in debts to Paris Club creditor nations.[32] Cuba also recognized a "frozen" or "passive" debt that had not been serviced since 1986, which some experts estimated at $8 billion.[33]

In the absence of detailed official data, in 2010 the European Union office based in Havana undertook the yeoman work of pulling together a more complete picture of Cuba's external obligations.[34] It uncovered $31.6 billion in Cuban external debt as of 2008, with each of these major country creditors owed $1 billion or more: Venezuela ($11.4 billion), Spain ($3.2 billion), China ($3.2 billion), Japan ($2.8 billion), Argentina ($2.0 billion), France ($1.9 billion), Romania ($1.2 billion), and post-Soviet Russia ($1.1 billion). These numbers give an indication of the scope and size of Cuba's external obligations.

In 2013 Russia agreed to write off most of the $25 billion debt Cuba had owed to the former Soviet Union. In late 2015 Cuba made important progress in reducing its debts to official government credit agencies when it reached an agreement with 15 wealthy Paris Club creditor nations, whereby $8.5 billion in debts was forgiven and $2.6 billion was restructured on more favorable repayment terms.[35] Earlier, China and Mexico as well as Japanese commercial creditors had also restructured outstanding debts on terms favorable to Cuba.

Moody's continues to rate Cuba "Caa2," meaning its "obligations are judged to be of poor standing and are subject to very high credit risk," even as the credit rating agency changed its outlook from "stable" to "positive" at end-2015, citing lower global oil prices, continued cautious reform momentum, debt restructurings, and the rapprochement with the United States.[36] Cuba does not publish data on its international reserves—one important indicator of creditworthiness—alleging its fear of exposure to U.S. sanctions. In 2015 the government was stoking rumors that it had accumulated as much as $11 billion in reserves, pointing to several years of hard-earned current-account surpluses; but no detailed data were available to confirm this claim, which was contradicted by reports of delays in payments on various transactions.

One informed source estimated Cuba's debt service obligations (principal plus interest) for 2016 at $3.3 billion, or 18 percent of anticipated total export earnings (goods and services).[37] If exports were growing handsomely, this would be an acceptable external debt burden. Cuba's export performance will have to show significant improvement if it is to service its newly restructured debts in a timely manner and gradually build a better sovereign credit reputation.

We can reduce these findings on the current status of the underperforming Cuban economy to four sharp points:

• The Cuban economy has increasingly become a low-productivity service economy. Industrial production has yet to recover its pre-1989 levels. Agricultural output, despite some gains, remains insufficient to feed the population, and imports of food staples impose severe pressures on the balance of payments.

• Merchandise exports are a paltry $5 billion per year, just 6 percent of national output, reflecting the low international competitiveness of much of Cuba's industry and agriculture. The weak export performance opens a gaping merchandise trade deficit that Cuba struggles to finance, often by accumulating payments arrears that irritate its international partners and undermine its credit ratings.

• Especially debilitating, national savings and investment rates are very low: they are under 10 percent of GDP, half of the Latin American average, and even further below strong Asian investment rates. The unhappy result is an ongoing decapitalization of some sectors, relegating Cuba to a low-growth trap.

• Cuba's past poor performance on servicing its external debts and its long-standing arrears on some commercial external debt obligations are a depressive overhang that impedes Cuban access to international capital markets. However, important progress in restructuring official debts will facilitate a fresh round of trade finance from some government credit agencies.

Big Challenges Ahead: Tough Structural Adjustments

Just how far does Cuba have to go to create an economic model of sustainable growth?[38] The answer depends upon just what type of development model Cuba wants to create, whether a more efficient state-led socialism, a hybrid mix of public and private sectors, or a full-blown open market economy. (In the final chapter, I consider possible scenarios for Cuba's future.)

But as the 2011 reform guidelines admit, and as the analysis in this chapter reveals, whatever the chosen end-state, many difficult reforms await policymakers and the apprehensive Cuban people. The following are among the necessary structural changes, many of which are listed in the 2011 reform guidelines but have been repeatedly postponed or initiated with considerable caution:

- A unified currency and a realistic exchange rate;
- A more decentralized pricing system that more accurately reflects supply and demand in both input and output markets;
- A revamped tax regime that raises sufficient revenue to balance fiscal accounts and that targets social expenditures toward the most needy;
- Wage policies that better reward productivity and ensure a living wage;
- Price and fiscal incentives to drive a much more dynamic and diversified export performance;
- Reforms in key social services (including health, education, and housing) that respond to changing demographics and that protect the most vulnerable sectors;
- Definition of property rights and a revamped commercial legal code; and
- More transparency in government statistics and policymaking.

Such structural shifts would strike at the economy's chronic failures in the critical areas of labor productivity, capital formation, and export performance. They would create a business climate more conducive to an expanding domestic private sector and foreign investment. Armed with new policy tools that rely less on central command authority and more on regulatory rules and price signals, a more market-oriented strategy would also demand a major overhaul of the state apparatus—to build a smaller but smarter government. Any path taken will require a careful sequencing of reforms and a communications strategy that generates realistic expectations among the general public. None of this will be easy.

The next three chapters drill down into three areas that are critical to Cuba's economic future and where the government has already taken important initiatives: the diversification of international commercial partners; the treatment of foreign direct investment; and the emerging small-business private sector.

Dancing with Many Partners
Good Balance, Poor Execution

Since Fidel Castro's victorious 26th of July Movement marched into Havana on New Year's Day 1959, the policies of the United States toward Cuba have focused heavily on bilateral relations between the two nations separated by less than 100 miles of choppy waters. Even today, after more than five decades, U.S. policies—whether debates and legislation in Congress or official statements and executive orders and regulations issued by the executive branch—implicitly assume that there are only two players in contention: Washington and Havana. Yet this conceit takes us very far from the realities of Cuba today.

Since the collapse of its former patron, the Soviet Union, Cuba has dramatically diversified its international economic relations. Initially, Cuba reached out to Europe, Canada, and a widening array of friendly states in Latin America. Over the last two decades, Cuba has forged valuable economic partnerships with major emerging market (EM) economies—notably China, Brazil, Mexico, and Venezuela. Spanish firms manage many of the expanding hotel chains in Cuba, which cater to over 3 million international tourists each year. A Canadian company jointly owns mining operations in Cuba's Holguín Province and ships valuable nickel to Canada for refining and to China for end use. In joint ventures (JVs) with Cuba's national petroleum company, large Chinese petrochemical firms extract oil from onshore wells visible from main highways along the northern coast. Most recently, a Brazilian construction firm has undertaken the

45

modernization of the Mariel Port so that it can accommodate very large container ships transiting the Panama Canal as well as attract international investors primarily targeting export markets.

Despite these important advances, the Cuban economy remains in the doldrums, expanding over the last half-dozen years at a sluggish 2 percent annually. Cuba has successfully established economic relations with a variety of capable commercial partners, many of whom would like to invest more capital in Cuba and would prefer to purchase more Cuban exports to correct the imbalances in their bilateral trade accounts. But these nations are frustrated by Cuba's poor economic offerings.

This chapter tells the story of Cuba's outreach to the dynamic EM economies—which also happen to be ideologically and geopolitically compatible—as seen from the perspective of Cuba and its Chinese, Brazilian, and Venezuelan partners. I examine these nations' motivations as well as their anxieties and frustrations. How does Cuba fit into their international economic and geopolitical strategies, and what are the domestic political drivers behind their friendships with Havana? Canadian and Mexican interests are also explored, as Ottawa and Mexico City sharply differentiate their Cuba policies from that of their North American ally. For context, this chapter first examines Cuba's international economic relations during the 1990s, in the wake of the Soviet Union's collapse.

Opening to the West in the 1990s: Mixed Results

In the 1990s, following the traumatic disappearance of COMECON (Council for Mutual Economic Assistance) and its Eastern European economic partners, Cuba turned first to western Europe and Canada to provide commerce and, most important, for direct investments that would bring capital, know-how, and access to international markets. Some valuable investments materialized, but not in sufficient volume and diversity to place Cuba on a firm growth trajectory. The number of firms—both flows and stocks—investing in Cuba declined after 2002.[1]

Within Cuba, there are diverse opinions as to why this experiment fell short. More orthodox central planners blame the behavior of international investors. Allegedly, foreigners sought quick and outsized profits, failed to deliver on promised technology and capital, and often engaged in corrupt practices.[2] Some smaller businessmen, it was said, traveled to the island primarily for sex tourism. And U.S. economic sanctions discouraged firms with major interests in U.S. markets.

More reform-minded Cuban economists argue that, in fact, many of the larger JVs succeeded—notably in tourism and nickel—even as many smaller ones failed. Other investment opportunities were lost owing to a variety of mistakes made by the Cubans themselves: inexperienced Cuban negotiators failed to adequately understand the workings of specific markets; Cuba failed to maintain orderly payments and access to foreign exchange; and the Cuban government did not take full advantage of the 1995 foreign investment law that allowed, for example, 100 percent foreign ownership of investments—terms that Cuban bureaucrats, narrowly interpreting "national sovereignty," refused to countenance.

The Canadian export promotion agency, Export Development Canada, publicly issued this warning to investors: "The rules for doing business in Cuba continue to be opaque and arbitrary. Cuban bureaucracy is notoriously slow."[3] Even among those European and Canadian firms doing business in Cuba, executives reported that the tough bargaining positions of Cuban officials could be time-consuming and tiresome. Some international investors reported that the low profit margins allowed by the Cuban government were tolerable only in light of a long-term corporate strategy, as farsighted firms sought a toehold in Cuba in anticipation of a brighter future.

Another negative factor came into play in 2003 when the European Commission, following a political crackdown in Cuba, adopted a "common position" that linked future European economic cooperation to an improvement in Cuba's political behavior. This critical diplomatic posture sent a negative signal to potential investors. It also irritated the Cuban government, always sensitive to international criticism, and cooled Havana's interest in doing business with Europe. (On occasion, the Cuban government has perceived the European Union as the soft face of the more overtly critical United States.)[4] From the Cuban security perspective, economic relations that carry political conditions are of questionable net value and of uncertain durability. Today, European governments have softened their posture and are less "common" in their attitudes toward Cuba, but European diplomats in general report that a wary Cuban government treats them as "less than friendly"—not unfriendly but not entirely friendly, either.

So the partial economic opening to the West, while not without its fruits, was not sufficient by itself to impart dynamism to the ailing Cuban economy. Political frictions and Cuban attitudes conspired to limit the gains. If Cuba is to compete more successfully for funds, technology, and marketing skills on international capital markets, it will have to create a more favorable investment climate, and one that reflects a more realistic appreciation for the interests of potential partners.

Cuba has continued to court some European and Canadian business partners. But in the last 15 years, the focus of its attention has turned elsewhere: to the emerging market economies.

The South-South Strategy

For decades, Cuba had nursed the vision of South-South economic cooperation among developing countries, as espoused for example by the Non-Aligned Movement (NAM), which Cuba helped to found and which it has participated in—and hosted—enthusiastically. But that South-South vision was largely an aspirational concept, and the NAM was at best a forum for coordinating diplomatic positions and postures. As EMs became the world's most potent engines of growth, however, suddenly the South-South vision morphed into a tangible reality. From the vantage point of Havana in the twenty-first century, a strategy that turned to EMs looked like a real economic and geopolitical option.

In contrast to its testy, uneven relations with Europe, the Cuban government is more comfortable with the economic systems and geopolitical postures of its key emerging market partners (Mexico being a partial exception, as will be discussed). While emerging market economies differ substantially among themselves, they have in common strong state sectors that command ownership of productive units (state-owned enterprises) and routinely intervene in private markets. Particularly in the case of Cuba's top two EM economic partners, China and Venezuela, official entities play a leading role in orchestrating international economic relations. In the case of Brazil, the Brazilian Development Bank (BNDES) seals the major Cuban transactions with its political weight and concessional credit terms.

While the geopolitical locations and strategies of the major emerging markets are diverse, they tend to share a certain "anti-imperialist" posture and a preference for a multipolar world where power is more diffuse. Even

Figure 3-1. Cuba Merchandise Trade with Emerging Markets, 2000–14

US$ billions

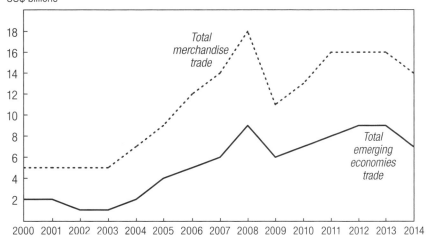

Source: International Monetary Fund (IMF), "Direction of Trade Statistics" (www.imf.org/external/pubs/cat/longres.aspx?sk=19305.0).

while they may assiduously nurture good relations with U.S. diplomats and businesses, EMs do not mind poking Washington from time to time. They certainly have had no problem voting for UN resolutions (opposed in 2015 only by the United States and Israel) criticizing U.S. economic sanctions against Cuba. Immersed in their national histories, the EMs share Cuban sensitivities to big power interventionism and harbor strong emotional attachments to the legal and emotive concept of national sovereignty.

Cuba's EM strategy does not exclude ongoing economic relations with Europe and Canada, who remain important commercial partners. But the current EM tilt signaled an important shift in Cuba's international economic outlook.

Today, approximately 50 percent of Cuban trade (merchandise imports and exports) is with major emerging markets: Venezuela, China, Brazil, Mexico, and Russia. As figure 3-1 shows so clearly, initially the EM strategy bore fruit: two-way merchandise trade soared from under $2 billion in 2003 to over $8 billion in 2008. But rather than being the early stage of a vibrant expansion in Cuban commerce, 2008 turned out to be a peak achievement, after which Cuba's EM trade fell backward. Cuba could not generate the exports required for balanced trading relationships, and its EM partners tired of extending credits that Cuba proved unable to repay.

Nor were its EM partners able to develop sufficient on-island investments to generate the value-added exports to anchor sustainable commerce.

Venezuela Comes to the Rescue

Like most of the small nations of the Caribbean basin, Cuba is heavily dependent on energy imports. During the Soviet era, Moscow provided a secure lifeline of petroleum on highly subsidized terms. When the Soviet Union dissolved and Cuba descended into what is euphemistically known as the Special Period, many Cubans literally went hungry. Then, as a phoenix arising out of a tar pit, Hugo Chávez ascended to power in 1998, and just as petroleum prices began to spike, oil-rich Venezuela extended a fresh lifeline to neighboring Cuba. Chávez idolized Fidel Castro, turning to him repeatedly for political advice and support. Before his death from cancer in 2013, Chávez's approach to governing mirrored that of the Cuban government in a number of important respects: the primacy of politics and ideology over economic results, the preference for presidential centralism, and the recourse to direct popular consultations and mobilizations.[5] Chávez's successor, Nicolás Maduro, has maintained his mentor's close ties to Havana.

Cuban-Venezuelan trade is politically driven, negotiated as state-to-state deals in the general context of the Bolivarian Alliance for the Americas (ALBA).[6] ALBA deals are nontransparent, but it is known that Venezuela provides its close ally Cuba with subsidized oil and partially offsets these transfers by purchasing Cuban medical personnel, teachers, sports trainers, and security advisers; upward of 40,000 Cuban professionals (including some 33,000 medical professionals) have been part of these deals.[7] Cuba records these exports of professionals under "services" but does not disaggregate them by type of professional or by country of destination. Nor do Cuban statistics list the prices of these professional service exports. What is known is that the Venezuelan government transfers funds to the Cuban government, which in turn compensates the skilled workers and their families while extracting a large tax.

Cuba today consumes approximately 150,000 barrels of oil per day; about two-thirds of this amount is from Venezuela, and the remainder derives from domestic extraction of crude oil and natural gas production. Under the ALBA agreements, Cuba must pay 60 percent of its Venezuelan oil invoice within 90 days of purchase in the form of bartered goods and services. The remaining 40 percent of the invoice is to be paid in the lapse of 25 years, at an annual interest rate of 1 percent. According to one estimate, the value of the oil received by Cuba from Venezuela over six years (2003–09) amounted to more than $14 billion, of which nearly $9 billion accounted for goods and services barter exchanges and over $5 billion in long-term debt.[8] Before the recent collapse in petroleum prices, reasonable estimates for the Venezuelan subsidy implicit in the "doctors for oil" program stood at $2 billion–$3 billion annually for Cuba—a vital sum for a country with annual merchandise exports of $4 billion–$6 billion.[9] Today, Cuba's leading expert on Venezuelan-Cuban economic relations estimates that by not having to resort to purchases on international petroleum markets at current low prices, Cuba saves $1.2 billion a year—still a very significant savings for Cuba's tight foreign exchange budget. Another leading analyst puts the value of Venezuela's oil subsidy at $1.9 billion (assuming an international oil price of $50 per barrel).[10] Also of note, Cuba receives 100,000 barrels daily at its Cienfuegos refinery (a Venezuelan-Cuban joint venture), which produces oil derivatives for re-export and earns Cuba additional hard currency.

Cuba's well-trained professionals work in poor Venezuelan neighborhoods as part of the Chavista programs to expand popular access to social services and have bolstered the Chavista political base and electoral results. The Cuban-backed social programs may have contributed the margin of difference in the critical 2000 presidential contest. In that sense, the swap of Venezuelan oil for Cuban professionals has paid off handsomely for the Chavistas, if not necessarily for Venezuela.

Venezuelan firms invest in Cuba, primarily in the petroleum sector. Notably, the Venezuelan state-owned petroleum giant PDVSA helped to manage the renovation of the idle Cienfuegos refinery, bringing its capacity to about 100,000 barrels per day. According to an authoritative Cuban economist, Omar Everleny Pérez Villanueva, Venezuela accounted for 15 percent of the roughly 220 foreign direct investments extant in Cuba in 2009. (Spain accounted for another 25 percent and Canada 14 percent).[11] The Cuban government does not release data breaking out revenues of foreign direct investment by country of origin. We do know that in 2009 the petroleum sector accounted for 27 percent of total foreign direct investment sales, suggesting a significant Venezuelan contribution.

The Cubans are well aware of the dangers of their dependency on Venezuelan largesse. They worry out loud that the Chavistas will not be in power forever. Due to the collapse of petroleum prices on international markets and massive economic mismanagement in Caracas, the Venezuelan economy has sharply deteriorated; and over the next several years the ability of the Venezuelan government to maintain its international subsidies will be constrained. Having suffered severely from the loss of one energy patron, the Cubans do not want to be shocked a second time. In 2012 Cuba sought to lessen its dependency on imported oil by exploiting what appeared to be promising offshore oil reserves, but drilling platforms failed to discover commercially viable deposits.

Venezuela has proven to be an invaluable partner for Cuba in the short to medium run. But Venezuela lacks the economic depth, and today the economic health, to meet Cuba's many other trade and investment needs in the years ahead. The Cubans are also well aware that Chávez's "twenty-first-century socialism" brand of big-spending populism is not sustainable over time, and that the Chavista experiment is endangered, politically at home and financially abroad. Even if Venezuela were a healthier economy, it could be a piece, but only a piece, of Cuba's emerging market strategy.

Most probably, one driver behind Raúl Castro's decision to accelerate improved relations with the United States was the increasing shakiness of his Caracas connection. Foreign exchange flows from U.S. tourists and remittances from Cuban Americans offered Havana a ready replacement for imperiled Venezuelan assistance.

China in the Kingdom of Minerals and Sugar

China has rapidly emerged as Cuba's second-most important commercial partner, behind only Venezuela and quickly outpacing Cuba's early post-Soviet leading trading partners, Canada and Spain. In 2010 China sold Cuba just over $1 billion of a wide variety of vehicles, machinery, consumer goods, and industrial inputs; by 2014 Cuba's growing appetite for Chinese products—financed by Chinese government credits and guarantees—consumed $1.3 billion. Brightly colored Chinese Yutong buses are visible throughout the island (despite maintenance problems). In return, China imported just under $800 million in Cuban goods in 2011, primarily nickel and sugar, although as commodity prices fell, Chinese imports of Cuban goods declined to $302 million in 2014. According to Chinese sources, these sugar purchases are driven less by economic efficiency criteria than by the mutual Chinese-Cuban interest in reducing the bilateral

Figure 3-2. Cuba-China Merchandise Trade, 2000–14

US$ billions

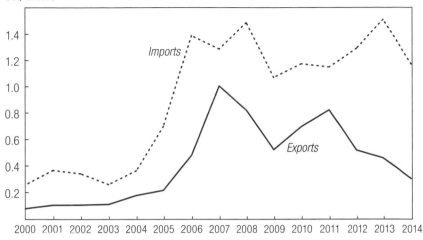

Source: IMF, "Direction of Trade Statistics."

trade imbalance (figure 3-2). The trade imbalance has resulted in a piling up of Cuban debt; in early 2015 China agreed to more lenient repayment terms, a necessity that did not instill confidence in Beijing in the economic prowess of its Caribbean trading partner.

Chinese firms have made a number of modest JV investments in Cuba. Taiji Farms grows rice for domestic consumption. Other JVs produce shoes, bicycles, and home electrical appliances.[12] Red Chinese flags fly over the Chinese National Petroleum Company–Cuban joint venture onshore oil fields on the north-central coast. Chinese-Cuban relations are given a degree of symmetry by Cuban state-owned enterprise investments in China, specifically in hotels, tourism, pharmaceutical production (cancer drugs and interferon), and ophthalmic hospitals. Bilateral educational exchanges allow Chinese students to study Spanish in Cuba and some Cubans to learn Mandarin in China.[13]

According to the Chinese embassy in Havana, over time China has undertaken 70 development assistance projects (separate from JVs) in Cuba, a combination of donations and low-interest credits.[14] These have included two hydroelectric projects, agricultural irrigation, a duck farm, blood bank equipment, housing construction, and donations of medicine and school books.

Chinese officials downplay Chinese interests in Cuba: they suggest that Cuba is just another commercial partner and that there is no special relationship, noting that even within commercial terms, the nearly $2 billion in annual two-way commerce is but a small portion of Chinese trade with Latin America and the Caribbean. In fact, China has long held a diplomatic interest in Cuba.[15] In the early days of the revolution, Cuba recognized the People's Republic of China—the first Latin American country to do so. Ché Guevara led an economic delegation to China in November 1960. But when Fidel Castro allied with the USSR, relations with China deteriorated. History took another turn with the passing of the Soviet Union. Chinese president Jiang Zemin visited Cuba in November 1993, and Fidel Castro paid a return visit to China in 1995. Raúl Castro has visited China at least three times and once spent 20 days touring six provinces. Today, Cuba backs Chinese positions on Taiwan and Tibet, and the two nations share similar views on "antihegemonism" and "nonintervention" along with preferences for a more multipolar world order.

For China, a growing presence in Cuba strengthens a friendly regime similarly ruled by a communist party and fits into a global strategy of expanding Chinese presence throughout the developing world.[16] Chinese officials assure U.S. diplomats that they have no intention of challenging U.S. security interests in the Western Hemisphere, but Chinese trade and investments have a de facto softening impact on U.S. economic sanctions against Cuba. Geopolitically, Beijing would prefer a reduced U.S. presence in its own Asian neighborhood and may imagine that a Chinese presence in the Caribbean serves as an offsetting asset—one that might someday be a useful bargaining chip in a global realignment of forces.

For Cuba the growing Chinese presence has obvious economic and geopolitical advantages. And China fits squarely into Cuba's emerging market strategy. More subtly, China may have helped to balance Venezuelan influence during Chavez's heyday and seems to offer a more durable partnership. Looking forward as Cuba reengages with the United States, China will continue to contribute to Cuba's strategy to diversify its economic and diplomatic relations.

Chinese-Cuban relations are not without strains. China is frustrated by the slow pace at which Cuba is dismantling its Soviet-era economic centralization. One former Latin American ambassador recounted to me how his Chinese counterpart "used to tear his hair out" at the slow pace of Cuban economic reform. The Chinese have been upset when Cuba, more than once, has suspended foreign exchange transfers on credits and investments. According to press reports, Cuba's external debt to China had reached $4 billion by 2010.[17] Various joint projects have run into serious problems, and other joint investment concepts have failed to materialize altogether: nickel extraction in Camariocas did not come to pass; the much ballyhooed second-phase expansion of the Cienfuegos refinery, along with an associated petrochemical complex and cross-island pipeline, was mothballed; and the construction of a well-publicized luxury hotel on Havana's Marina Hemingway has repeatedly been postponed. For the Chinese-Cuban partnership to fully flower, Cuban economic reform will have to proceed apace. The key constraint slowing Chinese-Cuban exchange is Cuban domestic economic policies. Neither partner has been fully satisfied with the results: the Cubans had hoped for more investment and more credit, while the Chinese had anticipated a more rapid reform process and a more reliable commercial partner.

Nevertheless, a senior Chinese diplomat expressed to me his confidence in the Cuban reform process, seeing it as irreversible and implying a distinct cultural shift that included an acceptance of private property, efficiency criteria, and rising inequality, as has occurred in China.[18] He also expressed the conviction that the improvement in U.S.-Cuban relations would enhance business confidence. The 2014 investment law and the opening of the Mariel Special Development Zone (ZED) had prompted Chinese firms to consider new investments, even as they were looking carefully at cost structures and "invisible" risks. But the reform process was likely to be gradual, and the diplomat counselled patience and respect for Cuban national pride.

Frustrated at slow progress in penetrating Cuban agriculture, industry, and energy, by 2015 China was refocusing its attention on tourism. In December 2015 Air China initiated three weekly direct flights between Beijing and Havana (with a brief stopover in Montreal). According to Chinese sources, the number of Chinese visitors is ramping up, from 8,000 in 2014 to 30,000 in 2015, and within 10 years could reach 500,000, including cruise ship passengers. To accommodate their tastes, a Chinese firm will open a high-end Chinese restaurant in Havana, and Beijing Enterprises is negotiating a JV to build a large tourism complex complete with an 18-hole golf course. Discussions on the Marina Hemingway hotel have also been revived. In addition, Chinese engineering and construction firms were engaged in modernizing port facilities in eastern Santiago and reportedly were participating in exploratory talks regarding the megaproject of converting Havana Harbor into a tourism destination. Also of interest, in 2015 the Chinese telecommunications giant Huawei inked a deal with ETECSA, Cuba's state-owned telecommunications provider, to sell its smart phones on the island.

Brazil and Its Near Abroad

Brazil's special interest in Cuba follows several motives. The Cuban economy has salient complementarities with the Brazilian—in the sugar industry, offshore petroleum, pharmaceuticals, and infrastructure construction—that attract Brazilian exporters and investors. In the diplomatic realm, the Brazilian drive toward hegemony in Latin America and influence throughout the developing world steers it naturally to Havana Harbor; Cuba is easily the largest of the Caribbean islands, and Cuba retains considerable prestige in certain circles worldwide. Brazil would cherish Cuban support for its overriding ambition to gain a permanent seat on the UN Security Council. Although Brazilian diplomats are quick to deny it, there has been fierce competition between Brasilia and Caracas for leadership throughout the Americas, and nowhere has this head-to-head rivalry been sharper than in Cuba.

There are also matters of ideology and domestic politics that contribute to Brazil's special interest in Cuba. Brazil touts its modern social democratic model of development, in contrast to Chávez's "twenty-first-century socialism," and if Brazil could nudge Cuba gradually toward its ideological direction, that would be a major diplomatic accomplishment. Within Brazilian internal politics, the more left-wing faction within the governing Workers Party has a historical affinity with revolutionary Cuba and wants Brazil positively engaged on the island.

The expanding Brazilian economy is spreading its tentacles throughout the Caribbean basin. Although still modest, Brazilian-Cuban trade has grown in recent years. Two-way merchandise trade hovered around $600 million in 2008–09 and surpassed $750 million in 2012, but fell back to $650 million in 2014. Brazil enjoys a significant trade surplus; in 2014 Brazilian exports reached $587 million against imports from Cuba of just $63 million (figure 3-3). Brazilian exports spanned a range of agricultural and industrial products, notably petroleum derivatives, soy, and meats,

Figure 3-3. Cuba-Brazil Merchandise Trade, 2000–14

US$ billions

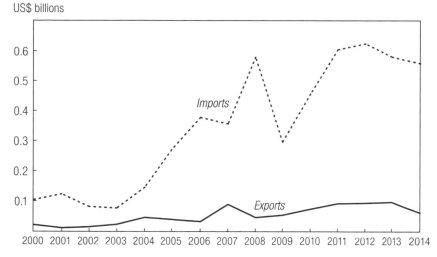

Source: IMF, "Direction of Trade Statistics."

while Brazilian goods imports were concentrated in Cuban pharmaceutical products and minerals.

In 2013 the Brazilian government contracted with the Cuban government through the Pan-American Health Organization for the services of some 11,000–12,000 Cuban medical professionals, for an annual payment of around $500 million. The Cubans are stationed in rural areas, and their study of Portuguese has earned respect among their thankful patients. Employing them costs the Brazilian medical service less than it would cost to employ Brazilian doctors, who have avoided practicing in poorer rural districts. In theory, Cuban participants each receive a monthly salary of around $4,500, but in fact they see only $1,245, the difference accruing to the Cuban government.[19] As with Venezuela's import of such professional services, the Brazilian agreement helps Cuba finance its large deficit in bilateral merchandise trade.

Brazilian businesses have shown keen interest in the island. For 15 years the small but successful JV between Souza Cruz and TabaCuba called Brascuba has been producing and marketing cigarettes (see chapter 5). In late 2015 Cuban government authorities announced that Brascuba would be moving its operations and building a new factory in the Mariel Special

Development Zone; among the eight deals approved for ZED Mariel in 2015, the $120 million Brascuba investment was by far the largest. But the most impressive Brazilian business deal in Cuba was the $957 million expansion and modernization of the strategic Port of Mariel, undertaken by the giant Brazilian construction firm Odebrecht. The Brazilian Development Bank, which promotes Brazilian exports with relatively long-term, concessional credits, provided financing up to $682 million (85 percent for Brazilian goods and services) in support of Brazilian participation. Ownership of the Mariel Port, however, will remain Cuban, in the hands of the Business Administration Group (GAESA) of the Ministry of the Armed Forces (MINFAR). (In contrast, Brazil was excluded from participating in the phase II expansion of the Cienfuegos refinery complex, the megaproject that was once assigned by the Cuban government to China but that in the end was mothballed.)

A number of Brazilian firms have been exploring investment opportunities in a variety of sectors and products. The state petroleum company Petrobras had been awarded a concession for deepwater oil exploration, but withdrew from the field. During 2012 other prospectors failed to locate commercially viable deposits, delaying Cuban hopes for near-term energy independence. Other potential investment initiatives have centered around powdered milk, fruit-based energy drinks, poultry hatcheries, aluminum cans, and flat glass, as well as the development and marketing of high-value-added medicines. Investments in sugar and ethanol have also been discussed; Brazilian experts believe that Cuban soil compares favorably to the best lands in Brazil, but so far Cubans, sensitive to a return to foreign ownership in the sugar industry, have authorized not a joint venture investment but rather a Brazilian management contract in a single Brazilian sugar plantation. Few of these other aspirations have come to fruition.

Brazilian diplomats and corporate executives would like to do more business in Cuba but are frustrated by what they see as Cuba's preference for political "control" rather than economic production, by the apportionment of projects by political as opposed to price criteria, and by Cuba's restricted export and payment capacities. One skeptical Brazilian diplomat opined that a change in Cuban attitudes toward foreign commerce "would require a change in the narrative that blames all problems on external causes." In late 2014 another Brazilian diplomat stationed in Havana told me he hoped that more Brazilian firms would eventually invest in Cuba but noted the obstacles facing Brazilian investors: uncertainties regarding important economic reforms, including currency unification and wage rates at Mariel; lack of transparency and shortage of information; low agricultural productivity; prohibitions on ownership of land; and the continuing dominance of the "gerontocracy" in leadership positions. In late 2015 the same Brazilian diplomat noted that negotiating and approving the transfer of the Brascuba cigarette facilities to ZED Mariel had taken the bureaucracy over a year and had required the personal approval of Raúl Castro.

Mexican Separation

In the early years of the Cuban Revolution Mexico and Cuba were proud of their close relationship, based on shared perspectives of international relations and approaches to political power. In the 1980s and early 1990s it looked as though these strong diplomatic ties might be complemented with economic exchanges. But in the last decade Mexico and Cuba have experienced a "difficult divorce."[20] And despite a formal diplomatic entente, each of the exes has become less interested in the other, moving on toward other horizons.

In the 1960s, among the Latin American republics, only Mexico stood by the young Cuban Revolution, voting against the 1962 resolution to suspend Cuban participation in the Organization of American States (OAS) and refusing to comply with a 1964 OAS resolution calling upon members to break diplomatic relations with Havana. In those years, Mexican diplomacy was rooted in the principles of nonintervention and national sovereignty and was eternally wary of U.S. coercive power. The governing Institutionalized Revolutionary Party (PRI) still recalled its revolutionary origins, and its own authoritarian governance was not offended by Castro's political style. Pragmatically, the PRI and Castro cut a deal: Mexico would not criticize Cuba, and Castro would not seek to incite the Mexican domestic left against the governing PRI. In retrospect, this mutual nonaggression pact suggested that the Mexican-Cuban marriage was not entirely romantic in nature, and that shifting political currents could cause each partner to reassess its interests.

At least two Mexican presidents found a useful friend in Fidel Castro. President Luis Echeverría visited the island in 1975 as part of his effort to project himself as a left-leaning leader in the Third World. A decade later, President Carlos Salinas welcomed Castro to his 1988 inauguration, pleased at this endorsement following the evident fraud in the presidential balloting. Salinas promoted trade and investment with Cuba; Castro had told the outgoing Mexican president, Miguel de la Madrid, that he favored Mexican investment in Cuba, and Salinas convened a dinner of leading Mexican business executives to meet with Castro.[21]

Mexican investments began to flow to Cuba, notably in tourism, textiles, telecommunications, and cement making. Mexican merchandise exports jumped from $104 million in 1990 to $432 million in 1995. But these new commercial flows and the promising economic partnership they augured did not consolidate the diplomatic marriage. The mid-1990s turned out to be a high point, after which relations quickly deteriorated.

For its part, Mexico began to change. The same Carlos Salinas who had courted Fidel Castro decided that Mexico's economic future lay with the United States, and in 1993 he approached President George Bush to negotiate a bilateral trade opening that became the North American Free Trade Agreement (NAFTA). While Salinas himself adhered to traditional PRI political forms, his economic reforms opened the path to political change. His successor, Ernesto Zedillo, a disciplined economist who insisted upon democratic norms, began to distance Mexico from Cuba. When Zedillo visited Havana in 1999, he spoke out openly in favor of democracy, and his foreign minister, Rosario Green, broke all previous protocol and met with prominent Cuban dissidents. Castro took these new turns as indications that Mexico was abandoning its "independent" positions in favor of a more pro-U.S. and therefore anti-Cuban posture.

If Castro was distrustful of Zedillo, his relations with Zedillo's successor, the more conservative Vicente Fox, occasioned a very public falling out. Fox's feisty foreign minister, Jorge Castañeda (who had himself journeyed from the Marxist left to social democracy), believed that Mexico could use its new democratic credentials to strengthen its diplomacy. Castañeda seemingly went out of his way to criticize Cuba's human rights policies. And famously, just prior to a 2002 United Nations summit on international development in the city of Monterrey, at the request of the White House Fox asked Castro to "eat lunch and leave" so as not to be around when President George W. Bush arrived—a phone conversation that an offended Castro made public. By 2004 both countries had recalled their ambassadors—the diplomatic equivalent of a nasty divorce.

Mexican businesses had already become disaffected with Cuban economic management.[22] Firms complained that there were no laws or fixed rules, and that Cuban officials felt no compulsion to honor agreements or make timely payments. Some firms felt the heat of what they believed was unfair or disloyal competition from state-owned enterprises. Others complained about legal and administrative insecurities, government regulations that were arbitrarily tightened to squeeze any visible profits, and sudden government audits intended to intimidate or extort—as well as constant wiretapping by Cuban authorities. Some felt that these antagonistic restrictions were politically motivated—payback for the Mexican government's criticisms of Cuban political practices. Some of the major Mexican investors withdrew; for example, Mexican telecommunications interests sold out to an Italian firm.

Mexican traders and investors also found that Cuban payments in hard currency were irregular. Mexican exporters discovered that letters of credit were not honored, and investors found their hard-currency accounts frozen. Even when deposits for dividend repatriations had been made in Cuban banks, the authorities would not authorize transactions in hard currency. As arrears accumulated, Mexico's semiautonomous export credit agency, Banco Nacional de Comercio Exterior (Bancomext), agreed to a restructuring of some $400 million in Cuban debts. As part of the deal, Bancomext reopened a revolving line of trade credits, but in small amounts, indicative of a loss of confidence in both Cuban capacity and willingness to service its external obligations.

At one point when Cuba was behind in payments to the Mexican national oil company, Pemex, it suggested that Pemex consider taking over management of Cuban oil refineries. Pemex declined, lacking confidence that Cuba would honor any agreement. (Moreover, Pemex may also have been wary of U.S. legislation imposing sanctions in U.S. markets on firms engaged in certain business transactions in Cuba. Further, unlike other national oil companies such as Petrobras and PDVSA, Pemex has concentrated its activities at home.)

In 2010 Mexican merchandise exports were only $307 million—below the 1995 peak (figure 3-4). Mexican sales of chemicals, plastics, fertilizers, and metals reflected Cuban priorities in procuring necessary inputs for agriculture, nickel, tourism, and other industries. These modest sales reflect Cuba's insolvency and the decision by the Mexican authorities not to provide subsidized credits. Mexican officials argued that to do so would contradict Mexico's market-oriented development strategies; they didn't see the logic in giving away money. Mexicans also felt that trade based on financial subsidies was not sustainable over the long run.

Figure 3-4. Cuba-Mexico Merchandise Trade, 2000–14

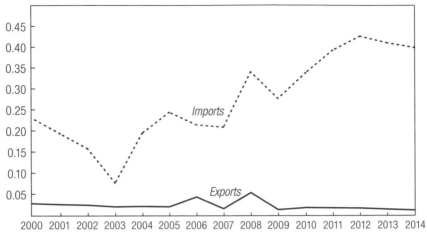

US$ billions

Source: IMF, "Direction of Trade Statistics."

Mexican imports from Cuba have been tiny, surpassing $50 million a year only twice since 1990 and falling to just $16 million in 2014 (figure 3-4). Mexican trade experts explain that the little Cuba has to export is often assigned to other markets, e.g., cigars to Spain or rum to Europe. Cuban pharmaceuticals represent a potential export, but Cuban firms have been slow to acquire the necessary patents and other Mexican government permits. Mexico has not shown interest in any large-scale purchase of Cuban medical personnel or other skilled professionals, as Venezuela and Brazil have done.

The two most recent Mexican presidents, Felipe Calderón and Enrique Peña Nieto, sought to reduce bilateral tensions, and both urged their ministries to enhance Mexican-Cuban economic exchange. But Mexican global trade now totals $854 billion and Cuba's small market has nearly disappeared from view: the romantic moment has passed and Cuba is now a low commercial priority. Mexico is closely watching developments in Cuba, but there is some skepticism among experienced observers about the current regime's ability to reform itself. Even one rather sympathetic Mexican official remarked to me, "How far will the reforms go, and how fast? It's all very uncertain."

The 1996 Helms-Burton Act has inhibited some large Mexican firms, such as Cemex and Pemex, which have big stakes in the U.S. market, from engaging in Cuba. (A Mexican law prohibits Mexican firms from cooperating with Helms-Burton, but doesn't alleviate the corporate headache from litigation in U.S. courts. Numerous international companies, including some Mexican ones, have sought to circumvent Helms-Burton sanctions by setting up legally independent entities registered offshore, as in small Caribbean islands.) Many of the Mexican firms doing business with Cuba are small and medium-sized enterprises with little or no exposure in U.S. markets. Observers feel that, in most cases where Mexican firms have decided against doing business in Cuba, factors other than Helms-Burton—country risk, credit risk, small and stagnant markets, political uncertainties—were decisive.

One notable exception to Mexican withdrawal from Cuba is Grupo Altex, whose joint venture flour mill company, IMSA, supplies much of Havana's daily bread consumption. The plant was once the property of Mexico's Grupo Bimbo, but the multinational food company feared that its large exposure in the United States made it vulnerable to Helms-Burton sanctions. Although associated with Bimbo, Grupo Altex is structured as a separate legal entity. As its profitability is ensured by cost-plus pricing (sales prices fixed by the Cuban government over the costs of inputs and production), Altex has maintained and even expanded its operations. But the Altex success story stands in sharp contrast to the wider Mexican restraint. Waves of Mexican corporate executives participated in fact-finding visits to Cuba in recent years, but few have inked investments. By November 2015 the Mariel Special Development Zone had announced two modest Mexican investments, Richmeat de Cuba (food processing) and Devox Caribe (paints and chemical additives).[23]

Mexicans interested in investing in Cuba report having been especially distraught when Carlos Lage and Felipe Pérez Roque, internationally oriented officials who represented a potential transition generation, were purged from their Cuban government posts in March 2009. Perhaps these capable Cubans reminded the Mexicans of their own generation of reformers that had moved Mexico forward in the last two decades. Public opinion polls show that younger Mexicans, barely aware of the 1959 revolution, are less interested in Cuba and less sympathetic to the regime in Havana than their elders were.[24] When Raúl Castro paid an official visit to Mexico in November 2015, Pena Nieto greeted the Cuban delegation politely—but met members in the provincial town of Merida on the Yucatan peninsula, distant from the capital and attracting modest public attention.[25] Mexico, like Cuba, now has other interests.

Exhaustion of the Emerging Market Strategy

From the perspective of the Cuban government, the new focus on emerging markets was a brilliant strategic move. While Cuba and its EM partners differ in important respects, they share critical economic and geopolitical interests. Cuba and its EM partners are comfortable with state-to-state transactions that include subsidized finance and other nonmarket elements. In particular, their large state-owned firms are accustomed to acting upon political direction and covering losses in politically driven transactions with cross-subsidies. Furthermore, Cuba and its EM commercial partners share a core geopolitical interest: building a more multipolar world where U.S. power is diminished. The Venezuela of Hugo Chávez and Nicolás Maduro has made that goal the core of its diplomacy. While China and Brazil seek cordial relations with the United States, there should be no illusions but that they also seek a diplomatic environment where their respective power grows at the expense of the United States. The Russia of Vladimir Putin, who has taken modest steps to reengage in Cuba, shares that geopolitical aspiration.[26]

The EM strategy yielded some important investments. With their stakes in Cuban refineries and onshore exploration and drilling, Venezuela and China are lessening, although not erasing, Cuban energy dependence. (Had their investments with other energy companies in offshore petroleum explorations and drilling born fruit, Cuba hoped to become a net energy exporter.) Also significant is Brazil's investment in the modernization and expansion of the Mariel Port complex, which beyond returning Cuba to its historic role as a transportation and logistics hub in the Caribbean could also help to make Cuba a cost-effective site for light industry and assembly plants integrated into regional markets. In addition, Brazilian and Venezuelan investments could revitalize Cuba's sugar industry by using the sugar for sweeteners or biomass inputs into alternative energy. Again, these EM transactions are not in opposition to Cuba's continuing relations with Europe (especially with Spanish hotel and tour operators) and Canadian mining and tourism. The new EM partners can coexist peacefully with the older Western partners.

Yet there is a disturbing pattern in Cuba's international economic relationships. With the passage of time, Cuba's partnerships seem to sour, whether due to the partner's own ill fate (the Soviet Union and—perhaps—the Venezuela of the Chavistas) or due to disenchantment, as partners find doing business with the Cuban state tiresome and excessively costly. In some cases, the commercial partner has evolved toward a more market-oriented model and has grown impatient with Cuban orthodoxy. Mexico, once an enthusiast of the Cuban Revolution, discovered that it had less and less in common with Cuban central planning. Already one feels that the latest set of new partners, China and Brazil, is dissatisfied with many Cuban commercial practices and attitudes.

In principle, the emerging market strategy could be a viable course of action for Cuba, providing it with a diverse and complementary set of international commercial partners and geopolitical allies. Geography and the complementary strengths of the U.S. economy dictate that exchange with the U.S. mainland will, one day, be the most efficient option, yet the South-South vision seemed to offer a reasonable second-best solution. And when U.S.-Cuban economic relations eventually reopen, for both economic and geopolitical reasons Cuba will still want to maintain a diversity of commercial partners.

But no international economic strategy will work unless Cuba can transform itself into a more efficient and reliable business partner. No set of geopolitical alliances will provide Cuba with the capital and technology it needs unless it creates a more welcoming investment climate. And no international alliances, by themselves, will be sufficient to provide the long-suffering Cuban citizens with the labor productivity and decent employment they deserve. As representatives of EM governments and firms have come to realize, Cuban policymakers hold the keys to unlocking deeper international economic cooperation.

Today, the exhaustion of the emerging market strategy—not only the slump in Venezuela—may suggest why the leadership of the Cuban Communist Party decided to accelerate a rapprochement with the United States. Since Cuba was not able to alleviate pressures on its balance of payments by lifting its merchandise exports, it turned instead to the United States for a quick spike in tourism and remittances. Not a long-term solution, to be sure, but probably sufficient for Raúl Castro, whose second and final five-year term in office will come to an end in early 2018.

Opening to Foreign Investment

New Portfolio Opportunities

At its birth, the revolutionary Cuban state defined itself in large measure in terms of what it was not: not a dependency of the United States; not a dominion governed by global corporations; not a liberal, market-driven economy. As the guerrilla army made its triumphal entry into Havana and the infant revolution shifted leftward, a hallmark of its anti-imperialist ethos became the loudly proclaimed nationalizations of the U.S.-based firms that had controlled many key sectors of the Cuban economy, including hotels and gambling casinos, public utilities, oil refineries, and the rich sugar mills. In the strategic conflict with the United States, the "historic enemy," the young revolution consolidated its power through the excision of the U.S. economic presence.

For revolutionary Cuba, foreign investment has been about more than dollars and cents. It has touched on key issues of cultural identity and national sovereignty, as well as on Cuba's model of socialist planning, a hybrid of Marxist-Leninism and Fidelismo, which has jealously guarded its domination over all aspects of the economy. During its five decades of rule, the regime's political and social goals have always dominated economic policy; security of the revolution trumped productivity.

Fidel Castro's brand of anticapitalism included a strong dose of antiglobalization. For many years, *El Comandante en Jefe* hosted a large international conference on globalization where he would lecture thousands of delegates on the many evils of multinational firms, which spread brutal exploitation and inequality around the world.

Not surprisingly, Cuba has received remarkably small inflows of foreign investment, even taking into account the size of its economy. In the twenty-first century, the globe is awash in transborder investments by corporations, large and small. Many developing countries, other than those damaged by severe civil conflicts, receive shares that significantly bolster their growth prospects. The expansion of foreign direct investment (FDI) into developing countries is one of the great stories of recent decades: FDI rose from $14 billion in 1985 to $580 billion in 2010 to $681 billion in 2014.[1] While FDI cannot substitute for domestic savings and investment, it can add significantly to domestic efforts and significantly speed growth.[2]

Today's ailing Cuban economy—whose 11.2 million people yield the modest gross domestic product (GDP) reported officially at $81 billion (and possibly much less at realistic exchange rates)—badly needs additional external cooperation, notwithstanding heavily subsidized oil imports from Venezuela.[3] As with any economy, domestic choices made at home and by Cubans will largely determine the country's fate. Yet as Cubans have been well aware since the arrival of Christopher Columbus, the encroaching international economy matters greatly; it can be a source not only of harsh punishments but also of great benefits. In an earlier work I explored the modest contributions already being made by certain bilateral and regional cooperation agencies and the larger potential benefits awaiting Cuba if it joined the core global and regional financial institutions—namely the International Monetary Fund, the World Bank, the Inter-American Development Bank, and the Andean Development Corporation.[4] This chapter explores the contributions that private foreign investments have been making, and could make on a much greater scale, to propel Cuba onto a more prosperous and sustainable growth path.

This chapter first reviews those sections of the official 2011 reform guidelines that pertain directly to foreign investment. The description of the formal legal framework for foreign investment, now based on the new foreign investment law (Law 118 of 2014), pays special attention to the exhausting approval process and shifting standards that have been applied by government ministries. The chapter then considers the formal legal setting to the broader concept of "business climate." In the 1990s an effort to establish foreign trade zones based on the formal legal framework failed miserably as investors judged that the business climate was overwhelmingly adverse. This chapter next attempts to survey the little available data to understand FDI in Cuba, past and present. Finally, the chapter examines the government's 2014 "Portfolio Opportunities for Foreign Investment," which lists over $8 billion in 246 specified development projects. The portfolio reveals much about the needs of the Cuban economy as well as the internal tensions within the Cuban establishment.

As we have seen, the reforms of the 1990s did yield some important results, as Cuba opened select sectors to foreign investment and commerce. By 2014, in partnerships with foreign hotel investors, managers, and tour operators, Cuba hosted 3 million international visitors yielding well over $2.5 billion in gross receipts. A Canadian nickel mining and smelter company, Sherritt International, is generating the largest single source of foreign exchange earnings, surpassing sugar. Other joint ventures (JVs) with major European multinationals are successfully distributing premium Cuban rum and tobacco in international markets.

These positive developments in international tourism, nickel and cobalt mining, and high-value-added agriculture (hand-rolled cigars and vintage rums) are foundations for future growth. They have not yet, however, sufficed to lift Cuba onto a strong sustainable growth path. To overcome the critical problems still confronting the Cuban economy, the Cuban government has repeatedly recognized that it will have to undertake more and deeper policy reforms.

The Benefits of FDI

There is a large literature examining both the various impacts of FDI on development and the best mix of national policies to maximize FDI's favorable impacts on the economy.[5] Many academic studies run aground because of certain methodological problems (for example, confusion over whether strong FDI is the result or the cause of successful development) and inadequate data (for example, insufficiency in cross-country or time series). Much of the literature is faulted for making generalizations based upon just one or a few country studies, or for failing to disaggregate among different economic sectors. Leading authority Theodore Moran notes there are at least four separate forms of FDI—in extractive industries, infrastructure, manufacturing, and services—and each generates diverse impacts and policy challenges. Still, too much research fails to make these critical distinctions.[6]

It would be foolhardy to imagine that all FDI provides net benefits to an economy, any more than all domestic investments do. Openness to FDI exposes an economy to the vicissitudes of global market trends and to decisions made by distant corporate boards. Large-scale FDI can affect wage levels and hence income distribution, in some cases creating "labor aristocracies,"[7] among other potentially contentious outcomes. Nevertheless, based upon the standard academic (neoclassical) economic growth model and much empirical work—and, I would add, common sense—it can be concluded that FDI can offer several very useful inputs to the host economy.

Investment capital is one such input. As a result of the global boom in FDI, investment inflows now frequently contribute as much as 5 percent of a nation's GDP, augmenting national savings (usually about 20 percent in developing countries) by about a quarter. This capture of external savings mitigates the trade-off between savings and consumption by allowing an increase in total savings and investment without having to squeeze popular consumption. But it is important that the capital inflows do not crowd out domestic savings, in the sense of relaxing societal efforts to raise national savings rates in favor of an unsustainable consumption orgy.

Another input offered by FDI is technology transfer. FDI is a composite bundle of capital stock, know-how, technology, and management practices that can diffuse knowledge throughout the local economy through various transmission mechanisms: the foreign investor can pass on best practices to its domestic suppliers regarding quality standards, low-defect reliability, and on-time delivery; local firms can learn via imitation and competition to supply FDI firms; and talented FDI employees can depart to form or join domestic firms, transporting their new knowledge with them. But these spillovers are not necessarily automatic. Smart, carefully targeted government policies, such as vendor development programs, can actively promote them.

FDI also offers the host economy employment and skills upgrading. Foreign investors typically pay higher wages than the domestic norm, reflecting greater capital intensity and labor productivity and, perhaps, greater interest in good labor relations and lower employee turnover. If FDI is of sufficient magnitude it may markedly increase the demand for labor and even place upward pressure on national wages. To fully benefit, governments and educational institutions can partner with FDI firms to provide well-matched manpower training.

Exports, too, are a benefit of FDI. Especially in smaller nations, FDI firms often target international markets and may integrate local production into global supply chains. The presence of FDI can also inspire local firms to think internationally and make that extra effort to search abroad for new customers. But it may take an active government policy to encourage FDI to grow *net* exports by seeking out and educating local suppliers to substitute for imported intermediate inputs.

Finally, FDI tends to improve consumer welfare. Consumers can benefit if locally produced goods are cheaper than imported equivalents. By increasing competition or by employing new organizational practices, FDI in the retail sector can lower prices and expand consumer offerings. FDI may also improve public health and reduce consumer risk by, for example, raising quality standards in food products.

Thus FDI offers great opportunities to capital-importing countries, but reaping the full benefits depends upon the country and policy contexts. Active national policies that maximize benefits can include high-quality education for technical workers, engineers, and managers; targeted incentives that encourage positive spillovers and technological learning; and carefully crafted programs that locate investments in poorer regions or that encourage hiring workers, including idle youth, women, and the handicapped, from less advantaged, high-risk backgrounds. More controversial are performance requirements—for example, mandating that FDI purchase a certain quantity of inputs from domestic vendors or meet export targets.[8] Cuba, with its relatively strong governmental institutions, educated population, and commitment to the welfare of workers and social equity, is well-placed to extract big benefits from FDI.

Shifting Attitudes

The rise and fall in the stock of JVs on the island has reflected the dramatic shifts in Cuban economic policies since the revolution. Over the last five decades five periods can be distinguished (figure 4-1). During the revolutionary 1960s, the regime systematically nationalized most foreign and Cuban-owned properties, beginning with large U.S.-owned properties and eventually extending to small-scale enterprises and even mom-and-pop retail outlets. The U.S. Foreign Claims Settlement Commission has certified 5,913 claims valued at $1.9 billion in seized U.S. properties (in 1960 values), including many by the marquee U.S. corporations of the era.[9] Just as consequential, much of the Cuban upper and middle class exited the island, eventually creating the prosperous Cuban American community

Figure 4-1. Five Phases of Cuban Policies toward Foreign Direct Investment

PHASE 1 Revolutionary 1960s	PHASE 2 Post-Soviet 1990s	PHASE 3 Conservative 2000s	PHASE 4 Socialist Mid- to late 2000s	PHASE 5 Ambivalent 2011–present
Nationalism and expropriation	Liberalization and welcome	Retrenchment and cancellations	SOE partners (Venezuela, China, Brazil)	Economic reform; anticorruption campaign

based in south Florida. In Cuba, Soviet-style planning came to dominate economic policymaking. In the second phase, the sudden loss of the large Soviet subsidy occasioned an interlude of liberalization, of warm welcomes to European, Canadian, and Latin American investors, often extended by Fidel Castro himself. But once the economy showed signs of recovery, Castro reevaluated the opening to foreign capital and ordered the closure of many JVs, especially smaller firms, amid a more general recentralization of economic decisionmaking. During the fourth phase, the Cubans turned toward state-backed projects involving Venezuela, China, and Brazil. The current fifth phase is one of ambivalence.

Since assuming the presidency in 2008, Raúl Castro has sent contradictory signals regarding foreign investment. In principle, Cuba's foreign investment laws and regulations (including Law 118 of March 29, 2014, which superseded Law 77 of September 5, 1995) offer favorable conditions, and—as the case studies in the next chapter reveal—some JVs are successfully navigating the Cuban economic system. But the government has been keeping many suitors waiting for the final green light. Projects for large golf and marina resorts have been pending for years. The owners of the prime commercial office space in Havana have been unable to secure authorization for next-phase construction. An international hotel chain that offered to refurbish the shabby downtown Habana Libre hotel was refused an equity share. Brazilian negotiators have been urging Cuba to allow large investments in sugar mills and associated ethanol plants, only to be frustrated by "political symbolism"[10]—lingering fears of compromising the sacred gains of the revolution and endangering national security. Even more alarming, major JVs have recently been shuttered or challenged by the authorities for failing to meet demanding performance requirements (as the case studies discuss). The much-anticipated passage of Law 118 created expectations of a rush of new approvals of important foreign investment projects, but as of this writing few have been approved. The new law seems not to have lifted the most serious barriers—ideological, bureaucratic—to foreign capital inflows.

If smartly marketed, however, FDI could come to play a more central role in increasing the productivity and competitiveness of the Cuban economy, creating new opportunities and higher wages for the Cuban workforce, and diffusing dynamism throughout the economy.

Reform Guidelines: The Roles of FDI

The 2011 "Guidelines for the Economic and Social Policies of the Party and the Revolution," as approved by the Communist Party of Cuba (PCC), contains 313 points, just 12 of which (numbers 96 through 107) directly address foreign investment—and these propose no major policy reforms. The relevant guidelines neither recognize the critical role that foreign investment is already playing in the Cuban economy nor propose that foreign investment become a central driver of growth. Nevertheless, in the internal debates during the drafting of the guidelines, the pro-reform drafters did manage to insert some positive language recognizing the potential contributions of FDI: "access to advanced technology, the transfer of management skills, a diversification and expansion of export markets, import substitution, the generation of new employment," and access to external finance.[11] This promising language eventually found its way into the 2014 foreign investment law, Law 118.

The more orthodox thinkers within the government and the PCC seem to have had the upper hand in drafting the section on foreign investment. The conservatives inserted language revealing their enduring distrust of foreign capital and underscored the need to carefully screen projects, as well as to monitor closely those projects that are allowed to proceed:

• Foreign capital is categorized as a "supplement" to national savings. While under any likely scenario domestic savings will indeed exceed foreign capital inflows, economists in Havana interpreted the "supplemental" label as demoting FDI to a secondary, nonessential role in economic planning. (In contrast, reformers such as Marino Murillo, minister of the economy and planning and chief of the Economic Reform Commission, have placed greater emphasis on FDI.)

- Foreign investments should be carefully screened to be "consistent with the National Economic Plan" and "to make sure that the foreign capital satisfies a host of objectives."

- The guidelines suggest that foreign investments be subject to both external and domestic performance requirements. Foreign-owned firms should purchase goods and services supplied by Cuban companies, as specified in their right-to-operate contracts.

- Approved projects should be subject to continuous and rigorous monitoring, to ensure that the foreign partner is observing its commitments. Existing partnerships should face "assessment and adjustment," to ensure consistency "with the country's requirements."

- A time limit should be set for approved foreign investments to commence operations, "to avoid their continued utilization of resources indefinitely with a resulting increase in inefficiency."

Amid these cautionary notes, the guidelines do contain some positive news for potential foreign investors. The guidelines call for "more expedient" assessment and approval procedures. Investments that target the domestic market rather than the high-priority export sector should nevertheless be considered where they provide "indispensable" products or substitute for imports. Special development zones that attract FDI and promote exports and high-tech projects should be created. The most important execution of this recommendation is the special development zone at Mariel (ZED Mariel), which later sections of this chapter detail.

The guidelines also call for an up-to-date portfolio of investment projects that might be of interest to foreign partners. After persistent expressions of interest from the diplomatic community in Havana, the Cuban Chamber of Commerce—whose leadership is appointed by the Ministry of International Commerce and Foreign Investment (MINCEX)—issued such a portfolio in December 2011. But the surprisingly short list broke little new ground and addressed a truncated number of sectors. The portfolio advertised these options: in tourism, three hotel sites, two of which could include golf courses; in petroleum, risk-sharing exploration contracts in Cuba's Exclusive Economic Zone in the Gulf of Mexico; in mining, a small nickel/cobalt refinery; in energy, projects in wind and solar; and in packaging, seven potential small joint ventures. Rather than signal a renewed interest in attracting foreign investment, the chamber's portfolio seemed to confirm that many Cuban economic planners saw FDI as at best a secondary supplement to more promising sources of growth. But much more encouraging (notwithstanding its own internal tensions) was the more fully elaborated "Portfolio of Opportunities for Foreign Investment" released in 2014 and amended in 2015, which will be examined shortly. The distance travelled between the 2011 and 2014–15 lists of offerings is striking, suggesting a gradual if still partial shift in power from the orthodox to the more reform-minded tendencies within the government and PCC, and encouraging to those who believe that only a concerted opening of the economy will bring greater prosperity to Cuba.

The Revised Legal Framework

As part of the post-Soviet economic opening, Cuba authorized a new foreign investment law (Law 77, 1995) that combined elements commonly included in national FDI frameworks with characteristics specific to the Cuban system. Law 118 of 2014 was a modestly modified version of Law 77 that contained several additional incentives to attract foreign investors. In its preamble, Law 118 affirms FDI's potential benefits: FDI will allow the country "to realize a sustainable development, to access external finance, technology and new markets, and to insert Cuban products and services into international supply chains and generate other positive effects for our domestic industry."[12]

Like its predecessor, Law 77, Law 118 stipulates that FDI may take the form of JVs with state firms or may be fully foreign owned.[13] Investors enjoy full protection against expropriation, "except for reasons of public utility or social interest" in which case they will be indemnified, and have the right to appeal to a mutually agreed-upon international investment dispute resolution entity.[14] Litigation over other disputes between FDI and state-owned enterprises (SOEs) or government entities is referred to the jurisdiction of national courts.

All sectors of the economy are open to FDI, excluding only health and education services and the armed forces (but not excluding the military's business enterprises). FDI firms can import and export directly (that is, without passing through a state wholesale company).

After exercising an eight-year exemption from profit taxes, FDI firms then must pay income taxes at a 15 percent rate of net taxable income (versus 30 percent under the old law), although reinvested income can be exempt if so authorized by the government. The old 11 percent wage tax was eliminated, but the 14 percent social security contribution remains. Profits and dividends are freely transferable abroad in convertible currency.

The legal regime governing FDI has permitted broad official discretion. In the mid-1990s the government welcomed and approved many JVs. But beginning in 2003, without any formal legal alterations, the government began to rigorously review existing firms and closed many that failed to meet its shifting standards, which now favored larger over smaller businesses and foreign SOEs over private partners.

With Law 118, it remains to be seen whether the amendments to the foreign investment regime signal—both to the foreign investment community and to the state bureaucrats who screen investor applications—a major change in attitude toward FDI. Will foreign investment remain under a cloud of nationalist suspicion and bureaucratic discretion, or will it be widely perceived as a welcome driver of national prosperity?

The Laborious Approval Process

Law 118, like its predecessor, requires formal approval by the Cuban government of each proposed investment. Authorized JVs must be registered with Cuba's Chamber of Commerce. But the registry is not made available to the general public (although copies are known to circulate informally). Similarly, FDI firms must submit an annual report to the government, but the submissions remain confidential.

For interested investors, an especially irritating peculiarity of the Cuban FDI system is the prolonged multilayered approval process. Except for some minor ventures that may be approved at the ministerial level, FDI proposals must gain the approval of the very top levels of government, either by the Council of Ministers or the Council of State. Reportedly, Raúl Castro himself must sign off on major projects. But first the foreign investor must draw up its application with its proposed SOE partner and the relevant ministry and present that request to the MINCEX and its Business Evaluation Commission. Second, MINCEX must then consult with all the corresponding agencies and institutions, which typically include the pertinent sectoral ministry, the powerful Ministry of Economy and Planning, the influential Ministry of Finance and Prices, the Central Bank, and the Ministries of Labor and Environment. Third, subsequent to these broad consultations, if MINCEX is favorably disposed, it makes a recommendation to the Executive Committee of the Council of Ministers (CECM), which is composed of several national vice presidents and pertinent ministers and formally chaired by President Castro.[15] Fourth, according to legal experts familiar with these procedures, the CECM normally accepts the recommendation of MINCEX, although CECM has been known to refer a proposal back to MINCEX for further elaboration.

This demanding screening process could be admired for its inclusiveness, but it also contains a plethora of veto points and opportunities for bureaucratic or politically motivated delays. In the past applicants complained that the process was a nontransparent black box, denying access to many of the decisionmakers or even knowledge as to which personalities were at the table. Many applications have simply languished unanswered; moreover, MINCEX has not felt obliged to provide a written ruling to applicants and may or may not offer an oral explanation. Once an application reaches the senior approval level, Law 118 (like its predecessor, Law 77) requires that applications be acted upon within 45 days; it remains to be seen whether the multilayered bureaucracy can indeed move paper with greater alacrity than in the past.

Law 77 allowed for 100 percent foreign ownership. Yet only half a dozen or so such wholly foreign-owned firms exist today: three in petroleum and energy, two in maritime transport, and one in the financial sector.[16] (In a possible departure from this trend, ZED Mariel in 2015 approved several small foreign investments with 100 percent foreign ownership.) Underscoring the wide degree of bureaucratic discretion in the foreign investment regime, government functionaries have chosen to largely ignore an important option that dominates FDI in most countries, which would allow foreign investments independent of Cuban SOEs. Interestingly, Law 118 permits joint ventures with state-owned enterprises, private farmers, and nonfarm cooperatives, but not with private entrepreneurs (*cuentapropistas*).

Another curious feature of the Cuban system is that FDI ventures are approved for a fixed time period—as short as 15 years—upon which time the contract is terminated, unless it is renewed by joint agreement of the parties and the government. As some FDI firms have discovered, renewal is anything but automatic, and the government may seek to alter the contract terms in fundamental respects. As we shall see in the contested case of the

Dutch-British multinational Unilever (chapter 5), the shifting demands of the Cuban state have sometimes set a bar too high.

In principle, the Cuban authorities have honored the prohibition against expropriation without compensation guaranteed in Law 77 (chapter 3, article 3) and reaffirmed in Law 118.[17] But many FDI firms have been closed when the state did not renew its contract, or, more precipitously, when the state placed the firm in an untenable position and forced the sale of shares to the state. The government has also seized the property of shareholders accused of corruption, as in the dramatic case of the successful fruit-juice manufacturing and distribution firm Rio Zaza (discussed in chapter 5).

The World's Heaviest Tax on Labor

An unusual characteristic of the Cuban FDI regime is the labor contract system. FDI firms are not generally allowed to directly hire labor. Rather, a state employment agency—typically a dependency of the relevant sectoral ministry (for example, tourism, light industry)—hires, fires, settles labor disputes, establishes wage scales, and pays the wages directly to the workers. The foreign investor pays the wage bill to the state employment agency, which in turn pays the workers. But there is a very special twist to the Cuban system: the investing company pays wages to the employment agency in hard currency, and the employment agency turns around and compensates the workers in local currency, an effective devaluation or tax of 24 to 1.[18] Thus, if the firm pays the employment agency $500 a month and the employment agency pays the workers CUP 500, over 90 percent of the wage payment slides into the state treasury; the effective compensation is instantly deflated to $21 per month. This could be the world's heaviest labor tax. It provoked one Cuban worker to remark informally to me: "In Cuba, it's a great myth that we live off the state. In fact, it's the state that lives off of us."

This labor system, which authorizes only one national union (Confederation of Cuban Workers, closely allied with the PCC), also violates many principles of the International Labor Organization, of which Cuba is a charter member. Most distressing for the average Cuban worker, it freezes Cuba into a low-wage, low-productivity trap: low wages deprive workers of positive incentives to raise their productivity, and their low productivity depresses their wages.[19] Low wages also dampen household purchasing power, to the detriment of business sales and economic expansion.[20]

The Business Climate

What drives the international investment decisions of firms? The literature devoted to explaining the over $1 trillion in annual worldwide equity investment flows differentiates among three major categories of investments: resource-seeking investments, efficiency-seeking investments, and market-seeking investments. All three categories are, or could be, relevant to Cuba:

• Cuba's natural resources include its inviting tropical climate, world-class vacation destinations, deepwater ports, valuable minerals (nickel, cobalt, and possibly petroleum), nontraditional energy sources (sun, wind, and waves), and arable soils.

• Efficiency-seeking investments are often attracted by relatively low-cost, competitive wages. Cuba could score in two categories: highly educated professionals with relatively low wages, and low-wage workers with relatively good education and hence favorable cost/productivity ratios. Still, Cuba would first have to overhaul its tax policies that elevate labor costs.

• The Cuban domestic market is modest in size but still interesting to some firms, including those multinationals compulsively seeking a presence in every market worldwide. For countries located in the Caribbean basin, the relevant export market is first and foremost the United States— not yet an option for firms operating in Cuba. Once U.S. sanctions are lifted some multinationals will use Cuba as a regional hub, serving the neighboring islands as well as the southeast United States.

Increasingly, literature on FDI focuses on what might be called the demand side: public policies of the receiving countries that affect the decisions of investors. Without negating the above-cited factors driving investment supply, governments should recognize that public policies "can tip the balance in favor of one country over another if all other factors are equal."[21] In *Investing Across Borders,* the World Bank presents cross-country indicators for practices, laws, and regulations affecting FDI in 87 economies.[22] While Cuba (which is not a member of the World Bank) is not included, the results of this survey are instructive; they indicate just how much of an outlier Cuba has become with regard to the treatment of foreign investment.

The 2010 edition of *Investing Across Borders* surveyed 14 Latin American and Caribbean countries.[23] Among the relevant findings for the region:

• *None* of the 14 countries requires special approval procedures for foreign, as opposed to domestic, investment. That is, foreign investment is granted "national treatment."

- Most economic sectors are fully open to FDI. In tourism, light manufacturing, construction, and retail, the 14 countries place *no* limits on foreign equity ownership. A few countries (Bolivia, Haiti, and Mexico) impose restrictions in banking, insurance, and telecommunications. Some countries protect their electricity sector.

- Starting a foreign business from scratch typically takes under six months, except in Haiti where it takes seven months. For example, it takes only two months in Costa Rica and 29 days in Chile.

- Countries around the world with smaller populations and markets tend to have *fewer* restrictions on FDI. Large countries—like China and Brazil—can offer their expanding domestic markets as bait to investors. In comparison, smaller economies, like Cuba, must compete more aggressively and make good use of the public policy tools at their disposal.

But Cuba, as noted above, seems to be doing the opposite. It requires all applications for FDI to pass through a complex and nontransparent review process, raising obstacles not present in many other Latin American and Caribbean countries. One key conclusion of the 2010 *Investing Across Borders* survey particularly relevant to Cuba's future: "Easily accessible and reliable information and efficient and predictable actions by public institutions help create a business environment conducive to investment."

Foreign Trade and Development Zones: Learning from Past Mistakes?

On the heels of the 1995 Foreign Investment Act, which aimed "to broaden and facilitate foreign participation in the nation's economy," Cuba introduced Decree-Law 165, establishing a framework for industrial free trade zones.[24] To attract assembly manufacturing that would create jobs and boost exports, the free trade zone law offered the standard mix of incentives common to free trade zones worldwide, including exemptions from tariffs and taxes for 12 years and unimpeded transfers of profits. While the main goal was to stimulate exports, investors were permitted to market up to 25 percent of production in the Cuban market.

To implement Decree-Law 165, Cuban authorities quickly opened four free trade zones, two in the Havana region (Berroa and Wajay) and one each at the port facilities of Mariel and Cienfuegos. A holding company of the Cuban military, Almacenes Universales S.A., was granted the concession to administer three of the free trade zones (Wajay, Mariel, and

Cienfuegos), while the fourth was awarded to CIMEX—the large state-owned enterprise in wholesale distribution and retail marketing.

Initially the government trumpeted the number of firms opening operations in the free trade zone. By the end of 1999, for example, the government reported there were 220 free trade zone operators hailing from 26 countries—notably Spain, Italy, Canada, Panama, and Mexico. By May 2000 the number was said to have jumped to 237 operators, with more than 23 others awaiting approval.[25] But it turned out that most of these firms were engaged not in manufactured exports, but rather in services and storage. In some cases, they were engaged in selling into the domestic market under special exemptions granted by Cuban authorities. The government reported that of 243 free trade zone enterprises registered at the time, 160 were trading companies and 49 were in the service sector, but only 39 were in manufacturing.[26]

Gradually the free trade zone experiment was abandoned, and in 2004 the free trade zones were relabeled special development zones and given an even more ambitious goal: the promotion of higher-value-added production. In fact, the free trade zones were closed or allowed to lie fallow. The permits granted to trading and service companies in the free trade zones were quietly revoked, and businesses were closed or transferred outside of the free trade zones.

Why the stark failure of the free trade zone experiment? Free trade zones work on the basis of two key incentives: lower production costs, usually based on relatively cheap labor, and access to external markets secured either through preferential trading arrangements (such as free trade agreements) or commercial channels opened through intrafirm transfers or supply chains. But Cuba offered neither of these key investment drivers: access to the major market dictated by geography—the United States—was closed by U.S. sanctions; and Cuban labor costs were dramatically inflated by the prohibitive government tax on labor. A 2000 United Nations study estimated the costs to free trade zone employers of Cuban labor at an average $1.75 per hour, versus $0.94 per hour in the neighboring Dominican Republic, and $0.50 to $0.75 per hour in Central America.[27] The Cuban government had simply priced itself out of the market.

Today, the Cuban government has launched a new initiative, the ZED Mariel, a combined special development zone and container port facility. It is not a free trade zone per se but rather has features typically associated with free trade zones: more favorable trade and tax treatments.

Mariel is being built by the Brazilian firm Odebrecht assisted by a Brazilian government line of credit, and is being operated by PSA International of Singapore. The official ribbon cutting for ZED Mariel was rushed to accommodate the January 2014 visit of Brazilian president Dilma Rousseff and occurred before basic infrastructure such as utility connections were in place. But during 2015 the Cuban Union of Military Construction (UCM) of the Ministry of the Armed Forces mobilized hundreds of workers equipped with Chinese machinery to prepare production sites. Nevertheless, it will now fall to the individual investors, who will be granted long-term leases on the land, to construct their own facilities.

Firms operating at ZED Mariel will continue to pay the wages of the workers to the relevant sectoral employment agencies at roughly the same rates as established in the JV contracts, or about $800–$900 per month on average. However, the regulations promise an important reduction in the implicit labor tax, such that the wages paid by the official employment entity to the workers will rise significantly, from the roughly $53 per month received by workers employed by JVs outside the zone to as much as $266 per month inside the zone.[28] According to ZED Mariel officials, the higher wages are intended to attract and retain a productive and stable labor force.

The nearby U.S. market remains closed to Cuban products unless produced by the emergent private sector, which is not yet being admitted to Mariel. In the meantime, the port facility is being dredged to allow for the very large container ships that will soon be sailing through the enlarged Panama Canal. Clearly the anticipation is that the containers will be off-loaded for transport to the Gulf Coast and Eastern Seaboard of the United States.

According to ZED Mariel officials, their planning allows for two scenarios: development without and development with the opening of the U.S. market. "We know the moment will arrive, we just don't know when," one ZED Mariel official confided.[29]

Estimating FDI Flows

Assessing foreign investment in Cuba is complicated by the scarcity of data. The Cuban government's culture of secrecy takes on extreme form when it addresses international capital flows. Incredibly, Cuba simply does not publish a capital account! Cuba releases no numbers on capital inflows or outflows, nor is there an official accounting of foreign reserves. And

Table 4-1. Foreign Investment Inflows to Cuba, 1993–2001

US$ millions

Year	Annual flow	Cumulative
1993	54.0	54.0
1994[a]	563.4	617.4
1995	4.7	622.1
1996	82.1	704.2
1997	442.0	1,146.2
1998	206.6	1,352.8
1999	178.2	1,531.0
2000	448.1	1,979.1
2001	38.9	2,018.0

Sources: Oficina Nacional de Estadísticas e Información (ONEI), *Anuario Estadístico de Cuba,* 2002 and other years (http://www.one.cu/CatalogoPublicaciones.html); and Jorge F. Pérez-López, "The Rise and Fall of Foreign Investment in Cuba," *Cuban Affairs Journal* 3, no. 1 (February 2008), 25 (www.cubanaffairsjournal.org).

a. The reported flows jumped in 1994, when the government decided to fold in flows from years prior to 1993.

offerings within the current account that record capital-related flows are presented in highly aggregate form: there is but one line for *renta* (income), which includes transactions (both outgoing and incoming) on interest, dividends, and profits, "among others."[30]

When pressed for an explanation, the Cuban government points to U.S. hostility, affirming that the U.S. Treasury might take advantage of greater transparency to harass Cuba's economic partners or seize Cuban assets. These fears may well be justified, demonstrating yet again how U.S. sanctions have engendered precisely the behavior pattern—in this case, extraordinary state secrecy—that the United States decries. In spaces where Cuba apparently feels less threatened, such as social indicators, or even the direction and composition of merchandise trade, statistics are made more readily available.

For a brief period, between 1993 and 2001, the Cuban government did publish some limited, highly aggregated data on foreign investment flows. Cumulatively, reported flows through 2001 totaled $2 billion (table 4-1).

This useful series was discontinued after 2001, when another emerging option caught Cuba's attention: the availability of state-owned capital in countries, notably Venezuela and China, which offered certain advantages from the Cuban perspective. As discussed in the previous chapter, these friendly powers were prepared to offer capital on subsidized terms and in ideologically comfortable state-to-state deals. These state-to-state deals are notoriously nontransparent and often not reported to the international agencies that track FDI. Thus it is extremely difficult to estimate actual investment flows; it is difficult to disentangle announcements, commitments, and on-the-ground implementation; and it is difficult to decipher whether the deal is structured in the form of equity (wholly owned or joint venture), as an arms-length service contract, or as a production-sharing agreement (often the case in the petroleum sector). The capital flows may not qualify as FDI at all, but rather as state banking loans. This has been the case with the Brazilian involvement in the Mariel port expansion and in the renovation of a sugar refinery in Cienfuegos Province—projects often erroneously labeled in the media as "investments."

Perhaps the best-informed estimate of the stock of Cuban FDI comes from an international financial consultant (who wished to remain anonymous) with privileged access to foreign investment data. This source noted that according to the Cuban Central Bank, FDI inflows as of 2001 totaled $1.9 billion (very close to the published figure of $2.02 billion, table 4-1) and further estimated that by 2009 the total stock may have reached $3.5 billion. The consultant added another telling estimate: 20 investors accounted for nearly $3 billion of the $3.5 billion; indeed, the top 10 investors accounted for the lion's share.

Joint Ventures: Number and Size of Firms

Cuban economists working on FDI have made use of data not on dollar volume of FDI flows, but rather on the number of joint venture projects broken down by economic sector and country of origin. These project numbers are generally sourced to unpublished government documents and occasionally to press reports in the official Cuban media. The aggregate numbers do not indicate the capital value or strategic importance of the projects, and lump together significant investments with very small ventures, including tiny brokerage firms. Nor do they make clear whether the investments are merely indications of intentions or whether capital has actually been transferred. They also lump together the top 20 JVs, which account for the lion's share of capital, with another 200 small to micro JVs. Even so, the aggregate numbers are extraordinarily small: as of 2011, the total number of joint projects stood at 245.[31] These 245 projects included

67 hotel administration contracts, 8 production and service administration contracts, and 13 production cooperation agreements. Moreover, not all of these joint projects included private partners; some hail from Venezuela as the source country, and presumably many of these projects engage not private investors but rather Venezuelan state-owned enterprises.[32] Compare the number of JVs operating in Cuba with the much larger number of foreign affiliates operating in other countries of roughly comparable size and development: 911 in Chile; 754 in Croatia; 5,387 in Ireland; 2,761 in Malaysia; 5,144 in Portugal; and 2,049 in Taiwan.[33]

The number of joint projects in Cuba peaked in 2002 at just over 400, then fell by half by 2008. This consolidation occurred for several reasons. The Cuban state closed down many JVs, having concluded that they were not living up to their original promises, were not advancing Cuban economic goals, were losing money, or were behaving illegally.[34] Some firms withdrew upon finding it impossible to carry on a successful business within the context of Cuban state planning; firms entering during the heady reform years of the mid-1990s were taken aback when Fidel Castro decided to halt and even roll back some of those hopeful market-oriented measures. In some cases, Cuban state-owned enterprises did not welcome competition from private firms that had certain advantages, such as superior access to foreign credit and therefore to imported inputs, and so used their access to government agencies to squeeze the JVs; hapless JVs reported that their electricity rates or real estate rents suddenly spiked, gasoline was no longer delivered on time, visas were denied to international experts, access to critical foreign exchange was blocked, and so on. Students of the political economy of state planning would not be surprised to hear of SOEs leveraging their political networks to disable private competitors.

In 1998 the Cuban government announced as a matter of principle that it preferred large-scale JVs to smaller ones.[35] Apparently, this preference remains in place. Yet this bigger-is-better prejudice flies against contemporary trends in international economic thought, which argue the opposite: that small and medium-sized firms are often more innovative and more flexible than very large firms and employ more workers per dollar invested. Nor is it necessarily an either/or proposition, as larger firms can benefit from being surrounded by efficient, specialized smaller suppliers. The Cuban government's opposition to smaller JVs seems particularly odd at a time when it seeks to stimulate employment, increase the availability of consumer goods, and actively promote small-scale enterprise.

Joint Ventures: Employment, Sales, Exports

Citing internal government documents, Cuban sociologist Mayra Espina Prieto estimated that in 2006 JVs employed 0.7 percent of the state's 4.9 million person workforce, or about 34,000 people, while a recent estimate suggested "more than 40,000."[36] These rather small numbers seems plausible, considering that some of the larger JVs are located in capital-intense mining and energy (Sherritt International), or else in international marketing (Habanos, Pernod Ricard), which has sales forces primarily located overseas and which does not directly employ the producers of tobacco or rum. Nor does this estimate take into account the large numbers of workers in hotels that are owned by Cuban SOEs but managed by foreign firms under hotel administration contracts.[37]

Some JVs are strategically placed in the vital export sector. According to Cuban economist Omar Everleny Pérez Villanueva (based upon his access to unpublished data), JVs accounted for $1.9 billion in exports in goods and services in 2008. He attributed 80 percent of these exports to just seven firms. Pérez Villanueva places these businesses in nickel, tobacco, citrus fruits, beverages, tourism, and communications, among others.[38] Based on the high degree of industrial concentration, these firms can be identified as Sherritt International (nickel), Habanos (British Imperial Tobacco, cigars), Havana Club (rum, beverages), Rio Zaza and BM (citrus fruits), and Meliá (tourism).[39] These businesses are the subject of the case studies in chapter 5.

De Facto Excluded Sectors

Law 118, like its predecessor, Law 77, allows for FDI in all sectors except health, education, and "the armed forces institutions, with the exception of the latter's commercial system." In practice, JVs have also been excluded from two sectors where foreign investors could make a huge contribution: sugar and biotechnology.[40] In the case of sugar production, the obstacles appear to be rooted in Cuba's revolutionary history. The expropriations of the large, often foreign-owned estates were a hallmark of the revolution; to return the land to foreign hands might seem an inglorious retreat. There is also the unresolved question of compensation to the former owners, necessary to free the lands from potential legal challenges by claimants and U.S. sanctions. Today, as officials reconsider FDI within the context of economic reforms, there is a sharp debate over whether and to what degree to further open food processing and agro-industry, including sugar-based biomass, to external capital. In an apparent victory for more favorable treatment for FDI after lengthy negotiations in late 2012, the Cuban government approved a joint venture, Biopower S.A., with British investors, to generate biomass from sugar derivatives; the roughly $50 million investment was to construct a 30 megawatt power plant.[41] The project has since been taken over by the U.K.-based Esencia Group, in a joint venture between Esencia's Havana Energy and Zerus, affiliated with Azcuba, the state sugar industrial group. The project was slated to begin operations in 2016.

In the case of biotechnology, government officials voice fears that foreign partners will take advantage of Cuban firms and pirate their innovations. Cuba's Biotechnological and Pharmaceutical Industries Group (BioCubaFarma) controls 16 enterprises that employ 21,000 people. But rather than turn to the European and Japanese multinational pharmaceutical giants to assist in marketing Cuban innovations and pharmaceutical products, Cuba has preferred both to seek state-to-state commercial deals with developing countries (notably Venezuela) and to attempt JVs abroad (notably in China), where Cuban firms are the foreign investors.[42] Cuba has had some success with these strategies, reporting pharmaceutical exports as surpassing $550 million (2012),[43] but has had great difficulty accessing promising markets in Europe, Latin America, and much of Asia. Yet it still chooses to avoid the pharmaceutical multinationals, whose knowledge of national patent regimes and distribution networks could take the Cuban biotech sector to another level of success.

In a sign of the thaw in U.S.-Cuban relations, the Roswell Park Cancer Institute located in Buffalo, New York, has entered into a collaborative relationship with Cuba's Center for Molecular Immunology (CIM).[44] To legally undertake this collaboration, Roswell Park obtained a license from the U.S. government (the Office of Assets Control within the U.S. Treasury). Roswell Park will partner with CIM to run clinical trials in the United States on promising CIM discoveries, including CIMA-Vax, a lung cancer vaccine that CIM claims extends life from 7 to 14 months for patients with advanced lung cancer. The vaccine is inexpensive and easy to administer. This could be a first step by Cuba's pharmaceutical cluster in reaching out to international marketing opportunities.

Also largely excluded from FDI opportunities are financial firms; state-owned banks retain a monopoly over most financial transactions. A legacy

Table 4-2. International Banks with Representative Offices in Cuba

Bank	Country of origin
Banco Sabadell	United Kingdom
Bankia	Spain
BBVA	Spain
BCPE International et Outre-Mer	France
Fransabanc	Lebanon
Havin Bank Ltd.	United Kingdom
National Bank of Canada	Canada
Republic Bank Ltd.	Trinidad and Tobago
Scotiabank	Canada

Sources: Banco Central de Cuba, "Sistema Bancario" (http:www.bc.gob.cu/Espanol/sist_bancario.asp); Fernando Capablanca, "Historical Importance of Cuba and Development of Cuba's Financial System from 1950 to 2015," slide presentation prepared for annual conference of Caribbean Central America Action (CCAA), Miami, November 16, 2015.

of the Soviet planning model, capital markets are severely repressed in Cuba. Those international banks allowed to open representative offices in Cuba (table 4-2) are generally restricted to international transactions that serve client needs.

FDI in Comparative Perspective

In countries roughly comparable to Cuba in size, or in those that share other similar characteristics, FDI flows have made substantial contributions over the last two decades. From 1990 to 2013–14, years in which Cuba was attracting altogether roughly $3.5 billion–$4.0 billion in FDI, Costa Rica attracted $22 billion, the Dominican Republic $27 billion, and Chile $199 billion (table 4-3). In Chile, the percentage of the population living in poverty was cut in half during those two decades. With a population under 3 million and persistent political unrest and criminal violence, Jamaica attracted over $10 billion. One Asian nation especially pertinent to Cuba, Vietnam, attracted over $80 billion. (Socialist Vietnam, like Cuba, retains a strong state presence in the economy and remains a one-party state). Ireland is also interesting, as it took advantage of its relatively well-educated workforce and access to European markets to attract over $250 billion in FDI. Of interest nowadays to other developing countries seeking to attract

Table 4-3. Inflows of FDI in Selected Countries, 1990–2013/2014[a]

Country	Cumulative FDI (US$ billions)	Average inflows/ GDP (percent)	Cumulative per capita FDI inflows
Chile	199	6.1	12,339
Costa Rica	22	4.1	5,277
Croatia[b]	34	4.1	8,001
Dominican Republic	27	3.3	2,531
Ireland	252	11.2	102,787
Jamaica	11	4.4	4,121
Malaysia	134	4.3	4,361
Nicaragua	7	4.5	1,297
Vietnam	82	5.9	897

Sources: For cumulative FDI: UNCTADstat, "Foreign Direct Investment: Inward and Outward Flows and Stock, Annual, 1980–2014" (http://unctadstat.unctad.org/wds/ReportFolders/reportFolders.aspx).

For inflows/GDP: World Bank, World Development Indicators, "Foreign Direct Investment, Net Inflows (% of GDP)" (http://data.worldbank.org/indicator/BX.KLT.DINV.WD.GD.ZS).

For per capita FDI inflows: World Bank, World Development Indicators, "Foreign Direct Investment, Net Inflows (BoP, current US$)" (http://data.worldbank.org/indicator/BX.KLT.DINV.CD.WD/countries).

a. Population data are from 2014 and FDI inflows are cumulative from 1990 to 2013.

b. For Croatia, data for cumulative FDI flow are available from 1993; data for FDI inflows as a percentage of GDP are available from 1992.

high-tech FDI with proactive investment promotion policies, Malaysia attracted over $130 billion, or over $4,000 per capita (as compared to Cuba's roughly $300 per capita).

In nearly all developing countries, most savings and investment are domestic in origin, yet FDI can still make a significant contribution. From 1990 to 2013–14, FDI as a percentage of total investment equaled about 6 percent in Chile, 4 percent in Costa Rica, 3 percent in the Dominican Republic, 11 percent in Ireland, 4 percent in Jamaica, nearly 5 percent in Nicaragua, and 6 percent in Vietnam (table 4-3).

To its own detriment, Cuba has largely neglected an important source of badly needed capital. Let us imagine Cuba had allowed FDI inflows equal to 5 percent of its GDP (the average for the countries in table 4-3) during the decade from 2000 to 2009, or roughly $2.5 billion a year. In that scenario, Cuba would have absorbed some $25 billion—many times the existing JV capital stock accumulated over two decades. The associated technology, management skills, and access to export markets could have transformed the business climate, catalyzed an atmosphere of dynamic change, and helped to elevate Cuba toward a sustainable growth path.

Open for Business: 246 Opportunities for Foreign Investment

In November 2014 the Cuban government issued a public appeal to international companies to invest over $8 billion in 246 specified development projects. The 168-page "Portfolio of Opportunities for Foreign Investment" offered fascinating insights into the current distressed state of the Cuban economy and into the competing development visions of its economic planners.[45] Within the lengthy document, there are many assessments and proposals that suggest that Cuban authorities are prepared to dramatically open their economy to international capital, yet there are also many provisos that suggest a much more cautious strategy.

This is not the first time the Cuban authorities have issued a wish list of projects open to foreign firms, but this edition is much more ambitious and reveals dramatic progress—and tensions—in officials' thinking about their nation's economic future. Careful reading of the publication, prepared by the Ministry of Foreign Trade and Investment, will leave potential foreign investors with few illusions: Cuba will remain a state-driven economy dominated by large government holding companies, and the authorities will dictate the direction and pace of change. Most foreign ventures will come with majority Cuban ownership. But it is refreshing to find this admission: "The growth rates of Cuba's GDP have been moderate and low, lower than the average for the region. In order to turn this trend around, accumulation rates higher than 20% are required to permit a GDP growth rhythm increase of 5 to 7 percent."[46] (Oddly, the details in this second sentence are omitted in the original Spanish version.) Given that current national investment rates have fallen to under 10 percent, to fill the gap annual foreign investment inflows must exceed by a large margin the $2.0 billion–$2.5 billion publicly proposed by the minister of foreign trade and investment, Rodrigo Malmierca.

The government publication provides remarkably frank, data-rich surveys, sector by sector, of current production capabilities and shortfalls—a must-read for specialists in the Cuban economy. It signals clear development priorities: energy (conventional and renewables), agriculture, and tourism (table 4-4). A consensus on priorities was probably easy to reach: tourism offers the only ready medium-term option for rapid growth in badly needed hard-currency earnings; Cuba is spending way too much of its scarce foreign exchange on food imports—creating a genuine food security crisis; and investment in domestic energy production is critical to lessen a dangerous dependence on a faltering Venezuela.

Table 4-4. Business Opportunities by Sector, outside ZED Mariel

Sector	Number of projects
Agro-food	32
Sugar industry	4
Wholesale business	1
Construction	6
Renewable energy	13
Industry	10
Mining	10
Oil	86
Transportation	3
Tourism	56
Total	221

Source: MINCEX, "Portfolio of Opportunities for Foreign Investment," 2014 (www.caribbean-council.org/wp-content/uploads/2014/11/Cuba-foreign-investment-projects-Nov-2014-official.pdf).

Tourism: Management Contracts and Golf Condo Destinations

The portfolio's tourism section is particularly revealing of the internal tensions among Cuban policy planners: many attractive projects are juxtaposed with well-delineated boundaries on the scope of foreign investment.

The potential tourism projects are sketched in striking detail. Cuba would like to build 21 new hotels in the Cienfuegos, Trinidad, Guardalavaca, Playa Santa Lucía, and Covarrubias areas. The state companies that own hotels throughout the island are seeking new management contracts, 19 for new hotels and 14 for existing hotels and facilities.[47]

Of particular interest to investors who might like to own condos on Cuban golf courses: a new government entity (belonging to the Palmares holding company), CubaGolf, will "promote the island as a golf-holiday destination." CubaGolf is currently in negotiations with several foreign partners to form joint ventures to build and manage tourism–golf condo complexes. One such potential joint venture in Holguín Province has a $380 million price tag and would boast two 18-hole golf courses, a five-star hotel with 170 rooms, and 1,300 housing units available for "in perpetuity" purchase (land ownership will not be transferable). Nightly hotel rates are estimated at $130 for a couple, and a game of golf will be priced at $70–$85.

Yet the government is setting aside some of the juiciest tourism opportunities for itself. In the high-return–low-risk locations of urban Havana and Varadero beaches, investor participation "will be the exception." The safe yields are reserved for state-owned firms, especially Gaviota (linked to the armed forces), which the document proudly remarks "is the fastest growing hotel holding company." Gaviota will restrict its foreign partners to management contracts and will demand that the partner provide not only construction financing but also international marketing, to ensure profitable occupancy rates. For example, Gaviota will own the luxury 200-room five-star hotel occupying the historic Gómez-Mena building complex, contracting the Swiss hotel chain Kempinski to manage the flagship enterprise when it opens in late 2016, and Gaviota will also develop the prized properties of the Prado, Malecón, and Packard hotels.[48] As highlighted during President Obama's March 2016 visit, Starwood Hotels and Resorts will manage the Hotel Quinta Avenida in Havana's fashionable Miramar district and a property owned by Gaviota.

Agriculture: Burdensome Restrictions

The agricultural policies outlined in the portfolio also suggest compromises between those planners who see the value of international engagement and private enterprise and those who fear that too many concessions risk undermining state controls as well as endangering the profitability of state-owned enterprises.

The section on agriculture makes this startling admission: of 6.3 million hectares of agricultural land, only 2.6 million hectares are being cultivated—despite years of official efforts to lure Cubans back to the land. But the document does not explore the adverse incentive structures responsible for this national catastrophe. Rather, it states that the nation's agro-industry is controlled by three large holding companies (GEIA, Cubaron, and Coralsa) overseeing 108 enterprises. Most land is firmly owned by the state, allowing just 15 percent for private farmers and another 7 percent for farmer cooperatives.

Nevertheless, Cuba now seeks joint ventures in cattle, pork, and poultry production, as well as in citrus, peanuts, and shrimp farming. Cuba would also welcome a foreign partner willing to invest $10.3 million to create a "leading brand on the international level" of premium coffee, grown in selected microregions in the hills of Guantánamo Province. Other opportunities in agro-industry include greenhouses for vegetables, hog production, soy processing, confectionary facilities, and dry yeast production.

Table 4-5. Business Opportunities in Industrial Sector, outside ZED Mariel

Project	Estimated investment (US$ millions)
Radial tires	223
Glass bottles	70
Aluminum cans	40
Footwear	20
Air conditioning units	15
Glassware	10
Subtotal	378

Source: MINCEX, "Portfolio of Opportunities for Foreign Investment," 2014.

Yet the sugar industry, however depressed, will remain firmly in the hands of the Cuban state. Only four mills will be open to foreign management contracts, expanding on the earlier management contract signed with a Brazilian firm to upgrade a sugar mill in Cienfuegos. The modest aim of each $40 million investment is "to recover" historic production levels.

The agricultural project list explicitly bars foreign investment from the tobacco and cigar industries (cigar marketing already being in the hands of Imperial Tobacco). Also excluded is lobster fishing and processing.

Energy and Industry Offerings

In the critical energy sector, Cuba is wide open to joint ventures in extracting petroleum from onshore and offshore blocks. But the goal is to raise the percentage of electricity produced from renewable sources from the current 4 percent to 24 percent by 2030. Foreign participation is welcome in hydro, biomass, and solar—and, exceptionally, Cuba will allow 100 percent foreign ownership in wind farms; it seeks investment of $285 million to generate 174 megawatts in Guantánamo Province and investment of $200 million to generate 102 megawatts in Holguín Province. These energy ventures, whether partially or fully foreign owned, will have to sell their output at prefixed prices to state distribution systems.

The proposed portfolio includes a wish list for joint ventures in industrial production. Foreign capital is sought in the industrial projects listed in table 4-5.

Cuban consumers have suffered from shortages of beer and soda, for reasons rarely explained by the authorities. Now there is a strong hint at the

Table 4-6. Business Opportunities in Mariel Special Development Zone

Sector	Number of projects
Biotech + pharmaceutical	13
Industry	6
Agro-industry	5
Energy	1
Total	25

Source: MINCEX, "Portfolio of Opportunities for Foreign Investment," 2014.

cause: shortages of aluminum cans! The proposed portfolio of investments features a joint venture ($21.8 million) to produce 577 million cans, the principal clients being two existing joint ventures: the beer firm Bucanero (In-Bev) and the bottled water and soda company Los Portales (Nestlé).

Cuba would also like foreign investors to help produce desktop computers and tablets. Current annual demand is estimated at a remarkably modest 75,000 computers (for a population of over 11 million), although this will rise to approximately 1 million in 10 years.

The Mariel Special Development Zone

As noted above, Cuba is opening the Mariel Special Development Zone west of Havana, facing the Florida Straits.[49] Supplementing Law 118, regulations governing Mariel promise some additional tax advantages, including a 10-year holiday on profit taxes followed by a 12 percent levy (versus 15 percent outside Mariel), exemptions from customs duties on capital goods imports, and greater flexibility in compensating employees. The material details will become apparent only once deals have been signed and firms are operating.

By the close of 2015, ZED Mariel had approved eight projects with a cumulative investment value of about $200 million, $120 million of which was accounted for by Brascuba, less a new investment than the transfer of the firm's cigarette factory from downtown Havana to a new, modern facility in Mariel.[50] ZED Mariel expects the approval of at least double the number of projects in 2016—that is, at least 16—with a cumulative value of at least $400 million.[51]

For ZED Mariel, the portfolio lists 25 export-oriented projects emphasizing medicine, agro-industry, and light industry (table 4-6).

Open for Business—but When?

As explained earlier, previous Cuban efforts to launch free trade zones floundered on the requirement of hiring expensive labor through government employment agencies and the continued closure of the most logical export market, the nearby United States. Eventually, Cuba will overcome these obstacles and render the "Open for Business" sign fully operational. The vexing question is when.

Overall, Cuba's portfolio combines enticing openings with many conditions and caveats:

• Firms must "guarantee" foreign markets, and their business plans must provide projections on the impact on the balance of payments.

• In the selection of foreign partners, the Cuban government will "favor the diversification of different countries."

• Privatization of state-held enterprises is ruled out (although the transformation of smaller state businesses into cooperatives in the service and construction sectors is proceeding apace).

• Foreign investment may partner with cooperatives but not with the emerging small-scale private enterprise. Readers searching the document for references to the much heralded self-employed *cuentapropistas* will be disappointed.

With its contradictory combination of frank analysis, attractive offerings, demanding requirements, and multiple barriers, the 2014 "Portfolio of Opportunities for Foreign Investment" opens an unusually transparent window into the ongoing struggles within the Cuban elites—those who wish to power ahead and integrate their economy into global capital and trading markets, those who adhere to the revolution's founding statist nationalism, and those who seek a middle road of carefully controlled change.

Missed Opportunities

To summarize the findings presented above: FDI added about $3.5–$4.0 billion to Cuban savings and investment over the last two decades or so, contributed handsomely to exports of goods and services, and accounted for roughly 7 percent of domestic output. JVs currently employ about 34,000–40,000 Cuban workers, or under 1 percent of the active labor force.

The flows of FDI to Cuba compare unfavorably to flows to other countries, whether countries of similar size and location in the Caribbean basin or in high-growth East Asia. In Cuba, the joint venture sector is small in terms of numbers of productive firms and numbers of Cuban workers employed. Yet in key export sectors, where foreign investors have been allowed to play a role, JVs have contributed critically to Cuba's economic survival. As the case studies in the next chapter make clear, once permitted to operate, JVs can be successful in the Cuban context. But whether by directly denying business permits to operate or by indirectly discouraging investors, the Cuban government has driven a wedge between Cuba and the vast ocean of savings circulating the globe and driving capital formation, technological diffusion, economic growth, and poverty reduction in developed and developing countries alike.

The new 2014 foreign investment law, the launching of the Mariel Special Development Zone, and the easing of tensions with the United States are all raising expectations of a new opening to foreign capital. In a few years the generation of the "*historicos*," the revolutionaries who descended from the Sierra Maestra to implant socialism in the tropics, will have departed power and passed the baton to successor generations. Sooner or later, Cuba will inevitably rejoin the global economy, of which it has been an integral part since the arrival of Christopher Columbus. In retrospect, the post-1959 revolutionary era of semi-autarkic development—with linkages to the Eastern European economic bloc led by the Soviet Union—will be seen as a historical aberration. The remaining questions are in what time frame and under what conditions will Cuba definitely reopen its gates to global business.

The Diaspora as Investors

The overseas Chinese and Vietnamese communities are two examples of diasporas that have made use of their kinship connections and cultural knowledge to help fund economic development in their home countries. As of the 2010 U.S. census, 1.8 million Cuban Americans live in the United States. Many of them have prospered and would invest in Cuba—if the two governments allowed them to do so under reasonable conditions.

According to Miami real estate lawyer Antonio Zamora, a Bay of Pigs veteran who has since traveled to Cuba dozens of times, there could be a booming condominium market for mainland investors and Cuban Americans looking to retire in a culturally comfortable environment that offers good health care and relatively inexpensive, secure living. Zamora also counts some 20 golf resort and boat marina projects on the drawing boards—of which four alone are cumulatively worth more than $1 billion—waiting for the green light from Cuban authorities.[52]

The future of investments by Cuban Americans is linked to Cuba's immigration rules, which currently deprive many émigrés of the right to own property. Senior Cuban government officials have been promising immigration reforms, which could set the stage for the release of pent-up Cuban American demand for housing and property on the island.

Through remittances, many Cuban Americans are already pumping money into their relatives' restaurants and other small businesses now authorized under the regime's policies for growing the nonstate sector (mini–private businesses, cooperatives, and private farms). U.S. sanctions do not yet permit investments—risk capital seeking a return—on the island, but do permit donations and (as of July 2015) in certain circumstances business loans. Today, the conditions under which remittances occur are known only to the parties to the transfer. They may lack formal legal protection, but as some Cuban Americans assert, "trust can be a stronger bond than written contracts." One informed Cuban American businessman estimated that some 80 percent of the larger *paladares* (restaurants) opening in Havana benefit from expatriate funding. Thus the September 2012 decision by the Cuban government to heavily tax gift parcels, including parcels containing materials for use by small businesses, was a setback to emerging private enterprise.[53]

Very few Cubans can accumulate savings from their meager salaries, and obligatory social celebrations quickly consume petty cash. Cuban state banks are accustomed to lending to medium- and large-scale enterprises, not to risky start-ups. New credit programs targeting the private sector have, so far, had very limited impact.[54] Hence aspiring Cuban entrepreneurs must rely on remittances or, in some cases, income earned during sojourns overseas. The financial constraint is a major obstacle to the blossoming of the small-scale private sector.

Under a project called Cuba Emprende, the Miami-based Cuba Study Group has partnered with the Catholic Church–affiliated Félix Varela Center to offer instruction to aspiring micro-entrepreneurs in subjects such as accounting, marketing, and composition of business plans. The project could be a prototype of cooperation between businesspersons in the diaspora and the emerging private sector on the island.

Larger investments by Cuban Americans, or by U.S.-based corporations, must await changes in regulations in both nations. The outstanding claims of properties expropriated in the early years of the revolution stand as another barrier to investment flows.[55]

As emphasized throughout this book, changes in legal frameworks, by themselves, will not be sufficient to unlock large-scale investment flows. Many U.S. individuals and firms will wait until they perceive a more attractive investment climate, with all that entails. Some Cuban Americans may exhibit a somewhat lower threshold, whether as the result of a "sentimental premium" or because they believe that their strong social networks, their "cultural capital," reduce their risks.

Joint Ventures in Cuba
Seven Case Studies

In the United States and in many other countries, observers benefit from large numbers of case studies of business organizations, both large and small, domestic and global. In addition to providing insights into management best practices, business case studies can tell us a great deal about how firms are adapting to the context in which they are operating, and about the business climate itself. For example, firms operating in a highly competitive industry driven by rapid innovation will behave very differently from firms enjoying a protected market experiencing slow technological change. Firms facing a restrictive, regulated market will behave very differently from firms operating in a wide-open, free market environment.

We have very few case studies of foreign firms operating in Cuba. Data are scarce, and few scholars or journalists have been able to interview joint venture (JV) executives. To begin to fill this void, this chapter presents seven case studies of leading JVs operating in Cuba. Sources include the published annual reports of the foreign investors; websites of the foreign and Cuban JV partners; interviews I conducted with foreign executives, investors, and diplomats (on a not-for-attribution or background basis); and other cited publications. In addition to making for colorful reading, the seven cases shed light on the unusual policy environment in which JVs must operate. The case studies reveal the special advantages and specific challenges that JVs face in Cuba and explore why some firms have succeeded while others have lost their licenses to operate. The studies also provide insights into how JVs perceive the current policy environment and where they would most like to see reforms. As a methodology, case studies are inevitably anecdotal, yet some of the findings are sufficiently robust to suggest recommendations for future policy, should the Cuban government decide it is in the national interest to attract more foreign direct investment (FDI).

The largest JVs operating in Cuba today, which account for the lion's share of the stock of FDI as well as of the nation's merchandise export earnings, are (in most cases) well-known global brands that have partnered with large Cuban state-owned enterprises. Most of the JVs were established in the 1990s, the heyday of Cuba's opening to FDI, when Cuba allowed some foreign firms to obtain 50 percent ownership (or even majority shares) and hence management control.

There is another type of JV that has populated the Cuban landscape: not the established multinational but rather the individual foreign entrepreneur with an unusually strong appetite for risk. Among the list of top JVs, Sherritt International is the prime example of this type of business venture. Sherritt's Cuban operations were the brainchild of a Canadian investment banker who cemented a strong personal relationship with Fidel Castro. Another partnership that until 2010 would have been on a list of top JVs, Rio Zaza, was the creation of a Chilean exile-turned-entrepreneur who was also a favorite of Fidel. However, Rio Zaza has since been seized by the Cuban authorities, making for a fascinating example of the perils of entrepreneurship dependent upon political connections. Yet even multinational giants are not immune to the shifting political currents in enigmatic Cuba, as the contested Unilever case underscores.

The seven case studies are of firms that are leaders in major sectors of the Cuban economy (see figure 5-1). In the mining sector, Sherritt is the leading producer of Cuba's most important merchandise export: nickel. Imperial Tobacco markets world-famous Cohiba cigars, exemplifying premium brand exports derived from Cuba's agricultural produce (a further example is the French marketing giant Pernod Ricard, which distributes Havana Club rum, the distillate from sugar). A visible presence throughout the island, Meliá, the Spanish hospitality chain, owns and manages many outstanding Cuban hotels and resorts. The four other cases (Nestlé, Souza Cruz, Unilever, Rio Zaza) distribute (or distributed) their top-selling consumer products in the domestic market.

Sherritt is also engaged in oil and gas, but this chapter does not consider in depth the petroleum production–sharing arrangements that may become important if exploratory drilling in Cuba's Special Economic Zone proves productive; these arrangements are a different animal altogether in

Figure 5-1. Joint Venture Case Studies, by Economic Sector

Foreign investor		Economic sector
Sherritt International	**sherritt**	Mining (nickel)
Imperial Tobacco	Imperial Tobacco	Brand exports (cigars)
Meliá	MELIÃ	Tourism (hotels)
Nestlé	Nestlé	Domestic ice cream
Souza Cruz (BAT)	SOUZA CRUZ	Domestic tobacco
Unilever	Unilever	Domestic household
Rio Zaza	RIO ZAZA	Domestic fruit juices, milk

their corporate and capital structures. Also not considered here are state-to-state investments, of the sort established between Chinese and Venezuelan state-owned enterprises (SOEs) and their Cuban partners. They, too, are also different creatures, and there is insufficient information on the public record to permit much outside scrutiny.[1]

Following the case studies, the chapter discusses general findings, including the advantages and disadvantages of operating within the Cuban system.

Case Study 1. Sherritt International: Betting on Cuban Nickel

In 1990, capping an 18-year career in investment banking in Toronto's equivalent of Wall Street (Bay Street), Ian Delaney engineered a hostile takeover of the Sherritt Corporation—a publicly listed old-line Canadian mining firm that had been a subsidiary of the Denver-based Newmont Mining Corporation.[2] The aggressive proxy battle solidified his reputation as the "Smiling Barracuda" of Bay Street.[3] At that time, Sherritt's nickel refinery in Fort Saskatchewan, Alberta, was shut down for lack of raw material to process. Coincidentally, the Soviet Union was collapsing and its demand for Cuban nickel was slumping. In a daring strategic move, Delaney flew to Cuba, met with Fidel Castro and his ministers, and began negotiating a series of deals that would result in a 50/50 JV between Sherritt and the Cuban SOE Compania General de Niquel to operate the underperforming Moa mining complex in the eastern province of Holguín. In a reciprocal arrangement, the Cuban SOE was granted a 50 percent share in the Alberta nickel refinery.[4] With these bold strokes, the Sherritt-Cuban partnership built a vertically integrated mining, smelting, and marketing operation—the Moa Joint Venture.

The Moa Joint Venture uses an open-pit mining process to mine lateritic nickel and cobalt ore at its Pedro Soto Alba plant. The ore is processed on site and shipped to the east coast of Canada. The minerals are then transported by train to Sherritt's Fort Saskatchewan facility for refining into finished nickel and cobalt. Currently, the Moa Joint Venture produces approximately 37,000 tons of nickel and cobalt annually at a cost of $5,000 to $7,000 a ton.[5] In 2011, when worldwide nickel prices were high, Sherritt's 50 percent share in the Moa JV led to reported revenues of $483 million and net earnings of $126 million, contributing substantially to the corporation's total revenues that banner year of $2 billion, and net earnings of just under $200 million.

For Cuba, exports of nickel and cobalt from Sherritt as well as from smaller, less efficient Cuban-owned operations averaged nearly $1.5 billion from 2007 to 2009, accounting for over 40 percent of the island's total merchandise exports (that is, excluding services), although more recently revenues are down due to falling global commodity prices.[6] Sherritt's mining operations are absolutely vital to the solvency of the Cuban economy.

Privileged Diversification

Building on the goodwill and trust that CEO Delaney garnered with the Cuban authorities, Sherritt has been granted concessions in an array of ventures across the island, even in some sectors where Sherritt had little or no prior business experience. (This pattern of privileged diversification is also evident in the spectacular case of the once well-connected Chilean investor Max Marambio, described below in the Rio Zaza case study.)

Sherritt's oil and gas division produced an average of 20,042 barrels of oil per day in 2013, contributing 40 percent of Cuba's oil production while employing a workforce of 300, 90 percent of whom were Cuban nationals.[7] In Cuba, all oil production is sold to the Cuban government, and Sherritt is allocated a share of oil production pursuant to its production-sharing contracts. For 2013 Sherritt reported revenues from its oil and gas sales to the Cuban government of $272 million. Looking ahead, Sherritt believes that there is potential for growth in Cuba's oil and gas industry. The corporation plans to grow its production through ongoing development drilling and by implementing heavy oil recovery technologies proven in western Canada and other jurisdictions.

In addition, Sherritt holds an indirect one-third interest in Energas, a JV established to process raw gas that is then used to generate electricity for sale to the Cuban national electrical grid. The remaining two-thirds interest in Energas is held equally by two Cuban agencies, Union Electrica and CUPET (Cuba's state-owned oil company). Sherritt provided the financing and technology for Energas's gas treatment and power generation facilities located near the Varadero, Boca de Jaruco, and Puerto Escondido oil fields. The three facilities currently have a combined capacity of 506 megawatts and supply a significant portion of Cuba's electricity. Sherritt operates the generation facilities under lease and service concession arrangements and is repaid from their cash flows. From its one-third share in Energas Sherritt reported revenues of $41 million and net earnings of $9 million in 2011.

But all has not been rosy for Sherritt in Cuba. In 2008, facing a severe foreign exchange crunch, Cuba fell behind in payments of $161 million of Sherritt's oil and gas and power receivables. The bulk of these arrears was rolled over into certificates of deposit issued by a Cuban government bank with a penalty interest rate of the London Interbank Offered Rate (LIBOR) plus 5 percent. In the event of default, Sherritt secured the right to receive payment from cash flows payable by the Moa JV, though Sherritt insists that notwithstanding delays and restructurings, in the end the Cubans paid.

Some of Sherritt's other ventures disappointed as well. In 1998 it acquired a 37.5 percent share of Cubacel, the cellular telephone operator in Cuba, for $38 million. Despite achieving a positive cash flow, Sherritt resold this investment, and the Cuban state has gradually assumed total control of the telecommunications sector.[8] In the excitement generated by the opening of Cuba to international tourism, Sherritt acquired a 25 percent share of the Meliá Las Americas Hotel and golf course in Varadero and a 12.5 percent share of the Meliá Habana Hotel—both of which were managed by the Sol Meliá enterprise. However, both of these investments were divested in 2009 for about $14 million.[9]

In 2006 Sherritt sold its 49 percent interest in a soybean processing business in Cuba for $43 million. The processing plant was dependent upon soybeans imported from the United States, so that the Cuban government may have been unhappy with its net impact on the balance of payments. Sherritt had warned that the business was performing "below expectations," and that distribution and market development for its product within Cuba was proving difficult.[10] Ultimately, Sherritt judged that the realized rate of return on investment was too low in light of the country risk. Placing value on soy-based protein and food security, the Cuban government was a willing buyer.

Sherritt Green, a 50/50 JV between Sherritt and an agency of the Cuban government, operated a small (200 hectare) fruit and vegetable farm in the early 2000s, and for several years the business received enthusiastic notices. But Sherritt's 2007 *Annual Information Form* suddenly omitted Sherritt Green; facing management and logistical issues, the project was closed down.

Most damaging, in 2009 Sherritt saw a long-term oil production–sharing contract with the Cuban government and Sherritt's Montreal-based partner Pebercan Inc. scrapped by CUPET, nearly 10 years before the contract's termination date. Neither Pebercan nor the Cuban government gave reasons for CUPET's action, although public documents indicate the SOE was well behind in its scheduled payments.[11] Reportedly the Cubans argued that the JV had fallen behind certain commitments, and there were disputes over cost deductions. In the coercive settlement, Pebercan received a net lump sum payment of $140 million from CUPET, $74 million of which was earmarked for Sherritt.[12] While it's difficult to evaluate the fairness of the deal, it reveals a pattern: when the Cuban state falls seriously into debt with an international partner, it may choose to close it down and wrap the arrears into a broader deal liquidating all assets. In that some compensation is offered and accepted, however grudgingly, Cuba escapes accusations of expropriation.

What the state gives, the state can take away. As Sherritt and other business cases demonstrate, foreign individuals and firms in good favor in Havana can gain privileged access to promising concessions. But as the Pebercan case suggests, if the business turns sour or the CEO falls out of favor, the unsentimental Cuban state shows little pity for former partners.

Alternatively, as in the cellular phone business, the state may decide that business opportunities are just too promising to leave room for private competitors.[13]

Corporate Social Responsibility

In conformity with Canadian business best practices, Sherritt maintains an active program of corporate social responsibility (CSR) in Cuba. The firm's annual reports frankly acknowledge that these programs help the corporation maintain its social license to operate. In cooperation with local Cuban authorities, programs focus on social and physical infrastructure in the communities in which Sherritt operates. Examples include street lighting and community sanitation, upgrades to senior housing and public schools, and the donation of materials to reestablish air conditioning in operating rooms at the main hospital in Moa. In other areas of CSR, such as worker health and safety and environmental stewardship, Sherritt's recent annual reports appear consistent with best practices.

While I have not attempted to rigorously evaluate Sherritt's CSR program, informal conversations with Cubans revealed some awareness of the firm's good corporate citizenship, and former employees express satisfaction with the treatment they received from the Canadian investor. The good will generated by a sustained, credible CSR program may not guarantee against government predation, but it raises its costs.[14]

Helms-Burton: Sherritt Shows No Fear

Prior to the 1959 revolution, the Moa mine had been owned by the U.S. Moa Bay Mining Corporation—now known as Freeport-McMoRan Copper and Gold Inc.—based in Phoenix, Arizona.[15] In November 1996, eight months after the Helms-Burton Act was passed, Sherritt CEO Ian Delaney received a letter informing him that he was on a U.S. State Department blacklist. Along with all directors and senior officers of Sherritt International and their families, Delaney was denied entry into the United States. But Delaney and Sherritt were undeterred. In its annual reports, Sherritt notes that U.S. presidents have repeatedly waived Title III of Helms-Burton, which would authorize damage lawsuits to be brought in U.S. courts by U.S. claimants against those "trafficking" in the claimants' confiscated property. "Even if the presidential suspension were permitted to expire," the corporation reassures its shareholders, "Sherritt does not believe that its operations would be materially affected by any Helms-Burton lawsuits, because Sherritt's minimal contacts with the United States would deprive any U.S. court of personal jurisdiction over Sherritt. . . . Management believes it is unlikely that a court in any country in which Sherritt has material assets would enforce a Helms-Burton judgment."[16] Governments of Canada and the European Union, among others, have expressed strong objection to the extraterritorial claims of Helms-Burton.

Sherritt concedes that the threat of possible litigation discourages some potential investors, lenders, suppliers, and customers from doing business with Sherritt. Nevertheless, the swashbuckling Delaney has remained confident in his Cuban investment, boasting at one point, "We have an amazing book of assets right now in Cuba. We've still got 25-year nickel assets, 12-year oil assets, and 15-year power assets."[17]

Case Study 2. Habanos: Premium Brands

Who wouldn't covet the exclusive rights to the global marketing of the legendary Cuban cigars? Many *aficionados* consider the Cuban cigar *"the premium puro"*—the world's best cigar smoke. Like French wines, the Cuban cigar can be mimicked but cannot be authentically reproduced elsewhere: it is a unique blend of *terroir* (soil and climate), carefully cultivated seeds, a secret combination of select tobacco leaves and wrappers, and patented processing techniques. Further, Cuban cigars are a lifestyle product, associated with sophistication and class, machismo and power (think Winston Churchill), and—with a little imagination—tropical sun, surf, and sex.

Initially, the Cubans came to the conclusion that while they had the product, they lacked the global reach of a major tobacco marketing conglomerate. Since Spain and France were major tobacco markets for Cuba, the Cubans sought out the Spanish-French firm Altadis as a partner. In 2008, when Imperial Tobacco acquired Altadis, the CEO of Imperial Tobacco immediately flew to Havana to reassure its new Cuban partners of the British firm's strong interest in its Cuban acquisition. For even though Cuban tobacco accounts for a small percentage of Imperial Tobacco's annual revenues, it is valued as a prestige brand that adds glow to the firm's entire portfolio: Imperial Tobacco's accountants have valued the goodwill of its Cuban cigar venture at £291 million. The world's fourth-largest cigarette company, Imperial Tobacco ranks number one as the largest producer of cigars.

Habanos is a 50/50 JV between Imperial Tobacco and its Cuban partner Cubatabaco. Imperial Tobacco reports good working relations with Cubatabaco, which takes responsibility for the supply chain—from the tobacco farmer through the manufacturing process. The partners evenly split the two co-presidencies and four vice presidencies, though the vice presidents of Imperial take responsibility for the strategic finance and business development portfolios. Imperial emphasizes that all key decisions are made by consensus and that both sides, pursuing common goals, take a win-win approach toward management decisionmaking. Habanos participates in an industry "regulatory council," whose membership includes Tabacuba, the world-renowned Tobacco Institute, and the National Association of Small Farmers whose members plant the tobacco. Working together, the Cuban tobacco industry seeks to maintain standards, plan annual production, and innovate new products. While the basic product, the cigar, may seem stable, new styles in terms of shapes, sizes, and blends are continually being designed and launched. Imperial, with its deep immersion in international markets, is well positioned to assist its Cuban partners in keeping abreast or ahead of market trends.

Reporting $400 million in revenues as of 2011, the Habanos joint venture had until this time maintained a steady annual growth rate of 7 percent or better, attaining or surpassing all of the key performance indicators (such as sales, market share, and profits) agreed upon in the joint venture contract and annual plan updates.[18] After switching to the proportional consolidation accounting method, Imperial stated in 2013 that the JV Corporación Habanos S.A., Cuba, reported Imperial's share of joint venture revenues as £51 million on total assets of £213 million, with after-tax profits of £15 million.

The basic economics has worked well for both JV partners. For Imperial, the direct labor component—250 Cuban employees contracted through a government labor entity—is pleasantly small when measured as a proportion of the cost of production or, especially, of final sales, even taking into account high government labor taxes. The Cuban partners take responsibility for purchasing tobacco from the artisan farmers, who either retain small, private acreage from prerevolutionary days or received their lands courtesy of the revolution. For the Cuban partners, the net foreign trade ratio is highly favorable: imports are a minor factor in production costs, while most of the output is sold overseas (or if sold in Cuba, in specialty shops where transactions take place in hard currency, at the exchange rate of US$1 to CUC 1).[19] Imperial takes responsibility for ensuring international liquidity and secures lines of credit from foreign banks. The Cuban partners are also entitled to half of the profits.

So far, Habanos's sales have represented a minor contribution to Imperial Tobacco's annual revenues, which in 2013 were £28.3 billion (of which tobacco accounted for £20.9 billion). And Imperial remains upbeat on its "Specialist Brands" of premium cigars: "Montecristo, Cohiba and Romeo y Julieta are our most prestigious Cuban cigars. Limited editions continue to support sales growth and through an expanding 'mini' range we're capitalizing on the growing demand for smaller luxury cigars."[20] At the moment, Imperial Tobacco assiduously brackets its Cuban operations from its U.S. activities, and its Havana-based executives stay clear of U.S. airports. But the firm is well positioned to surge into the United States—which accounts for some 80 percent of the market in premium cigars—once U.S. economic sanctions are dismantled. A glimmer of this potential appeared when President Obama eased travel restrictions in 2015 and allowed U.S. travelers returning from Cuba to bring with them up to $100 worth of Cuban tobacco and alcohol (a "sin allowance," in the words of a U.S. government official). As an executive with another major marketing multinational remarked to me, "Everyone in the consumer goods industries knows that eventually Cuban products will sell at a price premium in U.S. markets." When that day comes, Imperial Tobacco stands ready to provide the investment capital to boost cigar production by 50 percent in five years. Cuba has plenty of tobacco-friendly *terroir* to satisfy the demands of U.S. cigar aficionados.

Despite its good relations with the Cuban government and its commercial success, Habanos S.A. has not escaped from the broad brush of Raúl Castro's anti-corruption campaign (as exemplified in the case of Rio Zaza, described below). In 2010 Habanos's highly visible commercial vice president, Manuel García, and 10 of his staff were accused of pilfering genuine cigars and selling them at a fraction of their normal price to black-market distributors in return for bribes.[21] But the sudden removal of these seasoned distributors did not seem to materially impinge on the commercial performance of the JV.

Case Study 3. Meliá: International Hospitality

There is no escaping geography: international tourism is Cuba's overriding comparative advantage. Because tourism had become so closely associated with immorality and imperialism, the 1959 revolution largely shut it down. Yet beginning cautiously in the 1980s and then accelerating after the loss of Soviet subsidies, Cuba reopened its beaches to foreigners seeking tropical sun and surf. Cuba turned to European and Canadian hotel chains and tour operators who could help to build and manage hotels and resorts and organize tour packages and air transportation to ensure a steady stream of vacationers. For Canadians, Russians, and other Europeans of modest means, Cuban tourism offered good value and a relaxing week or two in a beautiful, warm, and secure destination. Cuba welcomed 3 million international visitors in 2014, up from 2.5 million in 2010; visitors jumped another 18 percent in 2015, following the normalization of diplomatic relations with the United States and the easing of travel restrictions.[22] International tourism contributes significantly to Cuba's balance of payments, generating over $2.5 billion in hard-currency revenues as of 2014.[23]

Among the international hotel chains invited to enter into JVs or management service contracts, the Spanish firm Meliá International Hotels has been the leader. As of 2015, it was operating 28 properties in Cuba (its worldwide total is about 310), divided among four brands, each appealing to different demographics or price points: Sol, with 10 properties, offering all-inclusive vacations for middle-income families; TRYP by Wyndham with 3 properties; Meliá with 12 for business travelers, including the urban Meliá Habana and Meliá Cohiba; and Paradisus with 3 upscale resort hotels. Meliá opened the 731-room, 1,000-berth Marina Varadero hotel complex in 2013. Meliá operates some of these properties as JVs with one of the major Cuban government hotel groups. In the majority of cases, Meliá has entered into management service contracts (contratos de administración hotelero) with the Cuban owner. On such properties, Meliá earns management fees that include a "basic fee" and an "incentive fee" based on performance.

In a survey completed in the mid-2000s as part of a study of Cuban tourism, executives of international hotel chains active in Cuba agreed that the Cuban tourism industry has produced above-average gross operating profits in most hotel groups, including Meliá. The study reported that "the island has consistently been Sol Meliá's most profitable market during recent years."[24] The study also noted that some hotel operators preferred service contracts rather than direct investments in order to minimize risk exposure in the Cuban market.

Meliá is quite happy with its Cuban workforce: educated Cubans flock to employment in the tourist industry, where they hope to gain access to tourist dollars, whether via hard-currency bonuses from their employers or tips from generous tourists. In the hiring process, the employment entity of the Ministry of Tourism (MINTUR) makes the first cut and then presents a list of candidates from which Meliá can make its selections. The government subsidizes the training that hotels provide to their employees. For that purpose, MINTUR receives financial transfers from the Ministries of Labor and Social Security.

The median worker costs Meliá about $900 per month, taking into account all expenses, including wages and bonuses, benefits, taxes, transportation, and food.[25] This wage bill consumes about 27 percent of revenues—less than in Spain but significantly more than in the Dominican Republic. According to some sources, the higher cost of labor in Cuba as compared to neighboring locations compels Cuban hotels to hire fewer workers per guest, which hurts the quality of customer service.

Many Cuban firms, both JVs and SOEs, pay a portion of profits into a Stimulus Fund for employee bonuses, which can amount to 30 percent of base salary (and reportedly more in some cases). The Ministry of Economy and Prices negotiates the nature of Stimulus Funds with each sectoral ministry (such as MINTUR). For the tourism sector, firms pay 3 percent of profits into their Stimulus Fund. If there are no profits in one period but superior profits in another, extra payments from the second period can compensate for the shortfall in the first period. Some JVs report that payouts from their Stimulus Fund are rather automatic, negating the goal of serving to stimulate performance. Some firms claim that their unions control the funds and simply distribute them equally among the employees, perhaps channeled by the political agenda or favoritism of union leaders. Meliá distributes its Stimulus Funds by the following formula: 50 percent according to disciplinary performance (that is, attendance, absence of pilferage) and 50 percent according to cost efficiency and client satisfaction. Stimulus Funds that are paid in hard-currency CUCs—as is the norm in the tourism sector—are much more enticing to workers than those paid in national currency.

The efficiency goals of President Raúl Castro are affecting the tourism sector. Earlier emphasis on employment creation—which was consistent with the national goal of full employment—has given way to a greater focus on cost containment. As a result, Meliá has engaged in staff reductions. Hotel operators are pleased at recent reforms in national labor practices, which have made it easier to hire part-time workers.

A chronic headache for hotels operating in Cuba has been reliability of supplies. For vital imports, JVs have the advantage when the foreign partner has ready access to external lines of credit. Most hotels have to rely on the annual import budget of the Importadora del Tourismo Hotelero (ITH), a dependency of MINTUR. ITH receives priority in the annual budget allocations since tourism is such a critical generator of foreign exchange earnings, but its resources are constrained by the nation's overall restricted hard-currency position. Hotels are also affected by decisions made by other Cuban government agencies (for example, decisions about allocating scarce fuels or sharply increasing electricity prices).

Irregularity in deliveries from domestic suppliers is another chronic headache. Hotels have long complained about the reliability and quality of farm products provided by FrutaSelecta, a MINTUR distributor. As a pilot project, the government has begun allowing some farm cooperatives to sell directly to hotels, which have welcomed the marked improvement in the variety and quality of fruits and vegetables (although transportation bottlenecks persist). Some hotels have also been allowed to directly hire self-employed workers for certain tasks, including construction and landscaping.

The quality of many local products remains a problem. To conserve foreign exchange and generate local employment, the government presses hotels to source locally, but hotels resist where poor quality would jeopardize customer satisfaction. For example, one hotel that caters to business executives refused the local producer of towels and linens in favor of a higher-quality importer.

Hotels operating in Havana are benefiting dramatically from the recent surge in tourism from the United States resulting from Washington's easing of travel restrictions. In response, occupancy rates and room rates have been rising, and in the winter high-season months the better Havana hotels are now booked to capacity. Americans making last-minute travel plans must seek shelter in private homes operating small bed-and-breakfast facilities, which the Cuban government licenses; the government estimates the number of such establishments at over 12,000, but there could well be more than 19,000 and rising.[26] Especially welcome are those Americans participating in the people-to-people programs (distinct from Cuban Americans visiting their families) authorized by the Obama administration. These visitors tend to be, in the words of one hotel operator, *gente de nivel* (higher-class travelers) as compared to the typical European or Canadian seeker of sun and surf. Airbnb now assists travelers in locating B&Bs; in ordinary circumstances, Airbnb might be considered competition to traditional hotels, but in Cuba's current booked-to-capacity context, the Internet website and the B&Bs it serves function as a useful complement in the hospitality industry.

Assuming that the surge in U.S. visitors continues, the big challenge for Cuba will be to build the accommodating hotels and other tourist-related facilities. Always short of resources, the Cuban government has regularly fallen well behind stated goals for constructing additional room capacity. Yet the government seems reluctant to allow foreign investors to take equity shares in new ventures. As of 2009, there were 65 hotel administration contracts—accounting for half of total hotel rooms—but only 14 hotels operating as JVs.[27] MINTUR and its associated tourism conglomerates (Cabanacan, Gran Caribe, Gaviota, and Islazul) prefer to retain ownership and control, and to limit foreign participation to management service contracts. According to a knowledgeable source, one international chain already active in Cuba offered $15 million to refurbish a major hotel property in return for equity, but MINTUR demurred. Similarly, a well-capitalized Middle East investment fund interested in a prime Havana location was rebuffed by Gaviota. Meanwhile, major international chains, including Meliá, Iberostar, Barceló, Sofitel, and Sandals are reportedly interested in investing more in the expanding Cuban market, as are some lesser-known investor groups. Senior executives from U.S. hotel chains such as Marriott International, Starwood Hotels and Resorts (owner of the Sheraton Hotel chain), and Hilton Hotels and Resorts have undertaken fact-finding trips, visibly salivating at the thought of entering—or reentering in the case of Hilton (former owner of what is now the celebrated Habana Libre)—the iconic and profitable Cuban market. During President Obama's March 2016 visit, Starwood triumphantly announced a first series of hotel management contracts. Returning from a brief trip to Havana, the CEO of Marriott International, Arne Sorenson, predicted enthusiastically: "If Congress acts to lift the travel ban, the number of U.S. visitors is likely to grow" from under 1 million today "to 5 million within just a few years."[28] Many elaborate plans are on the drawing board—some even visible on the Internet—poised to build golf resorts and boating marinas all over the island. One source counted 16 proposed golf courses at an estimated cost of $1.5 billion.[29] Some would-be (non-U.S.) investors have publicly trumpeted their belief that MINTUR approval is imminent.

International hotel chains such as Meliá see a bright future in Cuba. They are more than willing to continue to supply management expertise, but they would also like to take equity positions. Given that the scarcity of foreign exchange is hampering Cuban economic development and the construction industry in particular, equity partnerships would seem to be a reasonable bargain for all parties.

Case Study 4. Nestlé Ice Cream/Coralac

Nestlé, the Switzerland-based food and beverage giant, remembers when prerevolutionary Cuba ranked among its top five markets in Latin America and the Caribbean. Founded in 1867 and now with a twenty-first-century strategic vision of "nutrition, health and wellness," Nestlé has a long-term view of the Cuban market. Nestlé wants the Cuban consumer to associate its brand name with "good food, good life," guaranteed quality, and fun flavors. When the Cuban market eventually becomes more open and other global marketing firms are allowed to compete, the Cuban mind will already have been conditioned to select the Nestlé brands.

Nestlé regularly launches new products at the annual Havana International Fair. In 2010 it captured its fifth consecutive Gold Quality Medal with the launching of "Dolce Vita"—caramel popsicles coated with flavorful almonds. Then in 2014 customers could enjoy the new "Sensación Coco."

The company runs two JVs in Cuba: Coralac, the ice cream maker and distributor, and Los Portales, the bottler of mineral water. Los Portales markets the brand names Los Portales and Ciego Montero; plastic containers bearing those names are visible everywhere on the island. Both JVs partner with the Cuban government company Corporación Alimentaria S.A., or Coralsa. Nestlé holds a 50 percent share in Los Portales (with a capital of $24.1 million) and a 60 percent share in Coralac (with a capital of $6.4 million). Both firms fall under the jurisdiction of the Ministry of the Food Industry (MINAL).

Coralac enjoys a dominant market share in the hard-currency CUC market for ice cream products. Acting as a gatekeeper, the Cuban government limits the number of foreign brands that are allowed to enter the island

and that might compete with Nestlé's ice cream. Several state-owned firms compete in the domestic currency market, such as the renowned—and heavily subsidized—Coppelia brand. Yet some Cuban consumers remark that the quality of Coppelia ice cream has declined, perhaps for lack of new investment in plants and equipment;[30] these consumers now aspire to Nestlé ice cream, a special treat for Cubans without access to CUCs. Nestlé can look forward to the day when, upon unification of the dual currency regimes and an upward adjustment in wages, it sells its popsicles to all Cubans at competitive prices.

Coralac's sales have grown at a consistent percentage over the last decade, but its annual revenues are *de minimus* when measured against Nestlé's global sales of CHF 91.6 billion and profits of CHF 14 billion (2014). However, Coralac's profitability has been in line with its parent company's global performance. One financial plus of operating in Cuba is that there is little expenditure on conventional advertising: the state-run media eschew corporate ads, and roadside billboards are reserved for political messaging. Nestlé does brand its trucks, ice coolers, and wrappers; a 2006 consumer survey found that in the food category Nestlé was the most recognized foreign brand in Cuba.[31]

Coralac lives with the advantages and frustrations of a socialist system. In a market highly regulated by the government, the prices of Coralac's inputs and outputs are set within the state's annual plan. Prices are based on cost sheets for each product and any changes require approval by the Ministry of Finance and Prices, although price promotions are generally prohibited.[32] In effect, Coralac's profit margins are set in this formal extra-market negotiating process and hence are predictable and relatively stable.

As is true for many producers in the Cuban context, Coralac faces prices that are fixed by a government determined to restrain inflation and hence very reluctant to grant price increases. But there is a path around the inertia of existing prices. Coralac's factory produces more than 20 flavors of ice cream.[33] By innovating new products whose first-time prices may be set higher, firms can try to elevate their profit margins without necessarily affecting the consumer price index (which captures prices on an existing bundle of consumer items). Not surprisingly, then, each year Coralac spins new products into the Cuban marketplace.

Nestlé prides itself on quality control. It wants its local suppliers to meet its global standards, and Coralac therefore audits all of its suppliers. However, Coralac's ability to structure its supply chain is constrained by the government's direct control over the national dairy industry. In its global operations Nestlé typically engages deeply into upstream production, working with local farmers by providing training and expertise in milk supply, technical equipment, management, and finance. In Cuba, however, Nestlé is impeded from implementing its global "creating shared value" strategy, which involves collaborating closely with suppliers and with their rural communities. Thus the Cuban dairy industry is denied the full benefits of Nestlé's expertise in supply chain management. Cuban centralism inhibits Nestlé from diffusing its proven technological know-how throughout the local economy.

Although Nestlé holds a majority stake in Coralac, decisions are made collegially and by unanimity; at a general level there is agreement on the goals of sustainable growth. There may be more subtle differences, however, between the two partners. Nestlé's global market culture focuses on the consumer and brand loyalty, whereas Cuban partner Coralsa prioritizes employment creation and cost reduction.[34] The joint venture partnership encourages Cubans to think less in terms of material balances and input-output matrixes and more in terms of consumer welfare.

For foreign investors such as Nestlé, partnering with a Cuban government agency entails both benefits and challenges. At times Coralsa can carry Coralac's water, for example in negotiations with other government agencies whose powers impinge upon the joint venture's business operations. But Coralsa's loyalties run in two directions: it is loyal to the JV, but also to the government. The government's universal goals—conserving energy, reducing imports, and expanding exports—must apply to the ice cream industry, and Coralsa will seek to insert them into the JV.

Like all JVs, Nestlé must live with the labor system that governs foreign investment, in which workers are hired via a state employment entity. While the employment entity often assigns good workers, its priorities may not be fully aligned with those of the JV. The wage and performance guidelines set by the state limit Coralac's flexibility in establishing employment packages and incentive structures. Driven by the revolution's commitment to social equity, wage differentials among employment categories are remarkably narrow. JVs report many cases where promising employees decided to turn down promotion offers: "Why should I take on more responsibilities and headaches and possibly longer hours," a middle manager could reasonably ask, "when the increase in wages is so small?"[35] Recently, in response to charges that workers in JVs were becoming a new labor aristocracy, the government forced JVs to reduce expenditures on employee lunches (from $2.50 to $1.50 per day), to the detriment of employee morale.

Nestlé looks forward to currency unity, confident that it will be able to compete successfully against national brands that currently serve the local currency market. There is the worry of inflation, however, which is likely to be a by-product of currency unification and which could shrink consumers' purchasing power. Another impending challenge to the firm: the expanding private sector offering a wider range of consumer choices that will compete with foods and beverages.

Case Study 5. Brascuba Cigarrillos— Serving a Protected Consumer Market

Maybe it's the sunny Brazilian personality, but Brascuba Cigarrillos S.A.— the very first JV established under the 1995 foreign investment law—is unabashedly upbeat about its business and its ability to maneuver successfully in the Cuban environment. Only two of its managers are Brazilian nationals, but their buoyant personalities may be infectious. Or maybe it's the esprit de corps of Cuba's tobacco industry, which is proud of its fame on global markets. Or maybe it's the confidence that comes from knowing that the Cuban and Brazilian governments enjoy warm diplomatic relations.

Brascuba is a 50/50 joint venture between the Brazilian cigarette company Souza Cruz (owned by the U.K.-based British American Tobacco, BAT) and the Union of Tobacco Companies of Cuba (TabaCuba), a state-owned monopoly and dependency of the Ministry of Agriculture.[36] Brascuba's factory workers transform Cuban tobacco into cigarette brands that dominate the hard-currency CUC market.[37] Brascuba exports 10 to 15 percent of its production.

Brascuba has experienced steady growth since its inception, using 7,000 retail outlets across the island, and is widely regarded as one of the most successful JVs.[38] Souza Cruz is satisfied with its performance—even as its profitability falls short of BAT's global standards. Brascuba's profitability is capped by the prices for cigarettes as set by the Cuban government. The firm identifies these government-imposed price ceilings as its biggest challenge. With its modest profits, Brascuba was not able to invest in expanding production capacity as rapidly as it would have liked.

When asked what each partner brings to the bargain, Brascuba provides the same answer as many JVs: The foreign partner provides investment capital, technology, employee training (including in Brazil for some Cubans), exclusive brands, access to international markets, and international lines of credit. The local partner provides the land, the buildings, the workers, and, in the case of TabaCuba, an assured supply of high-quality tobacco and Cuban cigarette brands (Cohiba, U. Upmann, Popular). As a government entity, TabaCuba also provides channels to government ministries that help resolve problems as they arise. Indicative of its long-established working relations with the Cuban authorities, Brascuba's two Brazilian executives also enjoy direct access to senior officials in relevant government ministries.

The Cuban government wants Brascuba, like other established JVs, to improve its contribution to the balance of payments by importing less and exporting more. Thus the firm plans to substitute domestically manufactured cigarette filters for imported ones. Making use of BAT's global marketing machine, Brascuba already exports its cigarettes to over 10 countries, including Germany, Spain, Brazil, Mexico, and Japan. However, it has been struggling to hit the 20 percent exports and total output target set by the government without cannibalizing markets already served by other BAT production facilities.

A manufacturing firm, Brascuba is very concerned with the quality and cost of its labor force, consisting of over 500 workers operating in three eight-hour shifts. Like all JVs, Brascuba must select from among a list of eligible workers presorted by a government employment agency. Wage rates, set by a government salary scale, are permitted to vary only within a narrow band. Social equality rather than labor productivity remains the main driver of wage differentials. The controller general and chief anti-corruption prosecutor, Gladys Bejarano, warned: "It's an act of corruption when a manager earns 10 times the basic salary unit when the operators earn only two or three times the basic salary."[39] At Brascuba, median monthly wages have been 350 national pesos (at the exchange rate of 24:1, $15 dollars) supplemented by 29 convertible pesos (1:1 to the U.S. dollar), such that the value of the hard-currency bonus exceeds by a margin the base pay.[40] The terms and conditions of this stimulus award are negotiated with the Ministry of Agriculture. The established performance targets—for productivity, efficiency, and discipline—are set such that workers typically fulfill them and hence can anticipate receiving their all-important bonuses. Proportionally, these bonuses would exceed those reportedly authorized in other sectors, such as tourism (see the case study of Meliá).

However, although the bonuses are significant in size and may serve to improve employee morale and reduce labor turnover, such automatic payments are not optimal for incentivizing productivity.

Brascuba considers that motivating and retaining talent is one of the firm's key challenges. Beyond bonuses, the firm can offer some amenities, such as transportation, medical facilities for employees and their families, modest improvements in dining facilities, and opportunities for the employees to engage in conversations over coffee with senior management. An important stimulus is career promotion and training. For some managers this includes trips to Brazil, where they are exposed to the expertise and procedures of Souza Cruz and the parent firm, British American Tobacco. Brascuba managers take pride in their knowledge and application of high global standards of operation.

For a consumer market firm like Brascuba, the economic reform process presents a mixed picture. Brascuba would applaud currency unification because it would create a unified consumer market for its cigarettes and would reduce labor costs—assuming the lifting of the implicit heavy tax on labor levied by today's split currency system. A system of more flexible prices would be especially welcome, although on the downside, economy-wide price adjustments that eat into consumer purchasing power could hit cigarette purchases. Overall this Brazilian-Cuban JV has reason to feel confident that it could compete successfully in a more liberal market environment.

Brascuba estimates that U.S. economic sanctions raise its costs of doing business by some 20 percent. Inputs such as cigarette filters, manufacturing equipment, and spare parts, along with infrastructure such as information technology, must be obtained from more distant and perhaps less cost-efficient sources. Unexpectedly, Brascuba sees a link between the unwelcome emigration of skilled workers, whether to the United States or elsewhere, and U.S. economic sanctions.

The opening of the Mariel Special Development Zone (ZED) has provided Brascuba with an opportunity to modernize and expand its cigarette production. Brascuba negotiated a new 50/50 joint venture investment of $120 million, by far the largest in the Mariel development zone announced in 2015. The new JV has a 40-year expiration date, double the previous time frame—an important adjustment that the director of ZED Mariel emphasized had been approved by the Council of Ministers, "in recognition of the firm's good results over many years."[41] Brascuba will close its old facility in downtown Havana in favor of the new facility at Mariel, sharply expanding production and exports (primarily to Brazil, where Cuba-Mercosur trade terms will allow for favorable tariff treatment). Brascuba believes this is a good time for expansion: better-paid workers at Mariel will be well motivated, and the expansion of the private sector is putting more money into consumer pockets. Brascuba classifies itself as a fast-moving consumer goods company: its new investment in Cuba responds both to a short-term business opportunity and a strategic commitment to Cuba over the long term.[42]

Case Study 6. Unilever: Ouster and Reinstatement of a Marquee Multinational

With 2014 annual revenues of €48.4 billion and €8 billion in operating profits, Unilever is one of three world leaders in personal and home care products (the other two are Procter & Gamble and Nestlé). Unilever markets such diverse name brands as Dove soaps, Lipton teas, and Hellmann's mayonnaise in over 190 countries worldwide. Unilever's multiple research and development facilities spew forth a continuous stream of innovative products to bolster its portfolio of hundreds of differentiated "solutions." With its binational Dutch and British management, Unilever prides itself on its ability to operate in virtually every political environment in the world. The giant conglomerate is frequently recognized for its good corporate citizenship. As an example of its responsiveness to contemporary trends, by 2020 Unilever promises to source all of its agricultural materials in a sustainable manner.

In 1994 Unilever formed a 50/50 international economic association with Suchel, a Cuban state-owned company operating under the Ministry of Light Industry, which specializes in personal and home care products, including soaps and detergents. The Suchel Lever JV produced and marketed Unilever brands such as Lux soap and Pepsodent toothpaste, and it had annual sales of €25 million–€30 million and market shares of 50 to 60 percent in the hard-currency CUC market. Unilever was pleased with its Cuban investment. In the grand scheme of things, however, Unilever's Cuban operations were not worthy of listing in the corporation's annual financial statements: "those companies not listed are not significant in relation to Unilever as a whole."[43]

Unilever had multiple motives for operating in the modest Cuban market: it sought to establish its corporate brand names in the minds of the

Cuban people (much like Nestlé) and gain a beachhead in the Cuban market, anticipating long-term growth; it also sought to advance the corporate mission of a universal presence, and obey the competitive imperative of denying market shares to its major rivals. In Cuban markets, however, Unilever concentrated on personal and home care products, whereas Nestlé sold foods and beverages. This was a comfortable arrangement that avoided head-to-head competition between the two conglomerates. Both Unilever and Nestlé had gained a running start on Cincinnati-based Procter & Gamble and New York–based Colgate-Palmolive, excluded by U.S. sanctions.[44]

Unilever's operations in Cuba (from their beginnings in the mid-1990s to 2012) were not without problems. As in other JVs, Cuban labor regulations made it difficult for management to motivate the 400-strong workforce. Labor productivity in the Cuban JV reportedly was below levels registered elsewhere in Latin America and the Caribbean. Incidents of pilferage—which are common throughout the resource-scarce Cuban economy—may be especially common in firms dealing with consumer products. In Unilever's experience, the pilferage levels encountered in Cuba, of some 5 to 6 percent, measured about twice the global average. The unfortunate consequence of very low wages, severe shortages of consumer goods, and a deepening national culture of cutting corners and petty theft, pilferage is a cost of doing business in Cuba.[45] Furthermore, the labor system that regulates JVs makes it very difficult to fire workers. Cuban labor unions have tended to protect delinquent employees, arguing for remediation rather than retribution.

While enjoying a comfortable market share in the hard-currency CUC market, Unilever was largely excluded from the national currency markets, which are the preserve of state-owned enterprises. Unilever believed it was more efficient than its SOE competitors, not only because of superior management and operations but also because the firm's ready access to international credit gave it greater security of supply. Severe shortages of inputs often compel domestic SOEs to interrupt production, disrupting supply to retailers and consumers. Unilever looked forward to currency unification, when it would be able to compete head-to-head with the SOEs in a single national market.

Suchel, Unilever's JV partner, benefited from the bifurcated market. Suchel runs its own operations in personal and home care products, and has JVs with two Spanish firms: Suchel Camacho, which manufactures cosmetics and perfumes, including the popular "Alicia" brand (named for the iconic Cuban ballerina Alicia Alonso), and Suchel Proquimia, which places its bulk cleaning products in hotels. Suchel enjoys insider information on the technical formulas and corporate strategies of firms operating throughout the industry and thus has a serious competitive advantage.

Unilever was also constrained by the government's intrusion into its supply chain. The government expressed preference for local suppliers, although Suchel Lever could make the final determination; the JV tried to oblige the government preference but only if the local suppliers met Unilever's global standards. To its dismay, Unilever's offers of technical assistance to suppliers were often rejected, apparently because the government did not want to grant access to manufacturing facilities. Of course, government ministries fixed prices for inputs as well as outputs and had to approve spending and investment targets, all negotiated in the annual planning process.

When it came time to renegotiate the Unilever Suchel joint venture, the Cuban government questioned why Unilever had invested little in recent years. It did not care to recognize that Unilever's appetite for investment had been dulled by government-imposed disincentives, including the impending contract end-date and the 2008–2009 recession-induced payment delays stalling profit repatriation. No longer satisfied with a 50/50 partnership, Cuba pressed new contract conditions and sought a controlling 51 percent; Cuba also wanted the JV to export at least 20 percent of its output. But Unilever feared that granting Suchel 51 percent would yield too much control and could jeopardize brand quality. Unilever balked at exporting products made in Cuba, where production costs were as much as one-third higher than in Unilever plants in other Latin American countries, notably in Brazil and Mexico, where larger volumes allowed for more efficient production runs. Unilever did not want to in effect cross-subsidize exports from Cuba.

Frustrated at the negotiating process, Unilever professed an inability to discern government motives. Unilever was unable to penetrate the opaque decisionmaking process or to pinpoint the key decisionmakers (beyond assuming that President Raúl Castro had the final word). When Unilever CEO Paul Polman—a seasoned CEO accustomed to meeting with ministers and heads of state—visited the island he was granted access only to a vice minister, and that courtesy only after persistent lobbying by the British embassy.

Was Unilever the victim of a rigid application of Cuba's more demanding approach to JVs? Or did the state-owned Suchel seize the opportunity to edge out a foreign firm so as to reserve markets for itself? Or did the government's accumulation of some $25 million in debts tempt it to push out Unilever so it could renegotiate these debts with a subsequent investor on more favorable terms? Or was Raúl Castro's spreading anticorruption campaign responsible for freezing decisionmakers, who were now fearful of being accused of taking bribes from foreign businessmen?

As the negotiations for contract renewal dragged on, a Unilever company manager was quoted in the media in 2012 as saying: "We wanted 51 percent of the new venture and so did the Cubans. At this point, we are leaving, even though some discussion is still going on."[46] Frustrated by the stiff Cuban posture, Unilever opted to withdraw. The collapse of the Unilever contract renewal negotiations adversely affected investor perceptions of the business climate. If the Cuban government could not sustain a good working relationship with Unilever—a highly regarded, marquee multinational corporation with a global footprint—what international investor (at least one operating in the domestic consumer goods markets) could be confident of its ability to sustain a profitable long-term operation in Cuba?

In January 2016 Unilever announced that it had obtained approval to reenter the Cuban market, this time in the ZED Mariel—and with a majority 60 percent stake.[47] Again, the $35 million investment will produce personal and home care consumer products. In the old joint venture, Unilever executives had complained that low salaries, as set by the government, had contributed to low labor productivity. Now, in ZED Mariel, workers' income will be significantly higher: firms like Unilever will continue to pay the same wage scales to the government employment entity, but the entity's tax will be significantly smaller, leaving a higher take-home pay for the workers. Hiring and firing, however, will remain the domain of the official entity, not the joint venture.

The return of Unilever, under conditions that recognize the global giant's strategic operational requirements, suggests that Cuba is learning from its mistakes.

Case Study 7. Alimentos Rio Zaza: The Perils of Political Entrepreneurs

In February 2009 then-president of Chile Michelle Bachelet, President Raúl Castro, and their senior teams were hosted at the palatial Havana home of Chilean businessman Joel Max Marambio Rodriguez. The visiting

Chileans were impressed by their host's lavish lifestyle and by his apparently intimate ties to senior Cuban leadership. Yet the following year the Cuban Ministry of Justice would accuse Max Marambio of multiple deeds of corruption and seize his properties, most prominent among them the joint venture Alimentos Rio Zaza S.A., the island's leading producer of packaged citrus fruit juices and milk.

Rio Zaza began in 1993 as a 50/50 joint venture involving two Chilean investors, Marambio and Carlos Cardoen (a global arms dealer), with an initial capital estimated at just $2.5 million.[48] The business included upstream citrus plantations. By 2009 Marambio had bought out his partner; by then, Rio Zaza employed about 500 workers with annual sales of around $100 million. Rio Zaza's Tetra-Pak juices were a visible premium brand throughout the island. As democracy returned to Chile, Marambio relocated his primary residence there, but he remained a prominent figure among business circles in Cuba.

The story of Marambio and Rio Zaza is the stuff of cinematic drama.[49] As a teenager, Marambio's father, a militant in the Chilean Socialist Party, introduced him to Fidel Castro, who offered him training in Cuba's special forces. This unusual education prepared him to take charge of the personal security of Chilean socialist Salvador Allende upon his assumption to power in the early 1970s. When Allende was subsequently ousted in a military coup, Marambio returned to Cuba, where his relationship to Fidel and other prominent personalities opened the door to various bureaucratic and business opportunities. Solidifying his access to the inner circle, Marambio married a daughter of Antonio Núñez Jiménez, a participant in the historic Sierra Maestra guerrilla campaign and Castro confidant.

As an entrepreneur, Marambio did not limit himself to fruit juices. He opened a JV package tourism agency in close partnership with the Cuban national airlines, Cubana de Aviación. He owned a multinational real estate business that among other regular guests included staff of the Cuban airlines. Marambio even made a film with Gabriel Garcia Márquez, the famous Colombian novelist and close friend of Fidel's.

With his many business and political connections, Marambio seemed secure. Moreover, he and his brother Marcel appeared to be excellent entrepreneurs, with good noses for business opportunities and the managerial skills to execute successfully. So it must have come as a shock when government investigators from the secretive Department of Technical Investigation of the Ministry of the Interior began in 2010 to pick up his associates at Rio Zaza and his tourism agency. On April 13, 2010, the long-term general manager of Rio Zaza, Chilean national Roberto Baudrand, was found dead in his Havana apartment following lengthy interrogations by government agents; the exact cause of death was never clarified.

The Marambio brothers have been accused of "bribery of government officials, acts detrimental to economy activities and contracts, misappropriation of funds, counterfeiting of bank and commercial documents, and fraud."[50] Not surprisingly, they have chosen not to return to Cuba for trial. In such anti-corruption cases, there is little transparency or legal due process. The accused are not presented with precise charges until shortly before the trial, are interrogated without the presence of legal counsel, and may be held incommunicado for lengthy periods in unknown locations with only sporadic family contacts. Legal experts report that the most the accused can seek to accomplish is to plead for reduced sentences. In May of 2011 the Cuban courts sentenced Marambio to a 20-year prison term in absentia. A number of his alleged Cuban co-conspirators—business associates and senior government officials, including the long-time minister of the foods industry—are currently behind bars.

Rio Zaza was not officially expropriated, but the government "intervened" in the firm. Initially, Rio Zaza ceased operations and the familiar Tetra-Pak fruit juices disappeared from grocery shelves. It is now operational as La Estancia S.A. under the aegis of the Cuban joint venture partner Corporación Alimentaria S.A., a Coralsa dependency of MINAL. Marambio remains a fugitive from Cuban justice.

As is typical with corruption scandals, very little has appeared in the Cuban media about the Marambio case, fueling speculation on the government's motives. Following are four theories, not mutually exclusive.

Individual Indiscretion

Perhaps Marambio's flamboyant lifestyle was an embarrassment to the communist elite who live relatively austerely and discreetly. Marambio could irritate government officials; during the 2009 foreign exchange crisis, when the Cuban Central Bank froze accounts and Rio Zaza could not meet payments to international suppliers, Marambio reportedly expressed his displeasure directly and loudly to Central Bank officials. Nor did Marambio hide the fact that he paid his workers bonuses, above the officially set salary levels, during a time when such payments were not legal (although they were commonplace in JVs). Further, Marambio may have annoyed some Cubans when, during the 2008 Chilean presidential elections, he provided financial support to a third-party candidate who drew support away from the leftist ticket, leading to the victory of a conservative. In fact, Marambio's Chilean wife shared interests in the Chilean national airlines, LAN, with its principal shareholder—the rightist candidate Sebastián Piñera. This gave rise to accusations that Marambio plotted with Piñera to divide the leftist vote.

Intra-elite Power Shifts

As power shifted from Fidel to Raúl, Marambio lost his original patron. Some speculate that the institutional military, with which Raúl is intimately associated, never trusted Marambio because of his experience in Fidel's personal special forces. Throughout the government, Raúl has gradually replaced many of Fidel's loyalists with his own, and anticorruption charges can be part of that game. Perhaps real assets play a role: Raúl's team was able to gain 100 percent control over the lucrative Alimentos Rio Zaza S.A., renaming it La Estancia S.A. and renewing production.

Preliberalization Purification

This official explanation has two variants. The first is that the Soviet Union collapsed because of rampant corruption, so the Cuban Revolution must take preemptive measures and varnish moral legitimacy and principled concern for social justice. Alternatively, economic liberalization, however gradual, runs the risk of opening the gates to a post-Soviet-style corruption, so high ethical standards must be established beforehand. In either of these two explanations, however, the government's tactics seem ill-chosen. Absent information, citizens tend to see criminal accusations as arbitrary, because cutting corners has become commonplace in resource-scarce Cuba. Moreover, the prosecutorial campaign leaves untouched the obvious root causes of corruption: extremely low wages even among senior officials and lack of transparency in both economic and political spheres.

Terror and Control

The more cynical explanation is simply that communist regimes periodically undertake anticorruption campaigns. Such campaigns may seek to restore moral purpose, especially at a time of growing economic inequality (as in China today); they may be an instrument in intraparty factional and personal disputes; or, in the words of a Havana diplomat, they may serve "to remind citizens who is in charge." Such anticorruption campaigns can take on logic of their own, as zealous prosecutors become emboldened— the "revolution devours its sons" syndrome. But the current anticorruption campaign has also trapped within its widening net a number of foreign businessmen, including not only Chileans but also Canadians and Europeans operating high-profile businesses—from the distribution of premium Cohiba cigars in Europe (employees of the Habanos JV) to the remodel of a five-star hotel in downtown Havana (the Saratoga).[51]

The ill-understood anticorruption campaign, combined with the absence of standard legal protections, sent a chill throughout the joint venture community and deterred some otherwise interested investors. Rather than foretell a better business climate with higher ethical standards, the campaign has introduced an element of uncertainty and even fear.

Epilogue

Marambio exercised his rights to seek redress before the Paris-based International Chamber of Commerce's International Court of Arbitration, based upon the Cuba-Chile Bilateral Investment Treaty of 1996, and pursuant to both the Cuban FDI Law of 1995 and the Rio Zaza Joint Venture agreement. The three-member panel awarded Marambio $143 million for future loss of earnings and another $10 million for "moral pain and suffering." However, this decision was annulled by the court's appellate body. It seems improbable that Marambio will receive financial compensation for his losses.

Findings from the Case Studies

The seven case studies make clear that for foreign firms, there are significant advantages, and significant drawbacks, to operating within the Cuban socialist system. Firms are pleased at some of the recent economic measures and hope that reforms will continue and even accelerate after President Raúl Castro steps down in 2018 and a new generation of leaders emerges. There is no doubt that FDI is making valuable contributions to their JVs (FDI's contributions to the Cuban economy will be addressed below) and that foreign firms would be willing to invest more in Cuba if markets—domestic or international—were to expand. Even after the 2015 normalization of diplomatic relations and easing of some restrictions, the remaining U.S. economic sanctions deprive firms of certain U.S. technologies and other inputs, which raises the costs of doing business in Cuba by as much as 20 percent in some cases.

The seven JVs featured in the case studies all reported profitability. But many are lying in wait for the opening of the U.S. market: tantalizingly nearby, immense in purchasing power, and prepared to pay premium prices for exotic Cuban brands. Some JVs already have plans to dramatically expand their investments when that banner day finally arrives.

Advantages of Operating within the Cuban System

Capitalist corporations, one might imagine, constantly clash with socialist planning. In reality, JVs operating in Cuba discover that socialism, while not exactly a capitalist's paradise, offers a number of distinct advantages:

Market dominance. Once admitted, JVs are often granted full monopolies or dominant market shares in key market segments. The Cuban state restricts market entry by other foreign competitors or by national enterprises.

Guaranteed profits. Profit margins are in effect guaranteed by the state. A function of input and output prices set by government planners, profit margins are the outcome of a political bargaining process where JVs discuss with government planners the key business variables: prices and quantities.

Stability. The Cuban economic environment is relatively stable (some might say stagnant). The government sets prices, the labor market is tightly regulated, and competition and innovation are low. Nevertheless, in recent years global economic turbulence has affected the Cuban economy by dampening growth rates and consumer purchasing power, even as the surge in U.S. visitors and remittances lifted economic activity in 2015–16.

Power and influence. The Cuban JV partner serves as an avenue of influence in bargaining with state entities. Generally, the state, holding shares in the joint venture, wants the JV to succeed.

Party and labor union support. The Confederation of Cuban Workers and cells of the Communist Party of Cuba are embedded within firms. These politicized organizations impinge upon management autonomy and may represent workers' interests, for example, by arguing that social solidarity militates against layoffs. But these organizations generally align with the production goals of the firm and its associated state agencies. Management need not worry about militant strikes or work stoppages.

Disadvantages of Operating within the Cuban System

All seven JVs featured in the case studies claimed successful, profitable operations. Yet all have found it challenging to operate in the Cuban context. The top complaint by far is the labor contract system. Other common complaints include price controls that cap profit margins, state interference with the supply chain, and tensions with their Cuban partners over business priorities.

State control. In capitalist societies, there is constant jockeying among firms, governments, and workers' associations over the rules governing labor markets. For JVs operating in Cuba there is no debate: the state exercises total control. JV management bristles at its inability to set wages and bonuses to optimize productivity and labor discipline. Of even greater concern is the exorbitant tax on labor extracted through the dual currency system, which attacks profitability and seriously impairs international competitiveness. For some JVs, the high labor tax is patently inconsistent with the Cuban insistence on export performance requirements.

Limited profitability. Government price controls offer stability and predictability but also constrain profitability. To dampen inflation, Cuban authorities press JVs to improve their profit margins through higher productivity and lower costs rather than through price increases. In response, some JVs complain that their profit margins are too thin to allow for much productivity-enhancing investment or fret that the government will not allow them to expand sales at a sufficiently rapid rate to justify more investments.

Time-limited contracts. Another disincentive to investment is the time limitation on JV contracts. Facing a deadline that could result in the revocation of their license to operate, firms are prone to invest less and less as the contract end-date approaches.

Constricted supply chains. A multinational is only as good as the weakest link in its supply chain. Some seasoned multinationals, such as Nestlé, have always focused on the quality of their inputs, while others are becoming more conscious of the need to intervene further and further upstream to ensure quality control as well as compliance with social (labor, environmental, and health) standards. But in Cuba, some JVs noted, the state inserts itself between the JV and its suppliers. This creates risks for the JV and also deprives suppliers of the operational know-how that multinationals routinely diffuse throughout their supply chains elsewhere in the world.

Conflicting incentives. The Cuban JV partner may house contradictory loyalties. It has a stake in the success of the JV, but is also a dependency of the Cuban state. Some foreign investors reported being accustomed to placing more emphasis on consumer welfare and other marketing considerations, while their Cuban partners focus more on meeting planning targets set by the state.[52] Where the Cuban SOE also owns competing firms, it may face further conflicting loyalties.

Unstable rules. Notwithstanding the generally stable political context, JVs feel vulnerable to sudden changes in the rules of the game. The state can alter the environment, for example, with regard to prices of vital inputs such as energy and land. Tolerance for "gray area" practices can change, and the anticorruption campaign has retroactively accused unlucky executives of illicit practices. In extreme cases, government entities, ministries, or competing SOEs may decide to pressure a JV to sell or abandon its assets, to the benefit of better-connected Cuban interests. "One day you're welcome, the next day you're in jail," observed an executive with a large multinational waiting for more stable rules of the game before venturing into Cuban markets.

Mixed Signs

JVs would like to see major reforms in the labor laws and the dual currency system. Already they report some positive changes in these spheres as well as in others. Some workers are now permitted to hold two jobs and some employers can hire part-timers, adding welcome flexibility to labor markets. The government is also permitting some firms to reduce staff, giving greater weight to labor productivity over employment security. On an experimental basis, some tourist establishments have been authorized to purchase directly from local suppliers, without the intermediation of cumbersome state distributors, and at prices that imply a more realistic rate of exchange. Moreover, the new rules at ZED Mariel are encouraging; higher take-home wages for workers, management control for the foreign investor (for example, a 60 percent ownership stake for Unilever), and longer expiration dates (as in the new Brascuba deal) could all make a big difference if implemented widely and promptly.

At the same time, it is impossible for firms to ignore the Cuban government's steps backward, even as Law 118 of 2014 posted the sign "Open for Business." The 2011 reform guidelines suggest enduring distrust toward FDI within important segments of the Cuban state and society, and some new rules—for example, those dictating what firms can spend on employee lunches—manifest a deep ideological preference for equality over productivity. In addition, the persistence of delays in project approval suggests divisions within the state and, quite possibly, opposition in high places. Finally, although the ouster of Unilever (since reversed) was a rude shock to the JV community, it followed an established pattern of removing foreign firms from the Cuban landscape. In early 2011, for example, the state telecommunications firm, ETECSA, bought out its Italian partner, Telecom Italia, and deflected expressions of interest by Spain's Telefónica in order to retain monopoly control of a highly profitable and politically sensitive sector. And the takeover of Rio Zaza, the fruit juice firm, paralleled the quieter disappearance of the Israeli firm BM, also a manufacturer and distributor of citrus juices.

FDI's Contributions to the Cuban Economy

As routinely occurs every day around the world, FDI flows have arrived in Cuba bundled with world-class management expertise, new technologies, international product and process standards, and sustained product innovation. Joint venture expats, who are few in number in each firm, work hard to impart their management know-how to their Cuban colleagues. But much training also takes place formally and on a large scale. Meliá, for example, trains thousands of Cubans in hotel management and customer service, and Brascuba cycles Cuban staff through standardized training programs in home countries. According to Emilio Morales, a former senior executive of Cuba's large state-owned enterprise in wholesale distribution and retail marketing (CIMEX), the contributions of JVs "cannot be underestimated; they have been responsible for training personnel in accounting, finance, management, human resources, information technology, marketing and related fields. Some employees have been trained in Cuba and many have studied abroad."[53]

FDI is also the source of much product innovation. Firms like Habanos continually develop new products (such as premium cigars) for global markets, while Nestlé draws on its global R&D to launch new products in Cuba. Even more important, JVs such as Habanos and Pernod Ricard (Habana Club rum) gain access to global markets for premier Cuban products. Finally, FDI facilitates access to credit; multinationals draw on their global credit ratings to access international lines of credit at standard interest rates, well below what Cuban borrowers would have to pay on their own.

Further Evidence: European Investor Opinion

The findings from these case studies were bolstered by evidence gathered by the prestigious Center for the Study of the Cuban Economy (CEEC) of the University of Havana, whose economists surveyed the commercial attachés of members of the European Union in Havana regarding the perceptions of actual and potential investors from their home countries.[54] The survey, with both quantitative and open-ended questions, was limited to 15 diplomats and did not directly access JV managers, but the main findings are telling.

According to the survey, the Cuban business climate has a number of significant attractions, including political stability, personal security, a reliable workforce, and the possibility of eventually expanding into the U.S. market. While helping to explain some FDI decisions, these positive attributes require careful qualification:

• As of late, personal security has been jeopardized by the government's anticorruption campaign, which has jailed some foreign investors.

• There are concerns about labor discipline and motivation in the Cuban workforce. Just about any Cuban—whether manager or worker—will readily complain about low wages and weak incentives, while responsible government officials, including President Raúl Castro, routinely excoriate citizens for their poor work ethic.

• The PCC has provided remarkable political stability, but the advanced age of the current leadership and uncertainty regarding succession planning raise major questions about the evolution of Cuban politics over the long term.

Other survey responses cite inadequacies in protection of property rights and in the overall legal system; these weaknesses help to explain why the supply of FDI to Cuba has fallen far short of its potential magnitude.

Emerging Entrepreneurs and Middle Classes

Within the Cuban state socialist system, there is emerging a new Cuba—one defined by a dynamic independent private sector some 2 million strong, and by modernizing middle classes that could include half or more of the population.

The growing private sector is sopping up unemployment and offering alternatives to state employees while providing the Cuban public and international tourists with a widening range of more attractive goods and services. A common imagery fixes Cuba as a poor society whose middle classes departed in the wake of the revolution; yet Cuba today, like much of Latin America, has again become a society of emerging middle classes (albeit with depressed levels of private consumption). These tectonic shifts are unlikely to reverse as the Cuban socialist system becomes more heterogeneous and pluralistic. But it remains to be seen whether the powerful Cuban state is prepared to allow private businesses to extend their wings and grow into medium-sized and eventually large firms. Nor is it clear whether state entities will seek to partner with successful private entrepreneurs and a newly experimental cooperative sector, and—as discussed in chapter 4—take advantage of foreign (including diaspora) capital. Only then might today's modest economic gains accelerate into a genuine boom.

Since the collapse of the Soviet Union, Cuban socialism has indisputably failed to generate the savings and investment required to place Cuba on a sustainable path to prosperity. The decay of the urban landscape is on display in Havana. Factories and farms, suffering from prolonged decapitalization, are unable to supply the domestic market with sufficient goods and services to meet consumer demands and aspirations and (with some exceptions) are too inefficient to compete in international markets. Most painfully, the best-educated youth, the rising stars of the millennial generation, are exiting the island in alarmingly high proportions. In response to economic stagnation, the government has embarked on an effort to reform the state-owned enterprises (SOEs), but prior efforts in Cuba and frustrating experiences in Eastern Europe and elsewhere suggest the difficulty of the task. Rather, it is the emerging private sector that offers the best hope for a more dynamic and efficient Cuban economy, especially if it is permitted to partner with foreign investment and with the more efficient SOEs.

Of an active national workforce of 5.1 million, already over 1 million persons (or 20 percent) can now be classified as wholly within the private sector, including some 504,000 legally registered self-employed (of whom 143,000 are women) operating throughout the island. In the agricultural sector, there are some 575,000 farmers who own or lease their private plots, working individually or in service cooperatives, many of whom are prospering from the rise of market-driven agricultural markets. In addition, another 600,000 to 1 million (or possibly even more) workers can reasonably be labeled private sector. These include workers engaged in informal, gray area, or illegal full-time businesses and another, probably even bigger, segment of the population that this chapter labels GESPI ("government employees with significant private income" at least equal to their meager state wages), which is engaged in a plethora of creative activities. Altogether, as many as 2 million enterprising Cubans—40 percent of total employment—and possibly even more can be counted within the private sector. [1]

In-depth conversations with two dozen pioneering entrepreneurs and informal conversations with many others around the island suggest the energy and dynamism of the emerging private sector but also reveal people's frustrations—about the inaccessible state banking system, scarcity of critical inputs and of commercial rental space, burdensome taxation, and more generally the unsettled business climate, all of which must be remedied if private initiative is to thrive and the Cuban economy to emerge from its prolonged malaise.

Many of the small businesses will remain modest in size and ambition, but some could grow to become major generators of savings and job creation. In the specific context of Cuba's political economy, this study suggests four stages of capital accumulation during which private business can, step by step, add to household incomes, move forward to generate hefty profits, forge domestic value chains, and ultimately build alliances with efficient state-run firms and foreign partners. If the authorities establish a favorable enabling environment for business expansion, the private sector can eventually become a strong pillar in Cuba's new development strategy.

Observers are accustomed to thinking of Cuba in terms of a powerful state and a ruling communist party, lumping together the workforce as dependent state employees. However, since the collapse of the Soviet Union, Cuban society has become increasingly heterogeneous and complex. Just as analysts have recently discerned large and growing middle classes in Latin America and other developing regions, it is now possible to identify emerging middle classes in Cuba.[2] These middle classes overlap with the private sector, but as in other societies also include many public sector employees—managers, professionals, skilled technicians—who fit the various definitions of "middle class." Majorities of Cubans exhibit characteristics typically ascribed to the middle class: high educational attainment, marked female participation in the labor force and low fertility rates, and the security of home ownership and social security enrollment (but not the possession of many household consumer items). This chapter explores these phenomena.

Historical Background: The Repression and Rebirth of Private Enterprise

In its first few years in power, the Cuban Revolution defined itself by its nationalizations of foreign-owned enterprises and large domestic holdings. In March 1968, in what would become a motif of his rule (disregarding the lessons of Lenin's "new economic policies" when the Russian leader pragmatically allowed the resurgence of private property and markets), Fidel Castro launched a "revolutionary offensive" and nationalized the remaining 58,000 small businesses without meaningful compensation, leaving only some small farmers to hold private property. But then in a partial reversal in the mid-1970s, the government decided to allow some space for small-scale businesses called *cuentapropistas* (self-employed, working on their own account) whose numbers rapidly rose to 46,500 by 1981. Then another period of "rectification," of retrenchment and tightening restrictions, reduced the number of self-employed to 25,000 by the end of the decade. In response to the severe economic downturn of the

Figure 6-1. Evolution of Self-Employed, 1994–2015

Thousands

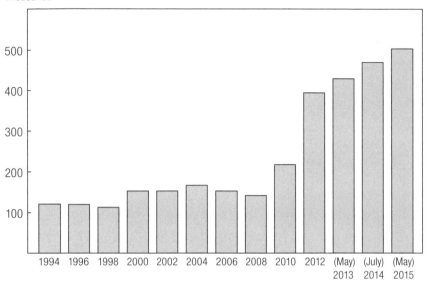

Source: Saira Pons, "Emprendimiento y Reforma Tributaria en Cuba," slide presentation prepared for the 31st Congress of the Latin American Studies Association, Washington, D.C., June 1, 2013; data for July 2014 are from CubaNow blog, August 29, 2014 (http://cubanow.us/blog/cubas_women_entrepreneurs_are_on_the_rise/); data for May 2015 are from *14 y Medio,* June 13, 2015 (www.14ymedio.com/englishedition/Number-Self-employed-Exceeds-Half-Million_0_1798020197.html).

post-Soviet 1990s, the government again relented and small businesses quickly expanded to 138,000 by 1995 (figure 6-1). The motif repeated: once the economy seemed to have stabilized, Fidel again railed against this reemergence of corrupting "petty bourgeois" behavior, imposed prohibitive taxes, and narrowed the types of tolerated activities.

It wasn't until Fidel's younger brother, Raúl, took the helm in 2008 that the government promoted the definitive rebirth of private business in Cuba, in the context of a larger strategy to modernize the economy. The Cuban authorities hoped that an enlarged private sector would absorb redundant workers being released from a bloated public sector, soak up mounting unemployment, and offer opportunities to an increasingly disillusioned youth, as well as provide more goods and services to long-suffering consumers. Memories of earlier policy reversals remain, but the forward-cascading momentum is much stronger today and is occurring within an international and domestic context that makes another reversal unlikely. Indeed, an impulsive effort to turn back the clock could endanger, not consolidate, regime stability.

A Panoramic View of the Emerging Private Sector

Cuba today is brimming with opportunity and ambition, as the long repressed entrepreneurial spirit is released and empowered. Urban streets—in Havana but also in Santiago de Cuba, Holguín, Cienfuegos, and smaller pueblos—are alive with new energies, as innovative restaurants open their doors, residents proudly repair and paint their homes, and vendors hawk fresh fruits and vegetables, cheap CDs, and cell phone accessories. Change is definitely in the air, even if corporate-branded billboards and the glare of neon signs are still absent from cityscapes.

At the heart of today's private sector in Cuba is the growing number of small-scale urban business owners or contract workers (*trabajadores por cuenta propia*, or TCPs) formally registered and counted in the official statistics (figure 6-1). They make up the heart of this chapter. Of the roughly 500,000 licensed TCPs, about 80 percent are business owners and the remaining 20 percent are contract workers employed with other TCPs. In addition, many other Cubans expend their energies in activities that can be classified as nonstate or private sector, participating in the still "informal" sector as public sector employees who also labor as part-time entrepreneurs or as temporary or migrant farm workers, independent artists, and religious workers.

In Cuba as throughout the developing world, many small businesses prefer to remain "informal," that is, beyond the reach of authority and taxation. In Cuba, this informal sector includes workers less visible to government inspectors, such as those reselling second-hand clothing in their homes, repairing broken household appliances, or serving as backroom assistants in their families' bed and breakfasts (B&Bs) and restaurants. As in informal sectors worldwide, some TCPs make this rational calculation: they prefer the risk of being caught and propositioning a bribe, or simply suffering confiscation and starting over again from scratch, to the burden of registering, paying monthly fees and taxes, and being subject to onerous government audits. Furthermore, private businesses that do not fall within the legally authorized categories have no choice but to remain extralegal and informal.

Interestingly, in Cuba today many public sector employees earn additional income from their private activities. Although the state does supplement wages with the provision of subsidized social services, this GESPI population seeks more disposable income for the purchase of life's necessities. In light of the extraordinarily low wages paid by government (median income in 2014 being CUP 584, or about $24 per month at the official exchange rate of CUP 24 to US$1),[3] this vital outside income can easily exceed official income. As one flamboyant TCP I spoke with quipped, "Now in Havana practically no one works for the state; and those who still do also have a private business on the side." The extra income may come from exercising their official profession; for example, ballet dancers traveling in Europe receive supplemental compensation, or fishermen can bypass a state wholesale monopoly to sell a portion of their catch on the open (extra-official) market. Some university scholars earn handsome honoraria lecturing abroad or in Cuba to visiting tourists; teachers tutor privately; and official tour guides offer their services after hours. Alternatively the extra income can come from an unrelated second job, be it fixing old cars, engaging in gray or illegal activities (such as selling goods stolen from state-owned enterprises), or—like the medical doctor who gained neighborhood fame for his fancy pastry creations—selling food. Many construction workers moonlight repairing and remodeling homes and apartments, in some cases cannibalizing materials from their day-job state employers. In the public health care sector, journalist and veteran Cuba watcher Marc Frank noted: "Doctors relied on patients' gifts, and sold them to survive. Nurses began caring for the better-off at home, and dentists engaged in private practice in clinics after hours or in their homes, using stolen tools and supplies."[4] In this category we might also include the many workers in the tourism sector, some working with foreign management companies, whose hard-currency tips well exceed their salaries paid in Cuban pesos.[5]

In more market-oriented economies, many of these persons would be working full-time in the informal, private sector economy, but in Cuba, where the government has pursued policies of full employment, they are allowed low-productivity jobs in the public sector and are paid accordingly; hence, they seek supplemental income elsewhere.

Estimating the Totality of Private Activities

According to official statistics, 1 million Cubans already work in the private sector, accounting for about 20 percent of the employed workforce

Table 6-1. The Cuban Private Sector, 2015

Thousands

Private sector employment	
Registered self-employment (TCPs)	505
Service and credit cooperatives	353
Land lease farmers	172
Private farmers	50
Joint venture employees	40
New urban cooperatives	6
Subtotal	1,126
Other private activities (estimated)	
Self-employed (full time, unregistered)	185
Self-employed (part time, GESPI)	400–800
Independent artists	Unknown
Migrant farm workers	Unknown
Religious workers	Unknown
Subtotal	600–1,000+
Total	1,700–2,100

Sources: Oficina Nacional Estadística e Información (ONEI), *Anuario Estadístico de Cuba,* 2014, "Empleo y Salarios," table 7.2; Armando Nova, "Cuba's Agricultural Transformation," slide presentation, Center for the Study of the Cuban Economy, May 2013 (unpublished); Camila Piñeiro Harnecker, "Cuban Cooperatives: Current Situation and Prospects," paper prepared for 31st Congress of the Latin American Studies Association, Washington, D.C., May 29–June 1, 2013; see also *On Cuba Magazine* (http://oncubamagazine.com/society/workers-of-foreign-investment-new-wage-regulations/); and author's own estimates as elaborated in the text.

of 5 million (table 6-1).[6] These numbers capture the burgeoning army of registered TCPs as well as farmers who own or lease their plots in usufruct, including those associated with service and credit cooperatives, and the employees working in international joint ventures and in the newly created urban cooperatives.

In the absence of official statistics or adequate private surveys, it is hazardous to estimate the numbers of "other private activities," but table 6-1 attempts a rough estimate by drawing on available data and conversations with knowledgeable Cuban scholars. According to official figures (2014), 1,991,700 Cubans of working age are not employed (the registered unemployed stood at 136,000, and another 1,856,000 citizens of working age are not in the labor market—that is, neither officially unemployed nor employed), and it is reasonable to assume that many of these survive through informal economic exchange (without reference to remittances sent from family and friends living abroad). Let's estimate that just 10 percent of these "idle" persons work informally, or roughly 185,000 persons.[7]

For reasons noted earlier, the GESPI category is also very large. According to a leading authority on the underground economy in Cuba, Archibald Ritter, there has been surprisingly little written on the subject, and within Cuba there appears to be no academic analysis of the problem. Ritter himself concluded that its scale appears to be "enormous" and writes that "it is unlikely that many people could survive on their *peso* incomes alone without additional sources of income," even as he does not venture a more precise estimate.[8] Here, the number of GESPI is conservatively estimated at 10–20 percent of the public sector workforce, or 400,000 to 800,000 persons.[9]

In addition to the GESPI category, several other categories of private sector labor, specifically artists, temporary or migrant farm workers, and religious workers, are worth noting. Cuba is remarkably rich in artistic talent. Thousands of professional dancers of ballet and salsa, singers, actors, painters, and writers legitimately earn income as "independent artists" when they market their products on the domestic market or overseas (although many open foreign bank accounts and fail to fully declare their earnings). As Cuba becomes more integrated into regional and global markets, many more Cuban artists will successfully monetize their talents. The creative industries could well become a hallmark of the new Cuban economy.

The number of migrant or temporary farm workers will vary seasonally, peaking at visibly significant levels, even as knowledgeable Cuban economists report the regrettable absence of official numbers or surveys. Those agricultural workers hired by private farms, including privately owned units as wells as service cooperatives whose members retain ownership of their land, are engaging in private-private contracts.

Another interesting category of private sector employment is religious workers. The Catholic Church is gradually reawakening, and Protestant churches are being renovated (often with external funding), their melodious songs resonating from their weekend assemblies. The more private Afro-Cuban practices of Santería are extremely popular and support a large supply chain that includes artisans who produce religious artifacts (and who may register as TCPs) as well as the animal husbandry that feeds the obligatory sacrifices. The Santería priests or *babalú* earn monetary and in-kind compensations that surely exceed whatever they might earn in those cases where they also hold public sector jobs. The aggregate number of religious workers in Cuba is not known but is not trivial.

In the future, the nonstate sector will likely expand to include many small and medium-sized private cooperatives producing both goods and services. In November 2012 the government (at the level of Council of Ministers) approved legislation allowing for the "experimental" creation of "nonagricultural cooperatives" (Decree Laws 305, 306).[10] Initially the government approved 271 cooperatives (concentrated among formerly state-run produce markets and in building construction but also in hospitality and transportation) in three tranches; by 2014 the government was reporting over 400 approvals with 5,500 workers, and by mid-2015 as many as 498 approvals, of which 347 were functioning, with 205 new proposals being studied.[11] Many more co ops will likely emerge from spin-offs of units of state-owned enterprises, from initiatives of municipalities to provide services such as child care or recycling, or from the decision of TCPs to formally join forces in a single business unit.[12]

Cumulatively, workers in "other private activities" add 600,000 to 1 million-plus workers or another 5 to 10 percent of the workforce, stretching current private sector employment to 1.7 million to 2.1 million workers, or up to 40 percent of total employment (table 6-1)—a much more potent force than commonly recognized.

In the future, the expansion of Cuba's private sector may be driven by several powerful forces: further significant reductions in public sector employment (as earlier announced by Raúl Castro), formalization of some still hidden informal workers, enlargement of private sector farming, private urban employment that expands beyond basic services into professional services and manufacturing, and tolerance of a new institution—medium-sized private firms (including cooperatives). And if the government follows through on liberalizing the foreign investment regime, employment could also rise in joint ventures. If GESPI and other private sector activities are included, in the next three to five years total private sector employment could reach 45 to 50 percent of the active labor force—and continue growing.

But if the private sector is to expand and become an efficient engine of growth, the government will have to address the problems confronted by today's pioneering TCPs, as enumerated in the next section.

Table 6-2. Authorized Private Enterprise

	Group description	Examples of designated activities
Group 1	Production and sale of food and beverages	Restaurants (*paladares*) up to 50 seats, snack shops (*cafeterías*), home delivery
Group 2	Production and sale of artisanal and industrial products	Artisanal crafts, pottery, shoes, religious articles including animals for religious purposes
Group 3	Personal and technical services	Repair of electrical and mechanical equipment, beauty salons, animal grooming, clothing rentals, event planning, photography
Group 4	Room rentals	Bed and breakfasts
Group 5	Construction and remodeling	Bricklaying, carpentering, electrical work, plumbing
Group 6	Transportation of persons and materials	Transportation via trucks, boats, and animals
Group 7	Other activities	Teaching of music and other arts, sports instruction, computer programming, flower sales, entertainment (clowns and magicians)
"Simple activities"	Activities benefiting from a simplified tax regime	Musical instrument repair, street vending (produce), care of seniors and the disabled, vehicle parking services, driving instruction, gardening, massage, messenger services, sales of household appliances, translation, accountancy, repair of timepieces

Source: *Gaceta Oficial,* no. 3, Special Edition, Resolution 21/2013 (January 29, 2013); *Gaceta Oficial,* no. 027, Special Edition (September 26, 2013).

Entrepreneurship in Cuba Today

In 2010 the government authorized private enterprise in 181 designated activities, which it expanded in September 2013 to 201 designated activities. For tax purposes the authorities have divided these activities into seven groups, plus an additional group that benefits from a simplified tax regime.[13] Some of the listed occupations, such as "artisan," are very broad, while others are comically bureaucratic in their specificity, such as "Benny Moré dance couple." These subdivisions, with a partial list of specific designations, are outlined in table 6-2.

So far, the most popular choices have been restaurants and snack shops, followed by B&Bs, transportation (taxis and trucks), construction, street vending of agricultural products, music sales (DVDs), recycling, and repair of household appliances. [14] This last one is a popular category probably because it benefits from the less burdensome tax regime. Enterprising Cubans are exploiting these opportunities with a growing variety of services and beginning to expand into small-scale production. Municipal authorities are empowered to grant the licenses in most cases, which are generally approved within a week or so. Authorities have incentives to act expeditiously: approved licenses are an immediate source of fiscal revenue and create employment and services for the local community.

To encourage Cubans to enter the private sector, the 2010 regulations and subsequent official announcements removed restrictive clauses that had previously governed private sector activities and added numerous incentives:[15]

• Government entities, including state-owned enterprises, can engage in commercial exchanges with TCPs.

• Some categories of TCPs can hire an unlimited number of employees (and not just family members, as had previously been the case).

• TCPs are eligible to enroll for social security benefits.

• TCPs are allowed access to bank financing and accounts and may rent government or third-party premises (as opposed to just operating out of a home).

• Restaurant seating capacity was increased—from 12 to 20, and then to 50—and the rental of an entire home as part of a B&B business is now permitted.

• Importantly, public sector employees are allowed to work in the private sector, legalizing the GESPI practice.

These reforms have opened exciting opportunities for aspiring entrepreneurs. Yet not all of these promises have fully materialized, and important restrictions remain.

Conversations with Entrepreneurs

To ascertain the impact of these new rules of the game, my assistant Collin Laverty (then a graduate student, now president of Cuba Educational Travel) and I conducted in-depth on-the-record conversations with 25 entrepreneurs. We also conducted informal conversations ("participant

Table 6-3. Cuban Entrepreneurs: Quick Facts

Industry	Number of entrepreneurs	Average time open (years)	Average number of employees	Average starting capital (1,000s of US$)	Number using domestic capital	Number using overseas capital
Entertainment and personal services	6	4.5	3.0	7.8	3	2
Retail	4	0.7	1.0	7.1	3	1
Construction	1	11.0	2.0	n.a.	1	1
Bed and breakfast	4	3.4	0.8	36.0	2	3
Transportation	4	2.9	0	21.9	4	3
Restaurants/snack shops	6	1.7	6.3	8.2	4	3

Source: Author conversations with self-employed in Havana and Cienfuegos, March 2012–April 2013.
n.a. = Not available.

observations") with many more Cubans working in a wide range of activities in Havana and Cienfuegos, including restaurants and cafeterias, bed and breakfast establishments, entertainment and personal services, retail trade, construction, and transportation. These conversations were conducted between March 2012 and April 2013, each lasting at least 30 minutes and often much longer. Although semi-unstructured and open ended to allow the TCPs to express their views without excessive prompting by questions that might color their responses, the conversations did emphasize financial questions; the responses to those appear in table 6-3. As noted, I conducted follow-up interviews with the highlighted TCPs during 2014–15.

We sought to establish some rapport with the respondents, and we eliminated cases where the respondents seemed to be very evasive or dishonest. While this sample is too small for robust statistical tests, the conversations did reveal experiences and perceptions that generally accord with other findings by Cuban scholars.[16]

Based on these 25 cases (table 6-3), the average start-up capital varies from about $7,000 in retail to the more substantial $36,000 in bed and breakfasts, where investment was required to remodel homes. These sums are larger than the tiny "micro" enterprises frequently encountered around Latin America, where start-up funds might amount to just a few hundred dollars;[17] these Cuban firms fall within the "small to medium" size category. Interestingly, slightly more than half—13 of 25 firms—had benefited from capital injected by overseas relatives, friends, and (in one case) an investor. Many of these same firms also drew on domestic sources of capital, including personal or family savings and the sale of assets (homes, cars). Not one of the 25 had accessed commercial bank loans, the entrepreneurs expressing dislike or distrust of the national financial system.

The illustrative conversations that follow convey the exuberance of today's pioneering entrepreneurs as well as their many vexations (see also box 6-1 for some specific frustrated ambitions). The conversations concluded by asking the entrepreneurs what changes they would most like to see in government policy, and their responses are also summarized here.

Paladares and *Cafeterías*

The cityscapes of Havana and other major urban centers are being transformed by the blossoming of privately owned high-end restaurants, called *paladares*.[18] These family-owned restaurants that typically operate within people's homes first appeared during the post-Soviet crisis of the 1990s, when the government allowed some private businesses to open, and they have flourished with the post-2010 reforms, growing in scale and sophistication. Much more than eating places, many *paladares* are creative imaginings of Cuba's history and culture: interpreting Cuban memories in a romantic garret (La Guarida), displaying the Cuban penchant for nostalgia for lost innocence and beauty (Bella Havana, Mama Inés, Tranvía in Cienfuegos) or for Soviet themes (Nazdarovie), advertising avant-garde arts (Atelier, La Guarida, El Cocinero) and late twentieth-century minimalist sophistication (Le Chansonnier), publicizing the bohemian and cinematic (Madrigal, named after a Cuban movie) or the invitingly familial (Doña Eutimia), and, increasingly, offering participation in plush elegance (Star-Bien, La Flauta Magica, VerSus 1900). Cuban *paladares* are expressions of the wide range of middle-class sensibilities found in today's Cuba.

A picturesque city on the island's south coast and the gateway to the colonial town of Trinidad, Cienfuegos is a tourist destination that also boasts a budding of *paladares*, including the medium-sized Las Mamparas, whose funding and operation are in some ways typical of this type of enterprise. Opened in September 2011, Las Mamparas—a reference to the restaurant's inlaid wooden panels—is a family business operated

---

Box 6-1. Frustrated Ambitions

The individuals interviewed asserted that current rules, regulations, and administrative practices were preventing them from realizing their business ambitions, in some cases entirely so. Out of ignorance or distrust, some may be underestimating the opportunities opened by the recent reforms, but the following snapshots give a sense of people's frustrations:

- A senior scholar specializing in the Cuban economy and associated with a prestigious think tank is anxious to form an international consulting firm with colleagues, but this professional service is not yet among the 201 authorized activities.
- A young architect selling artisanal products in Havana has been unable to find professional work in the sluggish construction market and refuses to work for "Stalinist" military-owned hotel chains where construction jobs are more plentiful.
- A restaurant co-owner, who formerly worked for the armed forces and served in Angola, would consider selling his primary residence to generate capital to open a private security firm, but affirms that the authorities would not allow private competition with official security agencies.
- A 31-year-old woman working in a state child care center wants to open a private day care center; she estimates high demand, but claims she would not be able to get a license, even though day care appears as one of the officially designated categories.
- A former biomedical researcher, now middle-aged, is working as a tour guide but without authorization. She says that her new profession is not yet a TCP category because the official Havantur travel agency does not welcome competition. She hopes eventually to form a tourism cooperative with friends who speak various European languages.
- Two publicists—one an accomplished media personality, the other a recent university graduate—are working as consultants to large restaurants. They are struggling to remake the existing profession of "social communications," which is focused on

---

within a spacious home propitiously located on Cienfuegos's beautiful, tree-lined main thoroughfare. For many years, Ms. Mei-ling Hernandez rented out rooms in another family home, and profits from that business were invested in this *paladar*, which is in the home of her husband. (Until recently, there was a very restricted market for residential properties in Cuba, and so homes tended to remain within families over the generations.) Her husband had experience working as a cook in Spain. (While not stated in this case, other restaurateurs have used savings from their overseas experiences as investment capital to open *paladares* in Cuba.) Seating

information flows within the firm; they want to create a more modern communications apparatus addressing customers and markets outside the firm. They make use of social media, including Facebook, TripAdvisor, and customized websites, but the government denies advertising access to TV and radio and to government-controlled print media.

- A seasoned fisherman, who lives in the shadow of the eighteenth-century fortress Castillo de Jagua in Cienfuegos, wants to form a fishing cooperative but believes that the cooperative regulations don't yet apply to fishing.

- Another successful fisherman invested the capital he earned fishing to open a modest fish restaurant; he now wants to expand his fishing business and purchase a larger boat—but cannot find one to purchase. He also wants to be able to directly supply his restaurant with his own catch but is required to sell his catch to state distributors who will turn around and resell his fish to his own restaurant.

- A former executive in a large state wholesale company, now a taxi driver with a 1995 air-conditioned Citroen, wants to open a retail store—but not until the government relaxes its monopoly on merchandise imports.

- Husband-and-wife owners of a successful neighborhood churros stand on their front patio would like to expand to a second space but report that they are unable to find necessary machinery at a reasonable price, and that renting retail space from government landlords involves "too many bureaucratic hassles."

- A gym owner with 18 years of experience is unable to find a larger venue to allow for more workout space, including a studio for group classes.

- The owner of a very successful beauty salon operating in her family home purposefully slows the growth and publicity of her business for fear of attracting attention and reprisals by authorities.

- The owner of a successful B&B in Cienfuegos who dreams of opening a small hotel in West Palm Beach, Florida, is frustrated by Cuban exchange controls and U.S. economic restrictions.

42 guests, Las Mamparas has a slightly bohemian decor, making it a favorite for the many performing artists that visit Cienfuegos. The interior remodeling and tables were crafted by hand by Ms. Hernandez's husband and daughter, Claudia, who also works the front of the restaurant. So the initial investment is a combination of family savings from another business (diversification), an existing family asset (the well-located home), and sweat equity (the remodeling). Such multiple sources of start-up capital are common among *paladar* businesses, while the more luxurious ventures may also benefit from a capital infusion from family overseas.

Ms. Hernandez, poised and self-confident, personally trains her employees. Some guests are her personal friends, but she reports that 90 percent are tourists—typical for the high-end *paladares*—and that she must cater to the foreigners' tastes: "Cubans don't like the cooking here—they prefer more lard and fat."

As the business approached the official 50-seat limit, Hernandez decided to open a *cafetería* (snack bar or diner) just down the street, under a separate license. Branded "The Big Bang," the food outlet caters more to Cubans, offering strong coffee and light snacks.[19] But the expanding entrepreneur has no interest in borrowing from a commercial bank, even though she understands that banks have relaxed their collateral requirements to include a wider variety of assets: "Bank loan procedures are very burdensome and they keep you waiting for two hours or more." She had a bad experience with an investment partnership in the past, and the absence of legal contracts means that such partnerships must be based entirely on trust. She prefers to go it alone and to expand gradually, saying "If it goes well, I benefit; if it fails, I fail." In the worst case, she will be left with a much-improved residence.

When asked what changes in public policy would assist her business, Ms. Hernandez replied that access to wholesale markets would lower her costs. Her kitchen also badly needs professional-quality cooking appliances, which are not easy to come by in Cuba.

In contrast, Café Madrigal, a popular tapas bar in Havana, caters to Cubans as well as foreigners. Owner Rafael Rosales, a well-known film director, offers moderate prices, soft classical music, and artistic wall hangings laden with historical references in order to draw an older, relaxed crowd. To explain his business model, Rosales offered this analysis: "I was among the first to recognize that the freeing up of economic forces is growing the middle class. My very first weekend, I watched actors, screen writers, business owners, tour guides, the families of employees in joint ventures, and many other Cubans with money in their pockets flock to the café."

Event Management: Party Planning and Catering

In 2012 Yamina Vicente began to transition away from her job teaching economics at the University of Havana to launch, with her sister, a business mounting decorations at private parties, a practice that has expanded to party planning. Now in her early 30s, she works with a network of some

18 private subcontractors to manage events, ranging from weddings to birthday parties to Halloween celebrations.

When she first ventured into the private sector, Yamina's friends questioned the wisdom of such risky behavior. Three years later, she reports, those same friends are begging to join her business. In one good weekend, Decorazón (the company's name is derived from the Spanish for decoration and *corazón*, or heart) can bring in more revenue than Yamina would have made during an entire academic year.

Over the last few years, the event planning business has become much more competitive, as many firms enter that space. Whereas Yamina was able to begin with $500 in capital raised from family and friends, today she estimates a new entrant would need at least $5,000 to compete successfully. To continue to expand her business, Yamina would like to purchase a large home and convert it into a banquet hall where she could stage her own events; she estimates this ambitious project would require $100,000, which she hopes to raise from investors. Currently, the state holds a near monopoly on large party spaces.

Decorazón's clients are mostly Cuban nationals, sometimes married to foreigners, who often finance their splashy affairs by means of remittances. The increasing interest in events such as baby showers and Halloween parties reflects the connections with U.S. culture and the growing ease of cross-Straits travel. Yamina herself flies regularly to Miami, where she acquires materials, most recently for a new line of business: face painting. Decorazón partners with other event planners to mount birthday parties for disadvantaged children, an expression of Cuban solidarity, Yamina proudly adds.

Another events-related company was started by Margaly Rodriguez, a whirlwind of energy who gained experience and contacts cooking at diplomatic missions in Havana and who gradually developed an informal catering business, Margalyfica, which serves primarily the expatriate community. In June 2011 she obtained a TCP license and her business has grown exponentially: Margaly purchased a car to help transport her culinary creations, and has found space to relocate her business outside of her home.

With her TCP license in hand, Margaly is able to contract with Palco, the large SOE responsible for organizing many international conferences, which pays her directly via official checks and which is willing to rent her catering equipment, including silverware and hot boxes. Margaly has catered meals and receptions at joint ventures and embassies and served appetizers for a reception of 250 people at the residence of the ambassador of the European Union.

Margaly candidly reports that in the catering business it's common to underreport earnings to reduce the tax burden. Procurement of vital business inputs continues to be a significant hassle, and her workers must exhaust themselves searching the city for ingredients.

Bed and Breakfasts: Composite Case

B&Bs—generally rentals within a home or apartment although increasingly in independent units—have become big business in Cuba. In Old Havana alone, some 400 B&B establishments provide as many rooms (600) as do the historic district's hotels; across the island as whole, as many as 18,000 rooms are available for rent, and the numbers are growing.[20] The Obama administration's relaxation of travel restrictions has resulted in a surge of U.S. visitors, and tourism from other countries has been rising as well, while new hotel construction in urban areas has failed to keep pace. Moreover, many tourists prefer the coziness of family homes, and B&B prices of some $20 to $50 per night are very competitive. Airbnb's website now facilitates bookings in Cuba.[21] Tourism is central to Cuba's economy, and bed and breakfasts are central to Cuban tourism (even though, apparently, official statistics fail to take into account the private B&B business in reporting tourism receipts). The bed and breakfast experience is summarized below, based on a composite of several actual conversations in Havana and Cienfuegos.

Previously, our composite García family had rented rooms in their home located on the outskirts of town, charging rates in local currency. With the sale of that home, their savings from rentals, and investment from a former Canadian boarder, the Garcías purchased a more centrally located and larger home and remodeled two rooms, with the purpose of charging rent in hard-currency Cuba convertible pesos (CUCs), primarily to foreign tourists. They also fixed up an interior patio for serving meals to renters and other tourists, purchasing attractive furniture made from recycled aluminum from a private local manufacturer. They plan to reinvest profits into adding another floor, making use of construction workers who are not registered as TCPs. They do not want to approach banks because they believe (erroneously) that debtors are prohibited from traveling.

Moreover, they have had problems with the authorities in the past, having been accused of renting to a sex worker (extortion, they assert), and they prefer to keep their independence and privacy. Their employees are all family members except for a cleaner, who is not registered as a TCP, although they may register her in the future so that she can become eligible for social security.

The Garcías would like the U.S. government to facilitate access to tourist visas for Cubans so that they could travel to Miami to purchase supplies, such as a filter for a planned swimming pool, an electric fly zapper, and a pump for their water system. (In 2015 and further in January 2016 the Obama administration relaxed restrictions on U.S. exports to private entrepreneurs, including B&Bs, but as of this writing the Cuban government had not yet opened channels for such commerce.) The Garcías also hope that the large state tourism companies will begin to book their clients directly with private B&Bs (as they have begun to do with *paladares*), and that telephone and Internet connections will improve.

Professional Services: Accountancy

Now in his early 50s, Mariano had a career working for the Ministry of Finance and Prices and brings knowledge of the tax and regulatory environment, as well as his government connections, to his private accountancy practice.[22] He works out of his home, and the small initial capital he needed to set up his office came from interest-free loans from his friends, which he has entirely repaid. All of his 40-plus clients are also small businesses, primarily from among Cienfuegos's B&Bs and *paladares*; indirectly, his business is heavily dependent upon the tourist trade. His prices are "negotiated," set not by the government but by private agreement. Mariano reports making a much better income now than he did as a public sector employee, in spite of not owning a computer.

The main constraint on his business, Mariano believes, is the size of the private sector in Cienfuegos, which in turn is limited by the sluggish economy and low consumer purchasing power. More tourists would definitely help. Mariano works on his own, although he has a network of other accountants he can call upon for specialized knowledge, and he may join with some of them to form a cooperative as the new regulations governing cooperatives become clearer.[23]

Retail Sales: Piscolabis Bazar-Café

Piscolabis (the old Spanish word for delicate snacks) is the offspring of three creative women who persuaded Eusebio Leal, the powerful director of the Old Havana district, to include them in a handful of pilot projects in his district.[24] In this new program, TCPs are being allowed to rent state property in prime tourist locations to open retail shops. Piscolabis sells the works of some eight Cuban handicraft makers, drawn from the co-owners' networks of creative talent. The partners work with the artisans in the design phase and encourage the use of recycled materials. The products are sold at a 30 percent mark-up over the price paid to the artisans.

The artisans' crafts and the store's interior design and furniture are entirely "made-in-Cuba with Cuban ideas," the founders proudly asserted. Most of the sales are to tourists, and the spike in U.S. tourists in 2015 has boosted business. While prices are beyond the reach of most Cubans, Piscolabis has noted an increase in purchases by locals with the disposable income being generated in the growing private sector. The business has five employees, who are paid a fixed salary plus a share of total revenues.

To prepare the retail space, the three TCP partners invested CUC 10,000 in equal shares. A designer, Sandra, and Vicky, an architect, had savings earned in home remodeling, while Claudia contributed earnings from waitressing at a prominent *paladar*. University graduates with some experience in private enterprise, they had written up a formal business plan, which impressed Mr. Leal. Their business plan projects expansions into other product lines and locations, including one designed to be more accessible to Cubans. By end-2015, the co-owners reported that they had met their financial goals, recouping the initial investment within three years. They have already added a modest sidewalk café to their customer offerings.[25] The young business partners could make good use of more capital, but banks are "complicated," one remarked.

In addition to this capital scarcity, another impediment Piscolabis confronts is a tax system that quickly slaps a 50 percent tax on profits while not allowing deductions for certain costs such as publicity, even though the company's publicity has been limited to e-mails, fliers, word-of-mouth, and, most recently, a website (http://piscolabishabana.com/?lang=en). A big problem is that the shop is not yet equipped to accept credit cards. Tourists who otherwise would make purchases leave empty-handed. Many establishments on the island are similarly not able to accept credit cards, which will slow the impact of U.S. regulatory reforms aimed at permitting their use.

Building Construction and Home Remodeling:
An Independent Entrepreneur and a New Cooperative

The greater availability of construction materials combined with the sudden legalization of home sales—adding dramatically to the valuation of family assets—has produced a boom in home remodeling in Cuba. The deteriorated Cuban housing stock is very badly in need of repair and expansion, and the opportunities for private construction firms are ample.

Jesus, in his early 50s, has been working as a TCP since the early 1990s. He employs two family members under his TCP license and draws on a wider network of construction workers as specific jobs require. He reports that friends and family—he has a brother working construction in Los Angeles, California—have brought him tools "as gifts—that's the Cuban way." For construction materials he does not use bank credit. Rather, he prefers for his customers to pay such costs in advance. Almost always, his clients pay for his services from funds they have received from relatives living abroad.

Business is brisk because building materials have become more readily available. But Jesus hesitates to grow his business. Speaking frankly and with direct eye contact, Jesus affirms that "the rules of the game are still very much in flux, there is much uncertainty about laws and policy." For example, prices of some building materials have been skyrocketing, but he still must purchase retail, as TCPs do not have access to the state-owned wholesaler, Almacenes Ferretería. And he recalls the monetary instability of the 1990s, when inflation and a sudden, sharp devaluation cost him dearly.

His two assistants (a brother and a cousin) report being paid a handsome CUC 5 per day (US$5). This is considerably better than the monthly income of CUP 250 (just over US$10 at the official 24:1 exchange rate) earned by some state construction workers or the official minimum wage of CUP 225 per month. The assistants add with pride that "Jesus is a very good construction worker."

Another experienced builder, Ricardo Veranes, responded affirmatively when the Minister of Construction asked him and other ministry employees whether they might be interested in leaving the ministry and forming a cooperative. With nearly 40 years of experience, Ricardo had managed

500 workers, earned the highly respected title of National Hero of the Republic of Cuba, and served as a deputy in the National Assembly representing Santiago de Cuba, his hometown and the nation's second largest city. Ricardo took up the challenge and selected 35 able laborers, initially hired as contract workers under his TCP license and then as members of a new cooperative named after a revolutionary martyr, Armando Mestre Martinez. As president, Ricardo is confident his cooperative can succeed based on several advantages: more flexible labor policies (easier to penalize or dismiss incompetent performers and avoid hiring redundant administrative personnel), freedom to select projects, and capacity to negotiate prices—even as the timely availability of construction materials and access to bank credit remain problematic. A further advantage is that in 2013, having just suffered a direct hit from Hurricane Sandy, Santiago was badly in need of reconstruction services, and business was brisk. The cooperative, which is governed by an executive committee and an assembly of all of its members, has set wage policies to stimulate productivity, and profits are also distributed according to measures of labor discipline and performance. Wages already exceed those paid to government construction workers by a wide margin. Consistent with cooperative principles of "solidarity and community," Ricardo offers discounted prices to some clients with less capacity to pay.

Electronics Repair

"Enrique Guerra Celulares" is the name of the repair shop for mobile phones and other electronic appliances located within the owner's home in Cienfuegos. An electrical engineer, Mr. Guerra spent his career working in a state-owned enterprise, but he also spent four years as a technician accompanying a Cuban medical mission in Venezuela, which enabled him to save some of the CUC 10,000 to CUC 15,000 he has invested in his repair shop.

His biggest problem is finding parts to repair his clients' electronic gadgets. He goes so far as to order parts on the Internet from China and has them delivered via DHL, working with friends abroad who make the payments. Friends also bring in parts, one at a time, when they return from travels abroad, to avoid having to pay heavy import levies on larger shipments. "It's an economy of ants," Mr. Guerra laments.

A roadside poster proclaiming "The Changes in Cuba are for MORE SOCIALISM" reassures Cubans that Raúl Castro's economic reforms are not forsaking revolutionary ideology. Cubans laboring under the national flag evoke patriotism and production.

Pre-revolutionary Havana evokes feelings of nostalgia and sadness. Inventive Cubans keep their classic cars running for tourists. Neglected buildings will either be restored for their architectural beauty or eventually replaced by entirely new construction.

Harvested sugar cane is offloaded for processing into sugar. Once the hallmark of the Cuban economy, sugar production is down sharply compared to pre-revolutionary levels. The remaining sugar plantations and mills will require huge investments in new technologies and logistics.

Nestlé markets its premium ice cream brands through posters and other visual displays, but state-controlled Cuban television and radio refuse commercial advertising.

The Carlos III is
an enclosed and
government-owned,
multitier shopping mall
in downtown Havana,
decorated here for the
2015 Christmas holidays.
It offers consumers
everything from
inexpensive perfumes
to branded sneakers, a
mixture of Cuban-made
and imported products.

Bursting from home fronts, private snack shops such as La Isabelita enliven Havana streets. The extra earned income raises family living standards as well as self-esteem.

An independent construction worker, Jesus specializes in home remodeling. Almost always, he reports, his clients pay for his services from funds they receive from relatives living abroad.

Dona Nora, a high-end *paladar* overlooking a main avenue in Cienfuegos, offers top-shelf Cuban rums in its bar, here shown with the proprietor on the right and a staff member.

An employee of Enrique Guerra Cedulares repairs electronic appliances, including cellular phones. This private shop is located in Guerra's home in Cienfuegos, and the owner reports that finding spare parts is the business's toughest challenge.

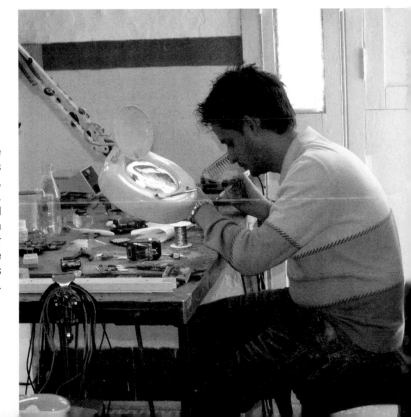

A roadside fruit and vegetable stand in the eastern provinces is dressed with a long braid of garlic bulbs. The prominent sign reads "Point of Sale: Supply and Demand." It also indicates market prices and that this is a property of a farmers' cooperative where the land is privately held but production is jointly managed by the farmers.

Hotel Inglaterra in downtown Havana, a storied venue since 1875 whose illustrious guests have included Sir Winston Churchill, the diva Sara Bernhardt, the prima ballerina Ana Pavlova, and two renowned Latin American poets, Gabriela Mistral (Chile) and Ruben Darío (Nicaragua). U.S.-based Starwood Hotels and Resorts has been authorized to convert and manage it.

The other problem is weak consumer purchasing power. With a healthier economy, more Cubans would have cell phones and other electronic equipment, Guerra asserts, and demand for his business would grow.

Transportation: The Business of Nostalgia

Julio and Nidialys Acosta are the proud founders of Nostalgicar, a fleet of gleaming 1950s model Chevrolets and other vintage vehicles. They count among their recent customers Beyoncé, Susan Sarandon, and well-heeled Cuban American business executives. "American clients are the best," report the couple, who previously worked as engineers for SOEs. "Americans are well-mannered, cultured, and interested in learning—and they tip well, too." Nostalgicar collaborates with licensed U.S. travel service providers to arrange outings for U.S. groups on cultural and educational visits. A friend living in the United States purchases replacement parts for the vintage Chevys and arranges for their transfer—via other friends, family, or mules—to Cuba. As a result of the relaxation of travel restrictions, they have also been able to directly pick up parts in Miami themselves. Excited by the recent surge in U.S. visitors, the Acostas have opened a workshop where they renovate classic cars and invite their clients to watch as they work their mechanical magic.

Although "Nostalgicar" is registered in Cuba as a trademark, it is not a legal entity but rather an informal association; each of the drivers must register as an individual *cuentapropista*, since Cuban law still restricts the quantity of cars an individual can own. The Acostas anticipate that new Cuban regulations will allow them to formalize their business as a cooperative: "We will be able to sign contracts with SOEs and get paid via check. The firm might be able to buy and sell cars—and maybe even import freely!" But the couple fears too fast an economic opening: "We won't be able to compete if the government lets wealthy foreigners come in and buy up a fleet of 40 classics without blinking twice."

The Acostas have partnered with various SOEs, including Havanatur and San Cristóbal, offering to serve their clientele; previously, the Acostas' main competitor, the SOE Gran Car, had monopolized contracts with the official entities. Meanwhile, the Acostas drive around Havana in their new Japanese model car, live in a spacious two-bedroom home, and enjoy a middle-class lifestyle, determined "to pursue our passion for restoring classic cars and progress economically by building our business."

Lessons from the Case Studies and Conversations

For early movers, profit rates can be very rewarding. Facing little competition, successful Cuban businesses can hope to recoup initial investments in one to three years—a 33 percent rate of return, at the outside. In competitive markets where barriers to entry are low there will be downward pressure on profits, and businesses will have to differentiate their products. Restaurants, for example, will want to enrich their menus with specialty cuisines as well as improve the quality of service; "VerSus 1900" invites customers to complete their evening at a rooftop bar where they can recline on canopied king-sized beds. At the same time, a favorable external shock—such as the surge in U.S. tourism resulting from the liberalization of U.S. travel regulations—will expand the consumer market and bolster business revenues and profits.

Some private businesses also benefit from the severe price distortions and implicit subsidies that characterize the Cuban economy. Entrepreneurs who can purchase inputs at repressed prices but sell their products at market "negotiated" prices can generate extraordinary rates of return. Establishments that receive revenue in hard-currency CUCs but pay workers in Cuban pesos valued at 24:1 are especially well positioned to engage in rent-seeking behavior. For example, income from one meal at a *paladar* could suffice to pay a waiter's wages—most likely less than CUC 30 monthly before tips—for a month.

Interestingly, Cuban businesses have proven able to tap a wide variety of sources for their investments. It is a common myth that Cuban households have no savings, but conversations revealed domestic capital accumulations with origins in sources as varied as savings from previous businesses; sales of assets such as cars, homes, or farmland; retained income from working as waitresses and bartenders at high-end *paladares*; and unspent bonuses received in CUCs by employees in joint ventures. Other entrepreneurs made use of savings earned abroad, in government-sponsored international missions, in postings as diplomats and military attachés, or as marketing representatives of Cuban SOEs. Capital is scarce, but not as negligible as sometimes believed, and can suddenly appear out of nowhere when opportunities beckon. Friends and families living abroad are also contributing seed capital, as donations or interest-free loans and occasionally as equity seeking profits, thus dodging both U.S. and Cuban legal restrictions. Although little commented upon at the time, under the July 2015 regulations further relaxing economic restrictions, the Obama administration permits loans—but still not equity investments—to private entities. Conversations revealed cases where foreigners, from Canada to Argentina, were willing to inject capital as "silent partners," for example to back what one investor hopes will become one of Havana's first fast-food home-delivery services. Increasingly, Cubans living abroad are returning to open businesses in their homeland (see the story behind Mery Cabrera's El Café Presidente in chapter 7). Resident foreigners are also investing, most visibly in some of the larger *paladares*.

Constraints on Entrepreneurial Spirits

Without question, Cuban entrepreneurs face many constraints.[26] The most glaring is the woefully underdeveloped national banking system. Accustomed to passively lending to large SOEs, state banks are unfamiliar with evaluating projects or taking risks, and loans of any size must be approved at banks' national headquarters. Three of the state-owned banks—Banco Metropolitano, BANDEC, and Banco Popular de Ahorro—are authorized to lend to *cuentapropistas*, but the financial resources that the central government has allocated for TCPs are earmarked primarily for agriculture and for home remodeling by the poor, leaving little for other business sectors. Furthermore, many Cubans are suspicious of state institutions, fearing arbitrary victimization or tax audits, and are unfamiliar with banking documentation and procedures and with formats for business plans.[27] Cubans are denied access to international banking by the Cuban government and by U.S. financial sanctions.

Another serious scarcity is inputs of all sorts: spare parts for repairs of appliances and mechanical equipment and transport vehicles, basic materials for construction, and vital ingredients for restaurant menus. Moreover, TCPs are denied access to wholesale markets and so are forced to pay retail prices, like any household consumer. The government maintains a monopoly on imports, and customs officials heavily tax goods imported by travelers that are above minimum values, even if they are "for personal use." Many TCPs report that custom officials often confiscate a portion of the goods they are seeking to import for their businesses.

One very visible exception to input scarcity is "El Trigal," the bustling new wholesale market for fresh produce located in the Boyeros district near the Havana airport. On high-volume days, some 100 privately owned trucks bring in bags and boxes loaded with fruits, vegetables, and grains—rice, beans, peanuts, malanga, gourds, potatoes, tomatoes, cucumbers, chilies, pineapples—that originate on private farms and cooperatives in neighboring provinces ("farm to table"). The buyers are other TCPs: vendors with stalls at the food markets, street hawkers with their carts, and *paladares* offering designer cuisine. The wholesale prices are set by supply and demand and with active haggling: buyers are willing to pay prices above those at government shops for the better quality or timeliness of supply.

An often overlooked constraint facing TCPs is the scarcity of commercial rental space. For an entrepreneur who wants to expand outside his or her home, or to select a location on the basis of market opportunities rather than on dwelling happenstance, there are few choices. There is no shortage of empty store fronts, but they are owned by government entities that have little incentive to rent: taxes on commercial rental income are high. Regulations governing public buildings and land use are still works in progress. An official publication admitted that the old colonial town centers, with their rich tourist flows, were only beginning to study land values in order to be able to rent to TCPs.[28] However, government entities have been disposed to rent to preexisting tenants, such as beauty salons, barber shops, *cafeterías*, and produce markets.[29]

More generally, the business climate remains very challenging. Many Cuban consumers lack purchasing power, and annual GDP growth has been lackluster at 2 percent (the 2015 uptick to 4 percent was temporary, as the government forecasts that growth in 2016 will fall back to about 2 percent). While the political system has been stable, the rules of the economic game are shifting *"sin prisa pero sin pausa"* (without haste but without pause) in President Raúl Castro's words, and the end-state that policymakers have in mind has been ill-defined (the April 2016 Congress of the Cuban Communist Party is to release a long-term-vision paper, which may lend some clarity to official thinking). As the system shifts from state control to a more hybrid system with a growing nonstate sector and market signals, regulatory mechanisms that protect the general public and consumers will be required—and these will take time. For example, the government has been considering new rules to regulate the burgeoning numbers of individual bed and breakfast establishments to ensure basic standards for tourists. Another example: the government will want to relax the narrow scope for business publicity, potentially creating a system that provides information to consumers while protecting the beauty of cityscapes—but it's anyone's guess as to just where this balance will be struck.

Looking forward, will the government continue to relax restrictions on capital accumulation and business growth? Legally, a person can still own only two houses (one urban and one rural or beach "vacation" home) and just two taxis (although additional taxis can be registered in the names of family members). Restaurants are still limited to 50 seats, and policies governing expansion into additional locations or franchises appear to be works in progress. Many businesses have had the limits removed on the number of employees they can contract, but if a private firm's payroll surpasses five workers the payroll taxes increase disproportionately, a clear disincentive to business expansion.

As firms grow, the tolerance of the state sector for competition will be tested. The government remains suspicious of "exploitation" in the private sector, even though private sector wages are typically far superior to those paid to public sector employees.[30] If the government is concerned that market mechanisms will increase inequalities, a much more efficient solution than repressing growth would be to implement progressive systems of taxation and social services.

The government is under pressure from its educated population to expand the authorized categories that would allow professionals, such as lawyers and architects, to exercise their talents on their own or in partnerships (cooperatives). Already there are positive examples of TCPs hiring professionals such as accountants, as permitted by current regulations. The construction of such value chains would give new hope to the frustrated middle classes and slow the damaging brain drain. Within the designated activities, Group 2—the production and sale of artisanal and industrial products—enumerates only 10 activities, discouraging entrance into manufacturing. Eventually, it is being proposed in academic circles, the government could move from its "positive list" approach to a limited "negative list" of just a few prohibited occupations or sectors. In the meantime, clarification or expansion of what occupations are allowed under existing regulations might encourage new entrants.

Beneath the surface, many TCPs grumble about the negative attitudes and petty—and sometimes not so petty—persecution by government inspectors and police. Disturbing stories of crippling fines and imprisonment for minor offenses, cancellation of licenses, and confiscation of assets are commonplace. Encounters with the judicial system are expensive, not because of formal legal fees, but rather due to the requisite under-the-table payments to soften penalties. Fearing retribution, some TCPs purposely restrain their growth so as to not capture the attention of the authorities. The population's simmering resentments are communicated by the ubiquitous gesture of two fingers tapping the shoulder: to signal military stripes and unaccountable, overbearing authority. President Raúl Castro has spoken out against lingering attitudes that discriminate against TCPs, and some business owners report a reduction in official harassment, but more remains to be done if the private sector is to feel fully legitimate and well protected in Cuban society.

Taxation: Learning by Doing

Like businesspersons everywhere, Cuban entrepreneurs complain about their tax burden.[31] Determining the actual tax burden, however, can be difficult, especially in the Cuban case where the government releases few relevant statistics. For many Cuban *cuentapropistas,* the effective tax burden is very much a function of the veracity of their reporting of revenues. In the absence of credit cards or some other reliable system to record sales, and the incapacity of the fledgling tax administration to properly audit returns, it is widely assumed that many firms grossly underreport revenues.[32] In such cases, effective tax rates would be lower than the legal rates and in practice less of an oppressive constraint on business success than they might appear at first glance.

TCPs face a number of taxes, including a monthly licensing fee that varies by occupation and must be paid regardless of revenues, and small contributions (generally CUP 87.5, or under $4 per month) to the social security system. But potentially the heaviest is the tax on net revenues (profits), which must be paid on a monthly basis and then adjusted at year end, and which rises quickly from 15 percent on net yearly incomes of CUP 10,000 to CUP 20,000, to 50 percent on net incomes over CUP 50,000, equal to about $2,000.[33] Many businesses receiving a significant portion of their revenues in convertible currency pesos (which must be converted for tax purposes at the 24:1 official exchange rate) would quickly surpass the $2,000 mark and fall into the 50 percent bracket. In fact, the effective tax rate on profits could rise even higher, because the authorities place various limits on the deduction of costs from gross revenues. Businesses can deduct from their gross revenues only 20 to 50 percent of costs, depending upon their placement within the seven TCP groups (table 6-2), and some expenses are excluded from eligibility altogether. However, only 50 percent of claimed expenses must be fully documented in tax declarations.

In addition to income tax, each month TCPs must also pay a sales tax of 10 percent on gross revenues.[34] In a reminder that some authorities continue to think in terms of a nonmarket economy, the sales tax is deductible against profits but "cannot result in an increase in retail prices."[35]

In addition, TCPs with employees must pay (light) social security taxes and a complicated payroll tax. There is no payroll tax on the first five employees. However, the base salary upon which the payroll tax is determined rises with the number of employees: for 6 to 10 employees, the average base salary is set at 1.5 times the regional average salary; for employees 11–15, at 2 times the average salary; and for any additional employees the base rises to 3 times the average.[36] This upward-sloping scale discourages business expansion and job creation (or encourages hiring off the books). At the same time, it is noteworthy that the tax code sets no limit on the number of employees and creates rules that apply specifically to larger firms, as though anticipating their creation.

There are also some smaller (some might say "nuisance") taxes. Businesses that wish to advertise their presence with signs or other commercial propaganda must seek permission from local authorities and pay taxes based upon the precise size of their advertisements. These taxes also vary according to district, ranging from CUP 30 per square meter per month in "urban service centers" to CUP 50 in districts "of high architectural value."[37] Approvals cannot be taken for granted, as authorities, including the municipal or provincial zoning office (Dirección de Planificación Física), will weigh requests against the public interest.

Taxes have been simplified for certain categories of TCPs (table 6-2) that are allowed no more than one employee. These TCPs simply pay a fixed monthly quota and social security taxes. But for some micro-entrepreneurs, such as patio snack shops, the fixed monthly quota, which must be paid independently of revenues and varies by type of activity, has been a killer and explains why many TCPs have fallen behind in payments or have simply given up and turned in their registration cards.

In comparative perspective, are Cuban TCPs facing a heavy tax burden? Without access to unpublished official data, or a good estimate of underreporting, this question is very difficult to answer. But even at 50 percent of net profits (allowing for some underreporting) plus labor taxes, the Cuban TCP taxes appear roughly comparable to those in some other developing countries. According to a survey of the International Finance Corporation, the total tax rate ("percent of profits rate") is defined as the sum of the profit or corporate income tax, labor taxes paid by the employer, and property taxes, and varies widely across countries: in Colombia, 75 percent; Brazil, 67 percent; Nicaragua, 67 percent; France, 66 percent; Venezuela, 64 percent; China, 64 percent; Costa Rica, 55 percent; Mexico, 53 percent; Sweden 53 percent; United States, 47 percent; the Dominican Republic, 42 percent; Vietnam, 40 percent; and Chile, 25 percent.[38]

In Cuba, business taxes have been modified repeatedly in recent years. Unlike in previous policy cycles, when authorities raised taxes to choke off business growth, now modifications have tended to reduce rates. Not accustomed to having to collect taxes on a large number of private entities, the tax authorities badly need to augment their collection and auditing capacities and to computerize what is still largely an antiquated paper process. A broader tax base would allow for more revenue and lower rates. A smart tax regime should discourage tax evasion and informality, encourage honest reporting and taxpayer participation, and incentivize investment and job creation.

Stages of Capital Accumulation

The majority of Cuban small businesses are new and fragile, and many have clustered around food and beverage services. These aspiring entrepreneurs are experiencing a shake-out period, and many will not survive. Some will learn from their failures and try again, in another line of business. Inspired by success stories, other Cubans will take the plunge and enter the unfamiliar domain of risk and reward, of personal initiative and accountability, of long hours and relentless 24/7 responsibilities—the constant struggle to locate necessary inputs and do battle against the many obstacles to profitability placed by hostile or indifferent authorities and by the demanding conditions of contemporary Cuba. (In some households, one breadwinner will hold onto the warm security of public employment for the guaranteed income and other perks.)

Figure 6-2. Stages of Capital Accumulation and Key Government Decision Points

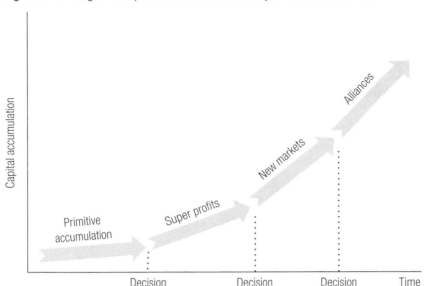

The new businesses can immediately add jobs and provide goods and services but cannot reasonably be expected to become major centers of capital accumulation overnight. Those who criticize the newly emerging private sector for not adding significantly to national savings fail to understand that the growth of the Cuban private sector will necessarily be a gradual process. But already there are firms that have surpassed the "micro" stage to become dynamic enterprises. In the specific context of Cuba's political economy, there are four stages during which select private businesses can, step by step, add to household incomes, move forward to generate hefty profits, forge domestic value chains, and ultimately build alliances with state-run firms and foreign partners (figure 6-2). If the authorities establish a favorable climate for business expansion, the private sector can eventually become a center for capital accumulation, domestic savings, and tax revenues, and a strong pillar in Cuba's new development strategy.

Stage 1. Primitive Household Accumulation

In these early years of economic opening, many new small businesses, self-financed or benefiting from modest injections of savings from family living abroad, typically have timid attitudes and modest goals. The owners do not think of themselves as business executives but rather as workers earning extra "pocket money" to lift family living standards. Many TCPs will never escape this early stage, their horizons narrowed by their modest aspirations and their proximity to the poverty line; any profits will be consumed to meet basic necessities, and even more so as the paternalistic state gradually cuts subsidies. Some who acquired their initial savings from illicit businesses, and without a record of paying taxes, are especially hesitant to deposit cash in state banks where they might face questions as to the origins of their assets. Fearful of authority and uncertain about the direction of policy, some micro-business owners will prefer to store any savings "under the mattress," or will invest in home improvements, new furniture, and household appliances. Of the case studies presented in this chapter, Jesus the builder would seem to fall within this stage of primitive household accumulation.

Nevertheless, some outstanding TCPs, whether from hard work and mounting ambition or great location and good luck, will begin to generate significant profits and raise their sights. As they develop a track record of honest income and healthy relations with government entities, they will gain the confidence to invest and grow.[39] If given the opportunity presented by an improving business climate, Enrique Guerra Celulares and Mariano the accountant could make this momentous leap forward. Some key decisions facing the government at this stage have to do with facilitating easier access to supplies and at wholesale prices (which it has promised to do) and making more retail space available for leasing or even purchase. Already the Cuban government has been modifying policies to make life easier for TCPs and could continue in the direction of lessening tax burdens (for example, establish net income rather than gross income as the tax base and remove artificial limitations on cost deductions) and relaxing the fixed monthly licensing fees for "simple" businesses.

Stage 2. Early-Mover Profits

Some small businesses enjoying early-mover advantage in underserved markets and with high turnover rates and wide profit margins can grow quickly. Some early-mover TCPs benefit from indirect subsidies, such as when they purchase inputs at low government-fixed prices, pay wages in national currency benchmarked against low government-set salaries, operate in markets protected from competition and imports, or compete with national state-owned enterprises that produce only low-quality alternatives. Some of the larger independent restaurants in metropolitan areas are visibly benefiting from these highly favorable market conditions; when *paladares* succeed in offering a well-branded dining experience with consistent quality, profit margins can be extraordinarily high. Other businesses benefit from these conditions, too; of the earlier case studies, Nostalgicar and Margalyfica could fit this mold, and the Piscolabis gift shop aspires to as well.

At this stage, government decisionmakers could begin to address the massive maze of regulatory burdens, so that a simplified regulatory regime serves to protect the public interest rather than to empower government inspectors prone to abusing their discretionary authority. The government could also issue new guidelines on public advertising, which would recognize that the circulation of information creates more efficient markets and better-informed consumers while also honoring legitimate concerns for the public interest and environmental aesthetics.

Stage 3. Growth and Diversification

Successful private firms—such as our composite B&B and potentially Piscolabis and the *paladar* Las Mamparas—will seek to expand and diversify their lines of business and points of sale. They may seek to invest in their own value chains—in businesses that supply their inputs or market their products. Successful entrepreneurs may also seek to diversify into new lines of business, including related ventures; restaurant owners might invest in transportation, just as the owner of a retail outlet might invest in the production of its sales items. This profitable private sector could rapidly move into a dynamic stage of growth and diversification.

At this stage, the government could eliminate disincentives to growth, such as the upward-sloping tax based on the number of employees, and arbitrary quantitative restrictions, such as on the number of seats in restaurants or the size of taxi fleets. The authorities should shake their suspicions of capitalist accumulation and their fears that robust private firms may escape official control and compete with SOEs. Rather, competition with SOEs should be welcomed as a driver to improving their performance. The legitimate goal of limiting concentration of assets and wealth could be better achieved through an effective, progressive tax system. (However, some restrictions might be maintained in the incipient real estate market, which remains very imperfect and subject to abuse.)

Stage 4. Strategic Alliances with State-Owned Enterprises and Foreign Direct Investment

Successful firms will quickly bump up against the many limitations of the Cuban reality. National capital markets are narrow to nonexistent. Domestic demand is weak. In many sectors technology lags badly behind global standards. And firms may run up against unfair competition by powerful SOEs. As they encounter such problems, firms may seek solutions in alliances with SOEs and foreign partners (foreign direct investment)—if they are permitted to do so. Only through such strategic partnerships will the Cuban private sector be able to access the capital, technology, and markets firms need to elevate productivity and create good jobs. Only through such partnerships will private Cuban firms be able to integrate into regional and global supply chains and compete on international markets, generating badly needed exports and contributing to Cuban prosperity.

State-owned enterprises are being granted greater autonomy from formerly powerful ministries. Beginning in 2014, some SOEs were allowed to retain up to 50 percent of their profits and to set some investment priorities and wage rates. Firms that persistently lose money will be allowed to close or be acquired by other firms, the government says, rather than be bailed out with state funds, as in the past. These more profit-oriented SOEs should be more inclined to seek alliances with efficient private firms, whether domestic or foreign owned, and would make for more compatible partners.

The Cuban government can accommodate rising entrepreneurs by offering them a level playing field where they can compete fairly with SOEs. Promoting active collaboration and strategic alliances between public and private entities would be to their mutual benefit. Furthermore, an opening to private domestic capital could help pave the way to welcoming investment by the Cuban émigré community—the Cuban diaspora living in the United States but also in Spain, Canada, and Latin America. Some diaspora entrepreneurs have access to large-scale investment capital and could integrate their Cuban operations into transnational value chains. Other diaspora investors could help to finance limited partnerships with relatives and friends on the island, jump-start small and medium-sized enterprises, and generate a business climate of renewed optimism and confidence in a better future. Taking advantage of Cuba's central location, these small and medium-sized enterprises could not only supply domestic demand but also sell into markets around the Caribbean basin and beyond.

Soft Landing for the Cuban Economy?

Successful business owners gain personal autonomy and self-confidence and develop an awareness of their business interests. These smarter executives learn how the decisions of government determine such economic variables as prices, taxes, subsidies, and interest rates, and how the results affect their own firms.

In the case of a socialist system, where government entities and state-owned enterprises control resources and markets, relations between the public and private sectors take on special significance in configuring business opportunities. Using their strong political connections and in many cases dominant market positions, SOEs are often capable of blocking the market expansion opportunities of competitors. In such circumstances, private firms can seek to marshal their own political capital to demand a level playing field where they can compete on merits, or they can seek to join forces and form public-private alliances with strong SOEs.

Looking forward, the Cuban political leadership will decide whether it is comfortable with a political economy that is open to collaborating and sharing benefits with a dynamic private sector, or whether it demands a closed system that seeks to maintain state monopolies and sets narrow limits on profitable options open to private competition. The economic and political implications of this crossroads decision will be very great.

An inclusive, open system can create perceptions of economic opportunity and mutual interest. If market forces are allowed to operate, over time the public-private balance of power will almost certainly shift in the direction of private enterprise, with its greater efficiencies and focus on profitability. But the power shift can be gradual and leave plenty of space for public ministries and firms—and their senior managers— to retain significant power and resources. Will the leadership of the Cuban Communist Party decide that its political survival is best served by sharing economic power? The final chapter explores various future scenarios in greater depth.

The Post-Revolutionary Middle Classes

In the immediate aftermath of the 1959 revolution, hundreds of thousands of Cubans—some 10 percent of the population—abandoned their homes and fled the island. The wealthier districts of Havana appeared to have been targets of a neutron bomb, one dissolving the people and leaving only the luxury villas and trendy apartment buildings. Those middle-class Cubans that chose to remain confronted the dilemmas captured in the classic 1968 film *Memories of Underdevelopment*, in which a disoriented intellectual struggles to adapt to the new socialist society.

The departing upper and middle classes left behind a Cuba of impoverished workers and farm hands. For many years the revolutionary government claimed to represent these workers and peasants, although in more recent times the government largely avoids divisive class distinctions and simply claims to represent the entire Cuban nation. But in the intervening decades—largely unnoticed—new middle classes have sprung up from within the revolution itself. By decapitating the social pyramid, the revolution had opened the doors to an unprecedented upward social mobility, and the government provided the educational institutions that equipped Cubans to seize the opportunities for social advancement. This seismic socioeconomic development—the rise of new middle classes within the post-revolutionary society—harbors important implications for the future course of Cuban economic and political development. Cuba today is very much host to large and growing middle classes, which overlap with (although are not identical to) the private sector.

There are several methods in the scholarly literature for measuring the middle class. In the method using per capita income or consumption, the measures can be either absolute or relative. In the method using absolute levels of per capita income, the thresholds vary from a low of less than $2 per day,[40] which essentially defines "middle class" as barely escaping poverty, to the more commonly accepted threshold of $10 to $13 of personal income per day, or $3,650 to $4,745 per year. The Cuban government does not release detailed data on the social distribution of income, reporting only an aggregated gross national income (GNI) per capita of $7,176 (2014) or $20 per day ($7,176 divided by 365 days).[41] In light of the relatively equal distribution of income and wealth in Cuba (where public sector wage differentials are very compressed and income-earning assets are few), by this measure a large number of Cubans would pass the $10 to $13 threshold and rank as middle class.

The World Bank declared that 30 percent of the population of Latin America and the Caribbean, or 152 million people, now fall within its definition of middle class.[42] The World Bank experts selected a per capita income threshold of $10 per day. Not being a member of the International Monetary Fund or World Bank, Cuba does not appear in these rankings. Pooling together five Latin American countries (Brazil, Chile, Costa Rica, Honduras, and Mexico), the World Bank study found that a middle-class household's daily income per capita in 2009 was $19.30, somewhat exceeding the $15.22 daily income for the average Cuban at that time and suggesting that the percentage of Cubans falling within the middle-class rankings might be somewhat less than the 30 percent displayed by this comparative group of countries. Among the countries surveyed, the size of the middle class ranged from 17 percent of the population in Honduras, to 37 percent in Costa Rica, to 42 percent in Chile.[43] However, the relatively equal distribution of income in Cuba could offset, at least partially, the nation's relatively low per capita product.

Other studies define thresholds in terms of relative incomes, based on certain income quintiles or deciles. For example, Easterly uses the middle three quintiles, Solimano the third to ninth deciles; for such relative income measurements the definition itself defines the size of the "middle" class.[44] Birdsall, Graham, and Pettinato prefer a range between 0.75 and 1.25 times the median household per capita income to define the middle strata.[45] The leading Cuban expert on social trends, Mayra Espina Prieto, places the Cuban Gini coefficient at 0.38,[46] which signals a distribution of income considerably more equal than in most Latin American countries, which hover around 0.50.[47] By this measure a large percentage of Cubans would likely fall within a range of the median income.

Alternatively, middle-class status can be defined not by income but by occupation. Cuban government statistics break down employment into five categories: manual workers (skilled and unskilled construction workers, mechanics), professional/technical (certified skilled workers including engineers, teachers, doctors, nurses), clerical (office employees), service workers (including barbers, restaurant personnel), and executives. Roughly speaking, if those who fall within the professional/technical (1,392,300), executive (291,000), and clerical (327,600) categories are defined as middle-class professionals (as they commonly are in the literature), then 40 percent of the occupied labor force (totaling 4,969,800 in 2014) would fall within the middle class.[48]

Finally, middle class can be defined by certain social achievements or values, such as educational attainment, women's participation in the labor force, indexes of economic security, and consumption baskets or aspirations:

• *Education:* For the Latin American middle class in the World Bank survey, the mean of education years is 10.4, signaling at least some secondary education.[49] For all Cubans, the mean of schooling years is nearly the same (10.2).[50] Thus, if educational attainment—possessing human capital—is given a large weight in defining middle class, as it often is, most Cubans would qualify.

• *Female labor force participation:* Female labor outside the home is a mark of modernity as well as a source of household income. In Latin American households considered middle class by the World Bank, roughly two-thirds of the women work. The female participation rate in Cuba is only moderately lower, at 60 percent.[51] More broadly, Cuba scores well in the Gender Inequality Index of the United Nations Development Program, virtually tied for best performance in the Latin American and Caribbean region with Barbados and Costa Rica.

• *Fertility rates* (or size of households): Lower fertility is associated with middle-class status, and Cuba displays the low rates characteristic of developed societies. Nearly 100 percent of Cuban women report access to contraception techniques, and fertility rates are the lowest in the Western Hemisphere.[52]

• *Home ownership and enrollment in social security systems:* In these two indicators of economic attainment and security, Cuba scores highly. Reportedly over 80 percent of Cubans own their homes—albeit too often in deteriorated status—and many have registered titles. With the mandatory inclusion of the TCPs and cooperative members in social security pensions, nearly the entire labor force is covered.[53]

So by several measures Cuba looks very much like a middle-class society. But there is one measure whereby Cuba would certainly not qualify: access to individual consumer items. One characteristic of middle-class values is an elasticity of demand higher than 1 (that is, the desire to spend more than one earns).[54] Frustrating for many Cubans is their lack of all the "stuff"—an up-to-date basket of final consumption goods—associated with middle-class consumerism. Few Cubans own their own cars or computers; any appliances they are lucky enough to possess are often in disrepair; and their access to well-stocked retail stores and private services is incipient only. As of 2013 a mere 11 percent of Cubans had fixed telephones and 18 percent had cellular service,[55] although in the past few years cell phones have become increasingly common sights on city streets.

Yet many Cubans display the middle-class trait of *aspiring* to consume. As one wry young man noted, "We're not *comunistas* anymore, we're *consumistas*."[56] Asked what her goals in life were, one Cuban in her early twenties blithely told me, "Of course we all want the same things: a car that starts, a smart phone, a computer with Internet access, and a decent home." Even if they cannot afford them, a surprising number of Cubans are aware of global brands, ranging from Nike shoes to Nestlé ice cream.[57] A common motivation for emigrating is the desire to experience the middle-class lifestyle associated with the consumer society.

There are few surveys of consumer tastes or of individual attitudes published in Cuba. But one academic publication based on 111 interviews confirmed what one might anticipate: that many Cubans are now pursuing strategies of upward social mobility. According to this study, these individualistic strategies seek advancement by moving into the private sector, by supplementing state incomes through moonlighting, and by using social networks. Upwardly mobile Cubans "offer an optimistic narrative, feel they are better off than their parents and will further improve their situations"[58]—perceptions and aspirations characteristic of the middle classes worldwide.

The emerging private sector—numbering as many as 2 million—and the middle classes   consisting of the majority of Cubans by some measures—are already defining the new post-Castro Cuba. The old narrative, that the Castros had to pass from the scene before real change could occur on the island, has been discredited by current trends.

As elaborated in this chapter, the private sector and middle classes overlap. Not all in the private sector qualify as middle class: some TCPs and small private farmers are doing poorly, and a select elite might have incomes that would elevate them into an upper class. And as elsewhere, Cuba's middle classes include many public sector employees. But there is large overlap, since many in the private sector, as broadly defined, are generating middle-class incomes. This rapidly expanding overlap category of middle-class entrepreneurs holds the keys—together with the leadership of the still powerful Communist Party—to the future of Cuba.

As noted in the discussion of stages of capital accumulation, the Cuban government can accommodate the rising middle-class entrepreneurs by offering them a level playing field where they can compete fairly with state-owned enterprises, and by promoting active collaboration and strategic alliances between public and private entities, to mutual benefit.

Over time the entrepreneurial middle classes will perceive government not just as an irritation but also as the necessary guarantor of a stable and productive business climate. They will want the government to remove the many aforementioned obstacles to TCP capital accumulation and growth. They will expect government to continue to guarantee public safety, to educate a workforce well adapted to labor market demands, to provide at reasonable cost the necessary business inputs (energy, transportation, computer information technology), and to adjudicate and enforce commercial contracts. Worldwide, many economic systems function reasonably well even when these systems are far from perfect, but the Cuban middle classes will want their government to demonstrate its intent and capacity to move forward toward better governance, especially with regard to business-related matters.

Emerging middle classes are generally perceived as modernizing forces demanding more open, transparent government and better public services for their businesses and families. Many scholars have also attributed to the middle classes strong pro-democracy preferences, but the Latin American historical experience has been mixed, very much depending on the political context. Middle classes who perceive their opportunities as blocked by authoritarian structures may advocate for democracy, but middle classes frightened by pressures from below—from poorer strata—may resort to authoritarian solutions (as arguably occurred in the Southern Cone in the 1970s). As a study by the U.S. National Intelligence Council concluded, "the rise of middle classes has led to populism and dictatorships as well as pressures for greater democracy. . . . Rising expectations that are frustrated have historically been a powerful driver of political turmoil."[59]

In the Cuba case, the emerging middle classes have been brought up under Cuban socialism; they may still honor egalitarian values and be rightly proud of the revolution's accomplishments in providing universal access to social services, but they also aspire to greater economic opportunity, individual autonomy, and material prosperity. They want to be able to travel and to explore the world—through the Internet and in person. It may be overly mechanical to predict that these Cuban middle classes will demand democratic capitalism, but it is safe to imagine that they seek a Cuba that is more "normal," more like other societies in the Caribbean basin where individuals have access to middle-class consumption patterns and have ample opportunities to realize their talents and pursue their careers independent of state control.

It seems probable that the political attitudes of the emerging entrepreneurial middle classes will turn on the capacity of the government to respond flexibly to their interests. If the government presents a closed system, unrest is predictable, and even turmoil is possible. But an open willingness to share power and resources can create conditions for a soft landing for Cuba, a gradual shift toward a more open and prosperous future.

Millennial Voices

Ambitions and Visions

I am often asked: What will happen in Cuba? What do younger people want? Rather than guess at an answer, I decided to allow Cuban millennials (aged 20–35) to speak for themselves. During the month of December 2015, I engaged in prolonged conversations with a dozen intriguing millennials living and working in Cuba's capital city, Havana. I presented each one with a structured set of 10 questions (see appendix B). Each lively exchange lasted about two hours. Altogether, I came away with a deep appreciation for the tremendous talent, bright intelligence, and driving ambition of Cuba's next generation. Some work in gray areas, testing the limits of government tolerance. But all have done battle against formidable obstacles that no American millennial can even conjure: a suffocating state bureaucracy repeating tiresome, dusty rhetoric, commanding a mostly run-down economy. The majority of Cubans can only dream of what their American counterparts take for granted: a smart phone and laptop computer with fast Internet access, their own bedroom apart from their parent's household, and an automobile with a reliable engine. From their daily struggles, Cuban youth emerge tougher, more resilient, more resourceful individuals.

These 12 millennials are not a random sample. I selected them from among the contacts I have developed over five years of visits to Cuba and from those contacts' social networks, searching for articulate, forward-looking personalities, rising stars of the next generation. Although some were born in the provinces, these millennials live in Havana and are well educated. They represent a diversity of professions, including TV and

Internet journalism, computer design and audiovisual production, the visual arts, restaurant management, government employment of various stripes (including a sociologist, foreign affairs analyst, and international economist), and two younger strivers, one temporarily earning his living in an upscale Havana restaurant, the other completing an advanced degree in the United States.

The millennials knew that their comments would be published, accompanied by their photographs. It is possible that some trimmed their remarks, anticipating that Cuban authorities would read them. But I think readers will find their narratives refreshingly candid, not at all what might be expected from within an authoritarian political system; indeed, their openness is an indicator of fresh winds blowing in contemporary Cuba. Certainly, these young men and women expressed themselves more freely than would have been the case when I regularly began to visit Cuba in 2011. The reader will notice an absence of fear in their voices.

In some respects, the Cuban millennials are similar to their counterparts around the world: alert, ambitious, hard working, postponing family for professional success, cosmopolitan in outlook and interested in world travel, measuring their own creativity and results against global standards. However, as a result of Cuba's relative poverty and isolation, most Cubans are far less digitally connected and more eager to acquire the consumer basics they have been deprived of, even as they are shocked at the overt, crass materialism so common elsewhere (Cuba's leadership avoids conspicuous consumption). As a result of Cuba's recent history and social experimentation, Cubans are hypernationalistic and acutely socially aware, attuned to economic inequalities and accustomed to expressions of social solidarity. They do not display the sense of entitlement or self-importance often attributed to millennials in the United States.

If these millennials are any guide, Cuba is not likely to lurch from socialist planning to unfettered market capitalism. In some Eastern European nations, socialism had been imposed by an invading Soviet Red Army; when the Soviet Union collapsed, their populations rejected anything that smelled of state activism, and the political pendulum swung abruptly to the right. In Cuba, the indigenous revolution has enjoyed more legitimacy, and has imbued the population with a belief in social solidarity and equality and pride in universal and affordable social services. Looking forward, Cuban millennials are less likely to endorse a U.S.-style free-market politics than a European-style social democracy.

Seven of the 12 millennials are female, reflecting the prominence of accomplished women in many sectors of Cuban life. One of the questions asked was, "Do women face additional obstacles?" In every case, the response was that not only are women able to aspire to leadership posts, but that women in Cuba face less discrimination—are freer—than many women elsewhere, including in industrialized societies. In Cuba's secular society, Cuban women do not have to contend with the patriarchal traditions of many established religions; and Cuba's health care system can freely administer to the sexual and reproductive needs of Cuban women. Furthermore, private ownership of guns is strictly banned, contributing to the low rates of violent crime and sense of personal security that Cuban women enjoy.

When queried, these young men and women denied any political ambitions. But readers should keep in mind that to overtly proclaim interest in official leadership positions could imply challenging the political monopoly of the Cuban Communist Party (PCC) and its controlling political bureau. A prediction: over the coming decade, as the Cuban political system evolves, some of these talented millennials will break out of their professional niches and leap to positions of national leadership.

Probably not all of the featured millennials will remain in Cuba. As several remarked, while they love life in Cuba and cherish family ties, they are open to transferring to where professional opportunities are brightest. If the Cuban economy continues to falter, many Cubans will vote with their feet and exit. The Cuban economy does not have to equal the wealth elsewhere to keep Cubans from emigrating, but it must narrow the gap in order for the brain drain to slow to healthy rates.

One imponderable is the impact of digital connectivity, coming slowly but inexorably to Cuba. One interviewee suggested that the more digitally adept 20–25-year-olds already feel themselves to be part of that larger connected universe. Whether that cyberconnection is sufficiently satisfying, or it simply whets their tastes and makes them yearn to be physically where the action is, remains a big, open question.

Every one of these millennials approved of the decisions by Barack Obama and Raúl Castro to normalize diplomatic relations. They hope that economic relations normalize as well, allowing a free flow of goods, capital, and people across the Florida Straits. The views of these young men and women reflect those of the general population (if not necessarily the leadership of the PCC), especially Cuban youth, who are ready to move beyond the decades of ideological Cold War confrontation. In a rare public opinion survey conducted on the island (without government authorization), the polling firm Bendixen and Amandi International found that a full 99 percent of millennials (in the survey, ages 18–34) believe that normalizing relations between Cuba and the United States is good for Cuba; 69 percent believe that the new relationship with the United States will change the economic system in Cuba; but only 37 percent believe it will change the political system.[1] The 2015 survey also found that 83 percent of Cuban millennials are dissatisfied with their economic system and 61 percent are dissatisfied with their political system. However, 67 percent are satisfied with the health care system and 70 percent are satisfied with the education system. Of the millennials interviewed, 79 percent would like to start their own business. All these findings are largely congruent with the views expressed below, even as the 12 young Cubans profiled here express themselves with more nuance and individuality.

For these dozen millennials, "normal" relations with the United States imply a powerful U.S. influence on the island. But Cubans also want to preserve their "Cubanismo," the unique national identity that blends centuries of complex interactions of many civilizations—refashioned and improved to meet the exigencies of the twenty-first century.

Meet the 12 Millennials

Among the millennials, Cristina Escobar (born 1987, Havana) and Elaine Díaz (born 1985, Havana) are already known media personalities. Both are working to promote more open, more responsive media. But Cristina is playing an inside game, working for the state television channel, pushing the envelope from within the system. In contrast, Elaine resigned her comfortable university professorship and crossed over into the unexplored riskier world of independent Internet journalism. Yet both women share these attitudes: they believe that in many significant ways Cuban women are freer than are women in the United States; Cuban women have every opportunity to triumph in journalism, even as many delay having children in order to pursue their professional goals; they express admiration for Barack Obama for being respectful of Cuban sovereignty; and they do not criticize those among their contemporaries who opt to emigrate, as angry Cuban politicians did in earlier years.

Yondainer Gutiérrez (born 1987, Ciego de Aguilas), Leonardo Rego (born 1992, Havana), and Giselle Garcia (born 1994, Havana) are digital designers and video production planners. They are launching commercial websites, producing audiovisual materials for foreign clients, and helping international film crews navigate Cuban logistics. In this new technological world, they are operating in gray zones not contemplated by existing Cuban regulations. For their fast-paced businesses, the Cuban bureaucracy is hopelessly cumbersome and unresponsive. Looking forward, they imagine a reformed Cuban state that actively promotes their industries. Yet they may choose to work and live abroad.

Lorena Gutiérrez (born 1987, Havana) and Mery Cabrera (born 1984, Pinar del Rio) are both highly educated and financially successful independent entrepreneurs, although they operate in very different markets. Lorena is a contemporary visual artist working in a range of mediums, selling her art works primarily to international collectors. Mery manages a visually appealing bistro-style restaurant catering to tourists and expats but also to the increasing number of Cubans with disposable income. Both women avoid direct confrontations with the authorities, even as they loathe the heavy-handed and arbitrary judicial and regulatory systems. Both enjoy international connections yet feel most comfortable in their native Cuba. It's a good bet that Lorena and Mery, talented and hard working, will achieve higher and higher levels of commercial and personal success.

Maidolys Iglesias (born 1987, Pinar del Rio), Marcos Galbán (pseudonym) (born 1990, Havana), and Ricardo Torres (born 1981, Villa Clara) work for state institutions. Yet all have found ways to excel and innovate. A sociologist, Maidolys works for the Office of the Historian, which is entrusted with renovating the largest Spanish colonial outpost in the Americas under the leadership of the legendary Eusebio Leal. Her cutting-edge challenge is to build linkages between Leal's office and the emerging social and solidarity economy (social enterprises and cooperatives). Marcos works in international relations, where Cuba hits well above its weight class but where, as a small country, it must constantly adjust to changes in its strategic environment. Ricardo is in the hottest seat of all: as an economist, he is called upon to advise decisionmakers on the critical issues of economic reform that will define Cuba's future.

Among the younger of these millennials, Manuel (Manolo) Valdes (born 1990, Havana) and Marla Recio (born 1991, Camaguey) are at comparatively early stages in their careers. Marla is completing a master's degree in international affairs and business in the United States, and Manolo also aspires to graduate-level studies. Both already have some private sector work experience, Manolo as a waiter in an upscale Havana restaurant—a high-income profession in today's distorted Cuban economy—and Marla in imported retail clothing (a line of private business no longer authorized). Both hope and expect that Cuba will become more integrated into the U.S. and global markets, and they are striving to prepare themselves to succeed professionally in that globalized business context. Both anticipate and welcome more normal relations with the United States as a great benefit for their generation and its families.

Here are the voices, personal aspirations, and collective dreams of these dozen millennials, among the top talents ready and eager to build the new Cuban economy and society.

Cristina Escobar Dominguez

At 28 years of age, Cristina Escobar is already a famous face throughout Cuba. Reporter, anchor, and political commentator for Cuban state national television, she first gained high visibility on an early morning show that allowed her 10 minutes for personal commentary. A savvy professional who knows how to seize opportunities, Cristina was the first Cuban journalist to ask a question at a White House press briefing when in the spring of 2015 she slyly queried: "In light of improving relations, might President Obama want to visit Cuba?"

Cristina believes that Cuban journalism should be more distant from official institutions and should rather act as a check on state power. Journalism should be less politicized and less biased, and should deal more with the pressing problems of greatest interest to the general population. Cubans should have the kind of media they truly deserve.

Many Cuban institutions and laws will have to change, Cristina believes. A new media law, currently under debate, will have to accept competition, an inevitable by-product of entering a globalized world. Cristina feels fortunate that the nation's vice president, Miguel Diaz-Canel, is leading the discussion on revising communications regulation. More broadly, generational change will yield new legislation in areas ranging from the electoral system to the family code; the latter will need to regulate the more complex forms of property in the emerging Cuban economy. Cuba cannot be stuck in time. The conditions exist for change, but it will not come over night; the battle will be ongoing. At her TV station, she's been fortunate to have the trust and support of her superiors as she executes her innovative media style.

Cristina is particularly passionate in describing how the Cuban Revolution has empowered women. She's proud to live in a country where women are among the freest in the world, she asserts. The majority of university graduates, including in the sciences, are women. Women are educated about their sexual choices and how to protect themselves, and have access to contraception and abortion. Violence against women is relatively low— in Cristina's experience, much lower than in Spain, for example. In her profession, women dominate Cuban media. If she's faced discrimination, it's been more on the basis of her relative youth than her gender. She points out, however, that in the structure of the Cuban family, women must still carry more than their share of the burden; for example, it generally falls to women to care for the elderly.

In the future, Cristina can imagine herself as a chief of programming and content, in command of more resources than Cuban TV can muster today. She plans to remain in Cuba, even if it might be easier economically to live elsewhere. Just as she doesn't criticize those who choose to emigrate, she also defends the right not to emigrate. Powerfully articulate and already a household name, Cristina denies any interest in entering politics, but she might consider working as a communications advisor or coordinator at senior levels of government.

Cristina is emphatic that the United States must learn to respect Cuban sovereignty. She attended the raising of the Cuban flag at the Cuban diplomatic mission in Washington in the summer of 2014, and was moved to tears: "Many Cubans died for us to see this proud day," she stated. She responds well to President Obama, whom she considers a very intelligent and sensitive leader, even as, on state television, she voiced criticisms of the major address he delivered in Havana. As the United States and Cuba move toward a more normal relationship, Cuba will have to develop a more nuanced assessment of U.S. politics, to focus less obsessively on the anti-Cuba lobby in Miami, and, most important, to seize the opportunities that the future will bring.

Elaine Díaz Rodríguez

The only Cuban journalist to be awarded a prestigious Neiman Fellowship, Elaine returned from her year at Harvard to launch her Internet-based magazine,

Periodismo de Barrio (Journalism of the Neighborhood). Forceful, personable, and with a winning smile, Elaine previously served on her local community council, where she concluded that government institutions were failing to solve the problems of their constituencies. Hence her publication, which will draw attention to the daily needs of "those left behind"—the average Cuban who is trailing the emerging middle classes, who doesn't benefit from the openings to private enterprise or receive remittances from abroad. *Periodismo de Barrio* will run features on what people want: more and better housing, higher salaries, less expensive and more varied foodstuffs.

Elaine eschews directly confronting the government. Rather, she advocates an independent journalism that provides an alternative to official media. *Periodismo de Barrio* intends to speak to and for the people—to scrutinize government activities and to rectify errors. In Cuba, the constitution defines media as social property, and the government owns virtually all media outlets, including print journalism, radio, and TV. But the Internet falls in a not fully regulated gray zone, and her publication has no formal legal status. Elaine chose to create a new reality that will force a change in the law.

Like many of her journalist friends, Elaine could easily have emigrated to the United States or Mexico. But she's a born optimist and fully anticipates important changes in Cuba. She's not afraid of uncertainty; on the contrary, she tolerates or even thrives on it. She also recognizes that her year at Harvard affords her international protection; when a conservative official blogger attacked her for taking a trip to Europe paid for by a German media foundation, the *New York Times* came to her defense. She assumes that the Cuban government is aware of her activities but does not feel physically threatened. Unlike the more directly critical digital outlet *14yMedio*, *Periodismo de Barrio* is not blocked by Cuban authorities. So far, she supports herself and her modest staff from money she saved from her Neiman and from small donations from European foundations.

In her vision of Cuba's future, the aging generation of leaders—whose revolutionary courage and triumphs earned them the right to rule—will pass, and the presidency and other centralized institutions will be less powerful, whereas local governments will gain in capacity and resources. New laws will establish frameworks for free media and free association, and unlike today the people will directly elect their legislature.

The Cuban people want closer relations with the United States, she believes, not only because they welcome the promised prosperity but also because they want to be closer to their relatives living there. A state visit by Obama to Cuba—she prophesied—would revive hope for changes within Cuba, especially in the economic sphere. She admires Obama because he is respectful, whereas Hillary Clinton is too interventionist, trying to dictate the type of democracy that Cuba should have. Elaine agrees with the Cuban government's decision to refuse Google's offer to quickly bring Internet to the island, for fear of exposing Cuba to surreptitious U.S. government surveillance.

Elaine is happily married and plans to have one child; any more would sacrifice her professional goals as a committed journalist. She will remain in Cuba, but she doesn't condemn those who emigrate; indeed, she feels personal pride in the accomplishments of Cubans who triumph abroad. The Cuban diaspora will play a big role in Cuba's future.

As a woman in Cuba, she welcomes the personal security resulting from the low crime rates. She felt more at risk in the United States. Elaine also objected to the machismo she encountered in U.S. academia, which seemed to become more and more pronounced with increasing rank and status.

Yondainer Gutiérrez Fernandez

A visual designer and entrepreneur, Yondainer Gutiérrez holds two jobs: as an independent contractor for mostly international clients (yon2x2.com), and as cofounder and CEO of the Cuban online restaurant directory AlaMesa. The consistent thread: to design visual solutions for websites and mobile devices and to improve the user experience.

A self-defined "free thinker" and a very hard worker who prides himself on getting by with little sleep, Yondainer focuses not on what cannot be done, but rather on what can be. Too many Cubans are held back by self-censorship, he believes. Of course, an individual should carefully study laws and regulations—but then take action and accept the consequences.

While completing his degree in visual communication design at the Superior Institute of Design, in 2011 Yondainer and his colleagues launched the website AlaMesa, which lists restaurants and private *paladares*. The website is a solution to the lack of local information about eating establishments, as well as the shortage of business advertising opportunities in Cuba. The restaurants do not pay for placement; his business model generates revenue from additional services such as publicity on his website or via social media. By December 2015 the award-winning AlaMesa had grown to 7,800 unique users per month, each averaging visits to eight pages, and 5,000 followers on Facebook.

AlaMesa fits within the authorized business category of "programmer of computer equipment." The firm consists of a core of six individuals, including programmers and a specialist in social media, and an additional eight or so occasional contractors. The firm serves individual as well as social goals: it generates income for the employees and helps create jobs in the hospitality sector.

Yondainer prefers to focus on solutions, but if pressed will note the many obstacles that face Internet-based firms such as his. First and foremost, there is little e-commerce in Cuba. Most Cubans still cannot connect to the Internet with any regularity. And U.S. economic sanctions have forced payment mechanisms such as Paypal to block Cuban sites. Nor are there many market studies in Cuba, so his firm visits trade fairs to observe how consumers are reacting to the various products and other stimuli.

In his eight years as a designer and five years with AlaMesa, Yondainer has been amazed at the lack of interest on the part of government institutions, even when he has approached them. "It's as though they are waiting for instructions from some higher god." In contrast, he notes much more interest from overseas, in both the U.S. and Europe. For example, several international firms, including Google and Everbright, recently hosted a "Start-up Weekend" in Havana. Such events not only provide useful training but also serve to build a community of local entrepreneurs. Why, he wonders, doesn't the Cuban government, or a collaboration among state-owned firms, offer assistance with legal and financial matters and funding for start-ups? Other governments in Latin America are providing such assistance to their local entrepreneurs. He's heard that the government has authorized the formation of one or two cooperatives of programmers but considers it absurd that the Council of Ministers should have to approve such business ventures.

Another issue for Yondainer is the work attitudes of Cubans, especially in state-owned firms. In his view, it's critical that workers feel good about their work, as means to provide for themselves and their society. At AlaMesa he strives to make the other employees feel very much part of the larger project.

Looking forward, Yondainer remains a committed optimist. There will be progress, he believes, so long as he and other Cubans engage in positive thinking and design solutions. He very much hopes that relations between

Cuba and the United States continue to improve. He looks forward to raising a family and prefers to remain in Cuba, where his businesses are located. But he is also open to other opportunities, to whatever presents itself. He lives by a phrase from the Cuban singer-songwriter Silvio Rodriguez: "*El sueño se hace a mano y sin permiso*" (Dreams should be hand-crafted and without permission).

Leonardo Fidel Rego Rivero and Giselle Garcia Castro

Leonardo Fidel Rego Rivero and Giselle Garcia Castro are students at the elite Advanced Institute of Art (Instituto Superior de Arte). They are enrolled in the program of communications and audiovisual arts, which includes radio, television, and film.

In earlier years the official Instituto Cubano del Arte e Industria Cinematográficos (Cuban Institute of Art and Industrial Film) generously supported Cuban filmmakers, and their movies gained international recognition. In recent decades, the national film industry has suffered from a scarcity of resources, driving filmmakers and other audiovisual artists to seek international funding and to form joint ventures with foreign production companies.

Today, in the world of film and other audiovisual mediums, including commercial advertising, Cuba is red hot, and many international production companies are descending on Havana. Taking advantage of this swelling demand, both Leonardo and Giselle are already working part-time as freelancers or contractors.

Part of a team of Cuban audiovisual artists, Leonardo has worked on editing and post-production for a variety of products, including video clips, animation, and documentaries. His clients are located in Latin America as well as the United States, especially in the religious sector. He has also worked on a children's mini-series that his associates plan to market internationally.

Speaking excellent English (she purposely studied for a year in the United States), Giselle has established herself as a go-to "fixer" or local production agent for foreign audiovisual productions. She advises her clients in accessing the necessary permissions from local authorities and makes logistical arrangements for them. Meanwhile, her university studies concentrate on audiovisual editing.

Government regulations in the audiovisual business have lagged behind technological change. Some of the work done by Leonardo and Giselle falls in a "hole" of unregulated activities and escapes taxation. Nor do current government rules allow them to form a film production company with legal standing, which complicates issues such as the legality of foreign funding, copyrights, and bank accounts. The government needs a new set of regulations that would create good labor standards, promote freelancing, and establish taxation rates. Smart regulation would create a framework for a thriving industry with many good jobs as well as a tax base for fiscal revenues—vital requirements for Cuba's future economic advancement.

Neither Leonardo nor Giselle believes that the socialist economic system is working well in Cuba today. Giselle notes that socialist central planning, imported from the Soviet Union, was never appropriate for an underdeveloped tropical island. Leonardo objects to a system full of inefficient cross-subsidies among sectors ignoring productivity. He thinks the country should focus on the most promising sectors, including the audiovisual industry.

Both recognize that international video productions are attracted to Cuba in part because of low costs. But they fervently object to being exploited and paid below international wage rates. For one of his productions, Leonardo was paid only about one-fifth of what he thinks it was worth at international prices. Giselle can earn in a single day what many Cubans earn in an entire month—but at rates way below what a similar task might be worth in Los Angeles. They want to be paid based upon the quality of their work, and they want to earn sufficient income to live well in Havana—in other words, to practice their creative professions without having to relocate to Los Angeles or elsewhere.

Looking ahead, Leonardo wants to be a director, even as he recognizes that to reach this goal he will first need to pass through a chain of technical experiences. Eventually, he wants to be successful enough to be able to select his clients and creative projects. Giselle aspires to be an executive producer of her own small production company; she hopes to choose her own projects and hire well-motivated personnel along with occasional freelancers.

Both are eminently confident that in the future they will be successful professionals, whether inside or outside Cuba. As Cuba becomes a more normal country, their decisions about where to live and work will not be an issue of politics or patriotism—as such decisions have been framed in the past—but rather of opportunities and personal preferences. Already, Leonardo considers himself "a citizen of the planet."

Lorena Gutiérrez Camejo

Lorena Gutiérrez is a graduate of the fabled art schools of Cuba: the National Academy of Fine Arts San Alejandro and the Advanced Institute of Art (Instituto Superior de Arte). She has exhibited at two of Havana's biennial art exhibitions, where entrance is highly competitive, and most recently in a prestigious group show of seven young Cuban artists at the Inter-American Development Bank in Washington, D.C. She works in a variety of mediums, including oil paintings, photography, and mixed media interactive installations.

Lorena defines herself as an independent visual artist. Art is her passion, a vital necessity and outlet for self-expression. She eschews purely commercial production, refusing to simply please the client—to offer souvenirs or decorations—or to prostitute her work for commercial gain. She is fixing up a new studio in an unoccupied home owned by her family, which she is planning to eventually sell so as to purchase space closer to the center of town and prospective buyers. She relies on curators and brokers to help market her work (she is not yet represented by a gallery), and most clients are foreigners, as few Cubans could afford her work.

The Havana art market is largely controlled by state-owned galleries; artists who exhibit in them must pay commissions and taxes. Fully private galleries are not yet permitted, even as some artists exhibit in their studios or in rooms within private homes. In Cuba, the arts are organized under the powerful Ministry of Culture, which houses the National Council of the Plastic Arts: to take advantage of the rising value of Cuban art, the council is now building its own institutional collection and plans to create an exhibition space. Lorena has applied for membership in the National Union of Writers and Artists, another important component of the Cuban art world. Perhaps these organizations could help to create a regulatory framework that would permit the emergence of a fully legal network of private galleries.

In many respects, Cuban artists have enjoyed a privileged position. Even before Raúl Castro lifted restrictions on travel for the average citizen, artists were allowed to liberally travel abroad and to exhibit overseas, where many of their works command substantial prices largely beyond the reach of Cuban taxation. In a country where other independent workers and firms struggle to acquire imported goods, Cuban state import agencies supply artists with their essential materials. The elite art schools that Lorena attended are fully free, financed by the state. Even before Raúl Castro allowed the expansion of small-scale private business, artists such as Lorena were licensed as "independent visual artists" by the Ministry of Culture.

Corruption is a central theme in Lorena's work. In Cuba, stealing from state-owned factories and retail outlets is a common means of survival, and petty corruption has spread through all levels of society, she feels. The mixed-media installation at the Inter-American Development Bank, "Upperworld," features well-dressed men and women wearing white collars surreptitiously engaged in illicit activities. An ominous stillness pervades the black-and-white setting. Another panel lists the extremely harsh penalties for various types of white-collar crimes as defined by the government, suggesting arbitrary and unfair legal proceedings.

As a child, Lorena traveled the world, as her father was a pilot for the Cuban airline and her mother was a flight attendant. She continues to travel freely to exhibit overseas. She's happy to live in Cuba, even as she has relatives living in Miami and Spain. Of her graduating class of about 30 from the Advanced Institute of Art, more than half have emigrated, though only a minority of these are able to continue working in the visual arts. She is not interested in emigrating herself, as she calculates that collectors today are hungry for art produced in Cuba. But she might live abroad for a while, if it benefited her career.

An only child herself, Lorena would like to bear at least two children, but not yet. For now, she is prioritizing her professional development, in part so she can have the income required to properly support her family. She does not perceive gender discrimination problems in Cuba's art world, where women enjoy considerable visibility and power. The arts are a risky profession, and Cuban women, hardened by struggle, do not yield easily.

Mery Cabrera

Born in Pinar del Rio, Mery Cabrera won a scholarship to study at the elite Lenin High School in Havana and went on to complete her studies at the leading university specializing in industrial engineering and business administration (the Polytechnic University José Antonio Echeverría, CUJAE). In search of a better business climate, she and her husband lived in Ecuador for six years, where she practiced capitalist techniques managing a retail outlet. When Cuba opened space for private enterprise, the couple gathered their savings, sold their home in Havana, and invested in a restaurant, El Café Presidente.

El Café Presidente enjoys a prime location on a major Havana thoroughfare. After just two years in business it's a huge success, attracting both foreigners and a few well-heeled locals. It offers the maximum 50 seats allowed by current government regulation. The design respects the building's prerevolutionary architecture (the space is rented from its private owner) and offers a sleek, contemporary, bright red-and-white interior. Mery's husband handles the finances while she serves as general manager, and she is evidently on top of every detail. Rather than hiring professionals from state-owned restaurants, who she feels do not appreciate client service, Mery personally hires and trains young, attractive Cubans, mostly male, with no prior experience in food and beverage but often with university education.

Mery selected the restaurant business, despite having no prior experience, not only because of its high profit margins. She also calculated that government authorities were less likely to close the restaurant sector, as they have other types of private firms such as movie theaters and clothing outlets. Still, the restaurant business faces serious obstacles. Born into a humble, provincial family, Mery lacks connections to well-placed families ("apellitos y papitos") that make starting a business that much easier. Taxes are high, and labor taxes increase sharply with the number of employees (she has 20). Finding critical inputs is a constant headache: private firms cannot import through normal channels, so she is forced to rely on individual travelers subject to the whims of customs officials, who once confiscated a blender because the box label said "professional use." Almost like SWAT teams, government inspectors arrive without notice and demand that her employees produce their identity cards in front of her customers. Once when she was in the hospital recovering from surgery, inspectors demanded that she make a personal appearance or they would shut the restaurant.

Mery dreams of opening other lines of business, such as professional firms for architects or engineers, but these are not yet permitted under regulations restricting private enterprise. She might also operate in Miami.

She wonders why the Cuban government doesn't allow private firms to flourish, to import and invest, and why, unlike Ecuador (even under the left-leaning president, Rafael Correa), Cuba doesn't offer businesses incentives and lines of credit.

Mery, who has a six-year-old son, doesn't feel women are discriminated against in Cuba. In the restaurant business, the leading figure is a woman, Lilliam, who runs a long-established *paladar* bearing her name and who has served as a generous mentor to Mery. Mery relishes life in Cuba, with its optimism, humor, and mutual assistance. She likes tropical weather: "I have hot blood," she says with a wide smile. As she has clearly demonstrated, given the opportunity, Cubans are capable of innovation and success, but the pace of change must accelerate. Virtually everyone agrees with that, Mery asserts, even the children and grandchildren of the top leadership, with whom she studied at her elite high school not that long ago.

Marcos Galbán

Since graduating two years ago from a specialized institute that feeds state ministries, Marcos Galbán (pseudonym) has been a government employee who prepares information memorandums for his principals. He works hard to close the gap between the theories of academia—which have long-term visions but lack information—and the practical, day-to-day crisis management confronting government decisionmakers. In his professional life, Marcos fully expects to succeed, while accepting that promotions will be gradual, based on his knowledge and hard work but also on age and seniority.

Marcos quotes José Martí: "The vain villager thinks the world is like his own neighborhood." The nature of his work will allow him to travel, giving him access to a world beyond Cuba without having to emigrate. While technological limits and government censorship restrict most Cubans to a local Internet, Marcos is privileged to have access at his workplace to the Internet, including Facebook and Twitter, but not yet YouTube, which occupies too much bandwidth for the current Cuban system.

Marcos is confident that Cuba will change, even if there are too many variables to predict the precise pace of change. President Raúl Castro recognizes that Cuba must be open to the world, as it always was in the past, and become once again a regional and even global hub for commerce. With the 2011 economic reform guidelines and the normalization of diplomatic relations with the United States, Marcos sees that changes are already under way.

More rapid growth will come with a more rational use of economic resources, Marcos believes. The easy growth will be in tourism, but Cuba must also diversify, for example into sustainable agriculture, where it holds natural advantages. Cuba must evolve from short-term crisis management—for example, searching for trade credits to meet basic import needs such as milk—to well-conceived projects designed with long-term business strategics. Even so, Cuba will remain a developing economy over the next 10 to 15 years, as it continues to struggle to overcome structural problems such as weak physical infrastructure, both inside the country and in its connections to the outside world (airports, seaports).

Marcos maintains that for Cuba's socialist economic model to endure, it will need to ensure the delivery of high-quality social services, which will depend on generating more wealth. Cuba cannot close its eyes to its economic problems, but should emulate China and Vietnam, which recognized their own problems and made major changes. For Marcos, the fundamental difference between capitalism and socialism lies in the distribution of wealth and the provision for the population's basic needs.

Politically, the historic generation that made the revolution is passing from the scene. Cuba will gradually evolve toward a rule of law and a regulatory state that oversees productive sectors; for example, there is currently a serious discussion of a new regime to guide the film and audiovisual industry. State institutions will be strengthened, including the judicial branch and a national legislature that must be professionalized (currently, deputies are in session on a part-time basis). Marcos is not worried that such a horizontal fragmentation of power might slow decisionmaking; he believes it will allow for the expression of conflicting points of view and the creation of an informed, legitimate consensus with shared responsibilities. "Cuba can do this," he says. "The 1940 Constituent Assembly produced one of the most advanced constitutions for its era."

In Marcos's view, the normalization of relations with the United States is irreversible, as it obeys the interests of various social and political sectors and reflects regional and global trends. Once the U.S. blockade is lifted, the Cuban economy will be able to function more normally: normal relations will allow for the two-way movement of goods and people and permit travel and migration to flow in both directions. Prolonged tensions between the United States and Cuba have distorted the actions and perspectives of government and citizens in Cuba. As relations normalize, Marcos anticipates, Cubans will be freer to focus more attention on other important questions facing his nation.

Maidolys Iglesias Pérez

A cancer survivor, Maidolys Iglesias graduated from the very top of her sociology concentration at the University of Havana, and hence was able to exercise her first choice: working at the Office of the Historian, which is in charge of the restoration of the colonial Old Havana (Habana Vieja). She serves as liaison between that office and the district's social enterprise start-ups, including cooperatives and purely privately owned firms.

While working, Maidolys is finishing her master's degree in social development, and hopes to tackle a doctorate program in the same field, or in the social and solidarity economy. Her office will allow her the flexibility to pursue her publicly financed higher education, just as the government fully covered the costs of her two years of cancer treatment for non-Hodgkin's lymphoma.

Looking to Cuba's future, Maidolys envisions an economy more diversified and more inclusive than today's, with cooperatives and private enterprise in addition to state-owned enterprises. Characterized by worker control (self-management) exercised through worker assemblies and relatively equal and generally higher wages, cooperatives are better fits for the Cuban economy than purely private enterprise. Where private firms exist, Maidolys believes, they should be encouraged to undertake socially responsible activities, including investing in their communities. Overall, Cubans operating in the nonstate sector should strive not just to enrich themselves but also to contribute to their communities as a whole.

The government must make it easier to form cooperatives, Maidolys says. Currently, each cooperative is approved at the very highest level of government—at the Council of Ministers, presided over by President Raúl Castro himself. Maidolys envisions approval at the municipal level instead. Most current cooperatives were born as spin-offs from preexisting state firms; but in the future, more should emerge spontaneously, as new start-up ventures organized from the bottom up. Sustainable investments will husband resources and keep in mind future generations. Overall, she believes, Cuba needs more of an "economic culture," where people are better educated about basic accounting and taxation, among other concepts necessary for entrepreneurship.

Having so personally benefited from universal social services, Maidolys feels strongly that they should remain a priority of Cuban development. But more attention must be paid to economic development; wages must rise (her own salary is CUP 450 plus CUC 10 per month, equivalent to just under $30) and household consumption must be bolstered. The economy must become more diversified by economic sector and should include international trade and investment in joint ventures with state-owned firms and cooperatives. "Eschewing taboos, Cuba should open to the world," Maidolys maintains. But the world should not overwhelm "Cubanismo": she defines these national character traits to include social solidarity, the capacity to joke and laugh when confronting daily struggles, an inherently happy disposition, and an inborn love of music and other performing arts.

Eventually, Maidolys would like to have two children, but for now she is focused on her professional development. In contrast, the majority of her friends from provincial Pinar del Rio already have children. In postponing a family for career enhancement, she considers herself more European in outlook. She has no complaints about gender discrimination: Cuba guarantees equal pay for equal work, and in her office the majority of managers are female, including her immediate superior and mentor.

In her work, Maidolys has had opportunities to travel in Europe and Latin America, but has never thought of emigrating. She cherishes being with her family and the warmth and security (low crime) of her beloved Cuba. She's happy and proud of the new U.S. relations with Cuba and looks forward to full normalization, when people will be able to freely visit and see the realities of Cuba with their own eyes.

Ricardo Torres Pérez

A leading young economist, Ricardo Torres is very much a product of the Cuban Revolution. His grandparents were rural laborers, the revolution educated both of his parents as engineers, and he was awarded a scholarship to study at the very selective Lenin High School in Havana.

Energetic and articulate, Ricardo enjoys teaching economics, inviting his students to examine the Cuban economy with a critical lens. He is also very excited about his research and advising to government agencies: the future of his country is being decided today. The economy will most probably grow, but whether it expands in a smart, sustainable fashion is a 50/50 proposition. Ricardo worries about a chaotic, unbalanced growth path, one focused more on sun-and-surf tourism and basic logistics but neglecting more sophisticated, knowledge-intensive industries. Such a distorted growth path is made ugly by growing inequalities, financial imbalances, and high debts.

Ricardo is forthright in grading his employer, the University of Havana. So far, the university and the associated think tank, the Center for the Study of the Cuban Economy, have supported his economics research, but should they interfere with his academic freedom, he would consider other alternatives: "I own my own life, and will not cede that freedom to any authority." The university also suffers from poor infrastructure, especially in IT. Salaries are low and funding for research is hard to come by, propelling many good members of the faculty to seek employment elsewhere, in the local private sector or overseas.

Many of his more capable friends from his university class have already emigrated and found good jobs in finance and business in Miami (although those with poor English skills are reduced to manual labor). As he contemplates his own future in Cuba, Ricardo thinks he might like to open his country's first truly independent think tank, which would contribute to a more pluralistic Cuba and to policy debates.

As a professional economist, Ricardo has given great thought to a new model for Cuban economic development. He can envision a rapidly expanding economy driven by vibrant private businesses, knowledge-based professional services, high-end tourism linked to a research-intensive biotech cluster allied with big international pharmaceutical marketing firms, and software firms also intertwined with local expertise. Building on local resources, Ricardo can also imagine a future Cuban economy featuring high-value-added, export-oriented agriculture in organic tropical fruits, as well as creative industries (film, music, fashion) with global reach and renewable energy investments in solar, wind, and biomass. But for this very sunny future to become reality, Ricardo recognizes, major structural shifts are needed: a much smaller state, smart regulatory institutions that promote rather than inhibit the expansion of entrepreneurship, functioning local credit markets capable of financing development, and much, much higher levels of capital investment.

People vote with their feet, Ricardo contends: the day when most bright, young Cubans decide to stay, "we will know that we mixed the right recipe."

Ricardo admits that such dramatic shifts will create not only winners but also losers. It's not about revenge against those who made mistakes, he says, but rather about doing what works. Providing a social safety net for displaced persons will be much easier in a rapidly expanding economy, and the same is true for preserving high-quality social services.

History and geography bind the United States and Cuba. Ricardo maintains that the two neighbors can become close friends, even allies, so long as the United States respects Cuban sovereignty. An explosion in bilateral cooperation is possible, as generations change and attitudes evolve.

Manuel (Manolo) Valdes

Twenty-five years old and with a degree in journalism from the University of Havana, Manolo Valdes is holding down two jobs. He's a "fixer" for the new Lebanese-Cuban Businessmen Council, helping its members navigate the exigencies of the Cuban bureaucracy. But his main income derives from his work over the last two years as a waiter at one of Havana's hippest and most expensive restaurants, El Cocinero (so named for its location in a former cooking oil factory)—where the Obama daughters ate lunch during their Dad's Havana sojourn. In a single evening, Manolo can earn over $20 dollars in tips, as much as what the average Cuban brings home in a month. What's more, he's had the treat of serving some of the international celebrities now descending on Cuba, including Mick Jagger, the Princess of Monaco, and Jimmy Buffett.

But Manolo aspires to much more, for himself and for his role in Cuba's future. A proud nationalist, Manolo believes that his country, once a crossroads of civilizations, can regain its former stature and become a hub of culture and commerce. A blending of civilizations, Cuba is a big stew, with its own special identity and culture. In his restaurant experience, Manolo has interacted with many foreigners, and he notices how much they enjoy their time spent with Cubans and just being in Cuba: they are free of annoying corporate advertising, and largely cut off from the Internet. Manolo realizes that Cuba cannot—should not—remain stuck in the past.

On the contrary, he imagines an open Cuba fully integrated into the global economy, even as the island maintains its cultural essence.

Manolo has been impressed with the business acumen shown by the Lebanese professionals he works with. Cubans need to learn to be more efficient and innovative, he believes. Cuba should not be mired in a geographic fatalism, limited to tourism and agriculture, but should instead build on its educational advantage and learn to specialize in a variety of products and services. This new business prowess should be leavened with a strong social consciousness. Manolo is attracted to the Scandinavian models of business innovation and social progress.

To help push Cuba forward, to be a protagonist in his nation's future, Manolo recognizes he needs more formal preparation. His goal is to gain a master's degree in international relations or business in the United States or the United Kingdom—some Anglo-Saxon culture—because Cuba's commercial future will inevitably be closely tied to the United States. His girlfriend is already on this professional path: she is pursuing a master's degree in business in the United Kingdom.

Manolo does not hesitate to express his political opinions. His grandparents fought for the revolution and then worked for the government. The anti-Batista struggle was necessary, but along with many others he sees Cuba as a country of lost illusions, of smashed dreams. It must transit from the current one-party system, where the parliamentarians vote by a 100 percent consensus, to a multiparty system with diverse voices and freedom of assembly. Millennials do not see themselves as well represented in the current political system, Manolo believes, and many object to the widespread hypocrisy, dishonesty, and loss of values   the results of many years of economic scarcity and daily struggles to survive.

Change will come. But the government must allow it, and the people must demand it. A danger is political apathy, Manolo believes, especially among the young, who prefer to focus on their own careers and families. The change is likely to be gradual: after the rapprochement with the United States on December 17, 2014, many Cubans expected or hoped that change would come quickly. But so far there's been no direct impact on the lives and pocketbooks of most Cubans. Nevertheless, in 10–15 years Cuba will enjoy normal relations with the United States. Foreign investment will flow in, administered by well-prepared Cuban managers. Havana will be completely transformed: Manolo can imagine the seaside Malécon promenade becoming a thriving regional financial center.

Marla Recio Carbajal

Marla Recio is the rare Cuban enrolled in a full-time master's program in the United States, in University of California–San Diego's School of Global Policy and Strategy. After finishing at the selective Lenin High School, Marla earned top grades in economics at the University of Havana. But she yearned for more: to broaden her horizons, to perfect her English, and to update her knowledge and deepen her expertise.

Both of Marla's parents held senior positions in government agencies. She is typical of the internal brain drain: the preference of talent to turn away from government careers for more profitable and rewarding private sector options. For a while, Marla ran a small private business selling imported clothing, until the government declared that private apparel stores could sell only items of domestic origin. But she has remained engaged with small business owners, helping to arrange visits to the United States where they can upgrade their skills.

At UCSD, Marla was honored by being named a "Dean's Fellow," a distinction achieved by only 10 percent of the student body. She feels that her Cuban education prepared her well for the quantitative classes, but that Cuban higher education has fallen behind both in educational materials, partly due to limited Internet access, and in teaching methods. English instruction, while widespread, is too deficient in quality for Cubans to be competitive in the global marketplace, where English is the common language. At the University of Havana, too many professors resorted to authoritarian, rote learning, whereas the better U.S. classrooms encourage critical thinking. At UCSD Marla has enjoyed soft skills development, participating in group exercises that encourage respectful interaction and creative teamwork. She believes that if work productivity is to increase, Cubans need to learn how to compromise and avoid aggressive posturing.

Marla's single biggest concern is the rising rate of emigration from Cuba. So many of her friends, especially the most talented and hard working, have already departed, and others are contemplating exit, to the United States, Spain, the United Kingdom, even Haiti! She's worried that the pace of economic change is too slow, and that wages will not rise fast enough to enable Cubans to attain comfortable lifestyles at home.

For Marla, however, Cuba is a golden opportunity. An economy that is just beginning to open up offers many niches where smart investors can jump ahead of the competition and earn very high returns. In Cuba today, some private firms, especially high-profile restaurants and bars, are posting 50 percent rates of return on investment. Upon graduation, Marla would like to build upon her social networks in both the United States and Cuba. She envisions herself as a bridge across the Florida Straits, encouraging educational and cultural exchanges and business opportunities. For her own start-up venture, Marla has several concrete ideas to embody these goals: a business to plan destination weddings in Cuba, a hostel to accommodate U.S. student travel, and a high-end villa rental property.

When Barack Obama and Raúl Castro announced the normalization of diplomatic relations on December 17, 2014, Marla says, she never felt prouder. Her Cuba was finally moving in the right direction; the government had opened its eyes to see the need for change. She is confident that this ship will continue to sail forward, and that she has acquired the analytical skills and social networks to make her own contributions to her nation's upward trajectory.

Scenarios

Dreaming in Cuban

Most social scientists limit themselves to predicting the past. It's convenient to have historical data, inevitably describing past trends. Economists and political scientists then develop models—relationships among variables—that best explain what happened yesterday and why.

It's a lot easier predicting the past than imagining the future. For one thing, the future has not yet given us data to crunch. Of course, data from the past can be used and simply projected forward. Yes, the future may look a lot like the past; there may be more continuity than change. And that makes for one baseline scenario worth investigating. But it deprives scholars of the opportunity to imagine discontinuities, to conjure up futures that substantially stretch beyond today's boundaries.

I asked a prominent Cuban intellectual: what scenarios can you imagine for Cuba's future? His quick retort: "Richard, that's way too hypothetical."

Perhaps. None of us has a crystal ball.

But Cubans in particular may have lost the capacity to imagine new beginnings. After all, for over 50 years now—two full generations—Cubans have lived within the communist paradigm as interpreted by one charismatic leader whose personality was so strong, whose presence was so deeply felt, as to crowd out alternative scenarios. Continuity, not change, was the norm. Indeed, during the regime's darker days, to articulate alternatives was supremely dangerous: one could be branded subversive, counterrevolutionary, a spy for imperialism and neoliberalism. Fidel Castro once famously said to a gathering of Havana intellectuals: "Within the Revolution, everything [is tolerated], against the Revolution, nothing!"[1]

The fictional narrator in Pico Iyer's lyrical love story set in Havana, *Cuba and the Night* (1995), wryly observed: "The biggest shortage of all, I always thought, was of a future; the government mass-producing images of the past, while people kept their eyes firmly focused on the present."[2]

But without at least a general sense of where you want to end up, how do you know whether it makes sense to move in this direction or that direction? Individual steps become arbitrary and hazardous unless they are moving forward consciously, toward a defined goal.

Cuba at the Tipping Point

For Cuba, if there were ever a time for imaginative futurology, for a stretching of the mind, this is it!

Oftentimes people do in fact have a general sense of direction, even if not fully articulated. They have a sense of self, shared social values, implicit goals. People may want more prosperity, more equal opportunity, or more security and stability. They may want individual autonomy or a stronger sense of social cohesion. They may prefer ethnic and religious homogeneity or rejoice in diversity. They may give priority to economic progress or give higher ranking to economic stability and personal safety.

Some Cubans—and Cubans are not unique in this respect—imagine that they are totally unique, that no society is similar to theirs and so they have little to learn from others. This is, in a sense, "Cuban exceptionalism." Thomas Piketty, the renowned French economist and author of *Capital in the 21st Century*, disdainfully refers to "intellectual nationalism"— the view that "there is nothing to learn from other experiences."[3] In her recent survey of Cuban writers, cultural critic Rachel Price writes: "Today, 'post-revolutionary' literature reimagines Cuba as transiting from a small island nation with delusions—however justified—of world-historical grandeur, to an archipelago on a shrinking planet."[4] Yet in their geography, history, and civic culture, Cubans do have some good grounds for their prideful boastings. Their island is by far the largest island nation in the Antilles. Sitting astride sea lanes with proximity to the North American mainland gives Cuba a privileged geography, rendering it a transshipment hub, whether for African slaves, Chinese merchandise, or European tourists. Historically, following centuries of loyalty to its motherland Spain, Cubans demonstrated extraordinary bravery and rendered many selfless sacrifices during the protracted and bloody independence wars. Cuba's socialist revolution—carried forward against the will of the dominant superpower—was among the most enduring of the twentieth century, and among the best articulated and most romanticized around the world. Civically, Cuba's combination of high-performance artistic culture, intellectual sophistication, and diplomatic prowess is impressive, as are the design and implementation of its universal social services.

But Cuba also exists within a world economy and a regional politics. For over 50 years, Cuba escaped capitalist development, choosing to join the centrally planned Eastern European and Soviet economies. That house of cards collapsed when the Soviet Union vanished. Cuba then deftly turned toward its emerging market strategy, negotiating a diversity of trade and investment deals with the rapidly expanding and (for the most part) ideologically sympathetic developing economies of China, Brazil, and Venezuela. As demonstrated earlier, while these negotiated arrangements have kept the Cuban economy afloat, they have not launched Cuba into a new era of sustainable growth. And the emerging market countries, while still economic powerhouses, are now grappling with their own economic problems, their capacity to bankroll international projects much diminished. Immersed in their own domestic troubles, they have less interest in underwriting Cuba with costly subsidies.

All the while, the ruling Communist Party of Cuba (PCC) has given first priority not to economic prosperity but rather to its own security, to maintaining its one-party monopoly and securing its intertwined bureaucratic control over all resources and decisionmaking on the island. In the 1990s, when its benefactor, the Soviet Union, suddenly vanished, Fidel Castro opened the economy a few notches, to let in enough oxygen for his revolution to survive (an outstanding example of what political scientists would label authoritarian resilience). But once Castro felt politically secure, he curtailed and even partially reversed his economic openings. Fidel reverted to his fiery denunciations of the injustices of global capitalism. In the more recent past, collaboration with like-minded emerging market economies gave Cuba a few more booster shots; but again, not enough to lift the economy onto a sustainable development path.

As the interviews with Cuban millennials in the previous chapter made so clear, few of that generation believe that this highly stratified top-down bureaucratic centralism is either desirable or workable, even if some of its fruits are well worth preserving. If their elders insist on maintaining their mid-twentieth-century system, many millennials will simply exit and seek to make their fortunes off-island.

Mapping Cuba's Future: Assets, Liabilities, Leadership, and Luck

In imagining the paths that Cuba could walk, first let us briefly review the available building blocks for the future edifice. Cuba is not an abstraction; it is not a virginal Garden of Eden. Rather, future scenarios must be well grounded in the island's specificities. From its accumulated historical experiences, Cuba boasts many assets on which to build, just as it also suffers liabilities that could stymie progress. As Cuba moves forward, the goal should be to build on the many assets and extinguish or mitigate the deleterious liabilities.

Among the chief assets:[5]

• Prodigious human capital, in the form of a remarkably well-educated, articulate, and self-possessed public with high self-esteem

• Spheres of excellence, specifically the creative industries, biotech research, and social service delivery systems, even if the health and educational systems are faltering for lack of resources

• Successful defense of its national sovereignty by a professionalized diplomatic service with global reach

• Varied natural resources, including tropical sunshine, endless beaches, stunningly beautiful bays, unspoiled coral reefs, multiple sources of untapped renewable energy, nickel and related minerals, and fertile soils, many lying fallow

• Civil culture, specifically low levels of violent crime and a proud nationalism

• Homogeneity, with muted ethnic tensions and tolerance for religious expression (so long as it does not overtly challenge the state)

• Social cohesiveness, involving empathy, interpersonal trust, and strong community-based social networks

• Regional diversity, with pride in local cultures and an array of differentiated resources and regional strengths: in western Pinar del Rio, striking vertical green mesas and tobacco plantations; in central Havana, high culture and colonial architecture; in "El Oriente" (the eastern provinces), rich Afro-Caribbean influences and history of fierce political rebellions

Among the chief liabilities:

- The heavy weight of bureaucratic centralism and top-down decision-making; excessive caution, inertia, and fear of risk taking and innovation
- Badly depleted capital stock and infrastructure, subpar national savings and investment rates, and low productivity, especially in agriculture
- Enforced isolation from valuable global currents, especially in technology and information systems
- Argumentativeness, machismo, and intolerance—counterproductive characteristics not unique to governing circles
- No tradition of compromise or tolerance for pluralism, in politics or personal life
- Incipient culture of individual consumerism fostered by images from nearby Miami that could swamp efforts to raise domestic savings and improve public services and infrastructure
- Attitudes in diplomacy that worked well in the past but that today are dysfunctional: playing the role of victim, of David versus Goliath, of the sardines versus the shark; projecting a negative defensiveness; refusing to graciously accept a "yes"

In building a better future, leadership will matter, as it has so often in history. What would the United States look like without Washington, Lincoln, or FDR? Mexico without Benito Juárez and Lazaro Cardenas? France without Napoleon Bonaparte? Unimaginable! For better or for worse, Cuba today is the outcome of the fiery imagination of Fidel Castro, who is Washington, Lincoln, and FDR—founder, liberator, social reformer—all rolled up into one larger-than-life personality. As an elderly lady confesses in a recent novel set in Havana: "Of course, [Fidel's] our father. Every father makes mistakes, especially stubborn fathers who want the best for their children. But he is our father and we love him."[6]

There are only intimations of who among the younger generations will be the successor leaders. In the medium term at least, the PCC's 14-member political bureau will select the president and other senior government officials and party leaders. The current first vice president, Miguel Mario Díaz-Canel Bermúdez, looks to be the heir apparent when Raúl Castro steps down in early 2018, as he has promised to do after completing his second five-year term as president. In his mid-50s, Díaz-Canel rose through the ranks of the PCC, serving as provincial party secretary and then as minister of higher education, where by all reports he earned the respect of the academics for his intelligence, integrity, and open-mindedness. But like other aspiring candidates, he is cautiously low-profile. There isn't enough known about him to confidently predict his future behavior once in power. Nor is it clear whether he will have to share power in a form of "collective leadership." Should Díaz-Canel and his generation fail to move Cuba forward, the restless millennials, who crave greater economic opportunities and normal relations with the United States, will likely exit the island in accelerating numbers. Alternatively, young leaders—who have yet to emerge but surely will—may seek to press their elders for more rapid reform, or even seek to leapfrog to power themselves.

In charting Cuba's future, luck will also matter. Will the international tourism market remain strong, or will virulent international terrorism deter travel? Will terms of trade and commodity prices bend favorably or adversely? Will offshore drilling rigs grant Cuba energy independence? Will Cuban scientists make a major commercial breakthrough in drug therapies? How high will the seas rise around Cuba's exposed shorelines? Will hurricanes become more common and more violent, and will the resulting storm surges overwhelm Cuban coastal defenses?

A comparatively benign international context could greatly benefit Cuba's changes. In a best-case scenario, external circumstances contain and mitigate climate change, spur rising levels of international tourism, offer good prices for Cuban commodity exports (nickel, sugar, alcohol, tobacco), and provide ready financial liquidity for bankable investment projects. The United States removes economic sanctions and the diaspora in Florida and elsewhere invests in Cuba, or returns to manage businesses or purchase properties for family vacations and retirement.

Three Scenarios: The Good, the Bad, and the Ugly

This chapter presents three possible future scenarios. But the purpose here is not to predict, not to order each of the three visions as having probabilities of "high," "baseline," and "low," even if some outcomes at this time appear more likely than others. Rather, the goal is to imagine various futures, rendered feasible because they are grounded in Cuba's existing assets and liabilities, and because there are already existing societies that resemble them. To the extent that the various key actors—Cubans on and off the island, the United States and other engaged governments,

Table 8-1. Three Scenarios of Cuba's Future

Scenario	1. Inertia	2. Decay	3. Sunny 2030
Economic reform	Slow motion	Uneven	Comprehensive
Economic situation	Stagnation	Stagflation	Growth
Institutional strengthening	Inertia	Decay	Systemic
Political reform	Continuity	Incoherence	Multiple paths
Popular mood	Disenchantment	Anxiety	Optimism
Overall social climate	Uncertainty	Volatility	Stability

multilateral financial institutions, international business, and globalized nonprofits—can better visualize their future choices, those choices are more likely to be smarter and more coherent. There are lessons to be drawn from the experiences of other transitional nations, though the specificity of the Cuban case must always be born in mind.

One important development that is very likely to occur by 2030 in any scenario is the widespread access to modern telecommunications. In line with trends throughout the developing world, many Cubans will own their own personal digital devices and smart phones (and whatever other telecom technologies emerge by 2030). But no one can know the political implications of this unprecedented technological transformation. Will it empower Cubans to organize and demand more open government? Or will Cubans be content to turn their attention predominantly to lighter fare such as messaging about daily activities among their friends and competing on video games?

Peering out to 2030, I imagine three scenarios: 1) stalled reform, where forces of inertia and immobility (*immobilismo* in Cuban parlance) maintain their grip and many millennials exit; 2) an ugly botched transition descending into economic stagflation and an explosion of criminal vices; and 3) a sunny soft landing, where comprehensive economic reform yields higher per capita incomes and consumption, and the political outcome is wide open (table 8-1). Let's call these end-states, even as we recognize that history is a continual flow and that change is ceaseless. For each scenario, I will venture some economic and social performance indicators drawing on precedents elsewhere on the planet (table 8-2). No two countries are exactly alike, but other experiences are instructive, offering lessons on what works well and what risks should be avoided. The more clearly alternative futures

Table 8-2. Performance Indicators

Scenario	1. Inertia	2. Decay	3. Sunny 2030
GDP growth	2%	1%	5%
GDP per capita[a]	$9,865	$8,426	$15,686
TCPs (self-employed)	750,000	1,000,000	2,000,000
Annual FDI	$1 billion	$0.5 billion	$5 billion
Crime	No change	Big jump	Slight rise

a. Projected from 2014 GDP per capita as given in Oficina Nacional de Estadística e Información (ONEI), *Anuario Estadístico de Cuba,* 2014, "Cuentas Nacionales," table 5.12, (http://www.onei.cu/aec2014.htm).
TCP = *trabajadores por cuenta propia;* FDI = foreign direct investment.

are envisioned, the more likely that the ship of state can be steered away from perilous shoals toward more felicitous shores.

Among the key variables that will determine Cuba's future political direction are the unity or fractures among the Communist Party leadership, the opportunities offered these *nomenklatura* to transit successfully to opportunities in the new Cuba, the organizational capacity and imagination of Cuban civil society, the interests and goals of the Cuban diaspora, and the creativity and engagement of United States and Latin American diplomacy.

Scenario 1: Inertia and Exit

In this less felicitous scenario, the forces of inertia and authoritarian resilience—the one-party monopoly and bureaucratic control—prove too powerful for those Cubans pushing for profound change. Fear of the unknown, paranoia about imperialist subversion from the North, the overwhelming desire on the part of the PCC leadership and cadres to maintain their authority and privileges—all these allow the imperatives of security and stability to trump the evident need for renewal. While some progress is made in economic reform, the generation that comes after the Castros proves too timid and too divided to take many definitive steps forward. The system's liabilities are amplified while potential assets are undervalued and underperform. Performance indicators are mixed at best. Cuba too closely reminds observers of other stalled transitions: the Soviet Union in the post-Khrushchev years, some Eastern European and Central Asian nations today, the perennially underperforming and frustrating Argentina.

Economic Reform

Economic reforms occasionally lurch forward, but orthodoxy forces incoherent compromises and at times backsliding. The resulting half measures prove disconcerting and create multiple distortions that spread throughout the economy. Some prices are government controlled, other prices are set by market supply and demand, still other prices are regulated by the government but are regularly adjusted to forestall shortages and long lines. This multitiered pricing system is wildly inefficient and confusing to the public and deters international investors. Cubans become experts at arbitrage and speculation. In the absence of international liquidity, government efforts at monetary reform result in the shortages of some essential goods and the bankruptcy of many inefficient state-owned enterprises (SOEs), forcing the government to inject credit to keep workers on the job—in turn causing outbursts of price inflation.

Institutional Change

Institutionally, there is a growing disconnect between authority and responsibility, between performance and accountability. Senior officials urge line managers to take initiative, but cautious middle-level managers are fearful of being accused of making mistakes or even of corruption. Agencies charged with oversight lack the expertise and authority to properly enforce regulations, and under-the-table payments too often drive decisions.

Political Reform

In this scenario, the PCC maintains its unity and stability, even as it tolerates more internal discussion of policy options. The state party apparatus gradually becomes more decentralized and internally competitive. As middle-aged cadres replace the generation that came to power in the 1960s, government and party take on a more normal, contemporary look. State-owned media become more animated and are challenged by nonstate Internet-based publications. By 2023, the end of the first post-Castro administration, the PCC begins to look something like the "big tent" socialist parties in Europe, with various ideological tendencies and personalities vying for influence, as internal coalitions shift depending on the issue at hand or the astuteness of political personalities.

There could be several bright spots in this overall gray scenario. Curiosity to taste the formerly forbidden fruit continues to drive tourism from the United States, even as many first-time visitors don't return due to the uneven quality of services. New hotels arise at beach resorts, more slowly in the major cities, as the state-owned tourism firms reserve the juiciest locations for themselves, preferring to engage foreign hoteliers as management partners rather than form joint ventures. This attitude restricts capital inflows and slows the construction of new hotels. Rather, the spectacular growth is in private B&Bs, which inadvertently become a hallmark of Cuban tourism. Enterprising Cuban families open boutique hotels and some even develop chains of guest houses with unique branding, eventually undertaking ventures on other Caribbean islands.

Confronted with the loss of subsidies from Venezuela, the government finally decides to act with urgency in the energy sector and approves a wave of foreign investment in oil and gas exploration. It takes seriously the pledge for renewable sources to provide 24 percent of energy by 2030, authorizing joint ventures and even some wholly foreign-owned foreign endeavors. In most other sectors, the foreign direct investment (FDI) approval process remains burdensome and slow. Overall, FDI inflows reach about $1 billion per year, enough to create some islands of dynamism but insufficient to generate a broad-based balanced growth.

The purely legal private sector of small enterprises peaks at 750,000 and remains closed to the middle-class professions. The government prefers cooperatives, compelling many private firms to join forces and adopt the cooperative legal framework. The larger cooperatives are controlled by PCC cadres, and while more efficient than state-owned entities (they can fire redundant workers more readily), few permit real participation by member-workers. Rather, government-succored co-ops become a tool for restricting the growth of a truly independent private sector. To restrain private accumulation of wealth, the government imposes harsher taxes on profits and personal incomes in the private sector business, even as some firms (notably those with political connections) flagrantly circumvent regulations.

Performance Indicators

In this stagnation scenario, GDP languishes with a barely perceptible growth of just about 2 percent per year, in line with the disappointing performance during the years 2010–14. Woefully inadequate national savings and investment rates barely surpass 10 percent. The capital stock continues to depreciate and the technology in most sectors falls further and further behind global standards.

In this disquieting world, some clever millennials unearth opportunities to develop their talents, but many decide to pursue their dreams off the island. The on-island population slowly declines and continues to grow older, placing mounting pressure on fiscal resources, social services, and pension funds.

In the schemata of the stages of capital accumulation (chapter 6, page 161), Cuba under this scenario is stuck in the stage 2–stage 3 range. Government wariness of change keeps a lid on openness and competition, to the despair of the more adventurous risk takers and innovators as well as those Cubans seeking access to global consumption baskets.

Nevertheless, it may just be possible that this scenario, with all of its risk avoidance and half measures, turns out to be the cautious prelude to a more energetic and definitive historical period. With hindsight, scenario 1 could come to be seen as simply the warm-up to a sunny 2045!

U.S. Reactions

U.S. policymakers will be disappointed at the tepid pace of this scenario. In U.S. politics, some in the Republican Party and the Cuban American community will work to maintain sanctions and even reverse some of the measures taken by the Obama administration to relax the economic embargo. Conceivably, some in the Cuban government purposefully maneuver to renew bilateral tensions. Irritants such as U.S. claims for compensation for nationalized properties remain unsettled. Even Democrats seek to employ remaining U.S. levers to foster more progressive and rapid change.

Precedents from around the World for Scenario 1

Relevant lessons for this scenario come from Eastern Europe, the Soviet Union, and Argentina.

Eastern Europe

Eastern Europe in the 1970s and 1980s was a gray region trapped in Stalinist-imposed institutions that ill fit national specificities. Reform factions emerged that pushed for modest economic reforms, but they were frustrated both by the dogged opposition of orthodoxy and by the failures of half measures to make real progress. Among the noticeable contradictions: markets where prices are half free and half controlled do not send clear signals, resulting instead in speculation and theft; and the heavy influence of the Communist Party and trade unions impedes efforts to make SOEs more efficient, compelling national treasuries to continue to subsidize otherwise bankrupt enterprises. In Eastern Europe, and especially in the Soviet Union, official ideology lost its grip on reality, especially among young people, many of whom emigrated to the West.

Soviet Union

In its last years, growth slowed in the Soviet Union and technological innovation (except in certain military-related sectors) increasingly lagged behind global trends. Efforts to renew Communist Party cadres and leadership fell flat. Finally, Gorbachev sought to reform the system from within, only for events to escape beyond his control.

Argentina

Argentina, the perennial underperformer of South America, suggests other pathologies of possible relevance to this scenario. For an immigrant departing Europe around 1900, it seemed reasonable to prefer Buenos Aires to New York as a gateway to new opportunities. Subsequently, Argentina squandered its natural wealth, in particular its rich Pampas grasslands, and the income gap between the United States and Argentina widened dramatically, even as the Argentine middle classes have enjoyed significant improvements in living standards. The legacy of Juan and Evita Perón still holds sway in Argentina: charismatic politics combined with an anti-imperialist rhetoric, populist boom-bust economics, a wasteful interventionist state, and institutionalized corruption. In the 1970s a brutal military dictatorship murdered and disappeared some 20,000 of its citizens accused of "subversion." When Pope Francis visited Havana and its Revolutionary Square in the summer of 2015, Raúl Castro invited the president of Argentina, Cristina Kirchner, to sit beside him on the podium. This gesture of hospitality recognized the nationality of the Pontiff (Argentinian) but also reflected the close diplomatic and ideological ties between

the Cuban government and Argentina's Peronist Party—disquieting intimations of one of Cuba's potential paths.

Argentina has experienced periods of good relations with the United
States, for example, during the years when the administrations of Bill Clinton and Carlos Menem overlapped, and possibly again with the election of
Mauricio Macri in late 2015. But the default in the presidential Casa Rosada
is to blame "imperialism" and "neoliberalism" for the nation's ills, to prefer
economic protectionism to open competition, to maintain state influence
over market economics, and to identify Argentina with global and regional
groupings that define themselves in antagonism to the United States.

Scenario 2: Botched Transition and Decay

In a second scenario that is closer to inertia than a sunny soft landing, Cuba
comes to look more like other Caribbean countries, manifesting many of
their less desirable traits. The opportunity for uniqueness is forfeited. Economic reform advances further than in the inertia scenario, but not far
enough to consolidate a new coherent system. The decaying bureaucracy
and deepening cynicism in official circles open gaping spaces for systemic
corruption and even organized criminal activity. Conceivably, internal
divisions within the PCC break out into the open, generating innumerable
scenarios for political instability and even violence. Performance indicators point downward; most millennials are discouraged and outmigration
accelerates, replicating the Puerto Rican pattern. Precedents for botched
transitions include the unhappy recent experiences of several countries in
Central America.

Economic Reform

The Cuban authorities attempt to take advantage of some commercial
opportunities made available by the U.S. opening, but lack the strong leadership and technical expertise to implement a coherent economic reform
program. Monetary unification is successful, commercial channels are
opened, and the private sector expands to at least 1 million authorized self-
employed as some restraints are removed, but the ministries and state holding companies battle to maintain a grip over most investment decisions.

Managers of SOEs and cooperatives misuse their enhanced authority to
strip assets and enrich themselves. Land and housing speculation becomes

a local and trans-Straits sport, surpassing billfishing as a main topic of cocktail conversation in elite circles. Many Cubans seize opportunities in international commerce not to build businesses but rather to gain access to kickbacks and capital flight. Firms that succeed in the private sector are vulnerable to "interventions" by envious and avaricious government authorities—all in the name of social equity. Whether for foreign investment, international trade, or building permits, access to government approvals routinely requires under-the-table transfers, driving many more mature multinational firms to stay away. Corruption at high levels becomes more flagrant and visible, enraging honest citizens. At the local level (provincial and municipal), undertrained and underpaid officials take advantage of their enhanced authorities to benefit their families and close associates. From time to time the government seeks to crack down on mounting corruption and jails some high-profile figures, but these campaigns only engender deeper cynicism when top anticorruption officials are themselves accused of wrongdoing. The anticorruption campaigns take on the color of political vendettas, useful for discrediting reformers and dissenters.

Institutional Change

The quality of state institutions seriously deteriorates, as they become infiltrated by competing factions of the PCC, increasingly mixed with criminal elements. The PCC loses some control, but technical experts are not empowered and regulatory decisions are too often driven by threats and bribes. The island appears to be sinking back into the grim 1930s or 1950s, characterized by gangsterism, political violence, even narcotics and organized crime. Cuba becomes a major transshipment center for illegal merchandise heading northward. The military stretches its tentacles throughout the economy as some active duty and retired generals develop their own fiefdoms, threatening the unity of the PCC and the integrity of government.

Political Reform

In this increasingly volatile atmosphere, foreshadowing outcomes is especially hazardous. One scenario: mounting popular discontent gives rise to a mass mobilization for change, but the PCC is divided over how best to respond, with one faction favoring accommodation and an acceleration of change, the other opting for repression. In the worst case, the PCC and security forces splinter, resulting in violence among factions that could become full-throated civil strife if it engages civilians. Under these circumstances, one possible outcome is overt military rule. While rule by the generals has become an outlier form of government in Latin America and the Caribbean, it is hardly without precedent. Some might justify a military junta "in defense of the revolution," or simply as a stop-gap measure to restore peace in the streets.

Performance Indicators

This volatile scenario could result in deepening impoverishment amid speculative wealth. GDP growth grinds to a halt, and some social indicators continue the deterioration they manifested in the final years under both Castros. Many private sector ventures close their doors, even as some fortunate entrepreneurs prosper. Foreign investors limit their exposure to projects with virtually guaranteed returns, such as in well-situated holiday resorts and energy-producing projects benefiting from government contracts with fixed returns. Most distressing, crime statistics converge with regional averages. Outmigration also surges, causing population contraction to fall further below current trends.

U.S. Reactions

In this scenario, U.S. policymakers are likely to turn away from Cuba, as yet another poorly governed impoverished nation in the Caribbean basin. The search for stability could lead the United States to support the security forces as a shield against international crime. Only select U.S. investors would venture forth, if U.S. government regulations allowed. In the worst-case scenario of severe civil strife and bloodshed, pressure would mount for direct U.S. military intervention, a tragic reversion to the practices of a bygone era.

Precedents from around the World for Scenario 2

Botched transitions and decay accompanied by explosive vice are all too common in the developing world. Precedents include some states of the former Soviet Union, the Northern Triangle of Central America (Guatemala, El Salvador, Honduras), to a certain degree the neighboring

Dominican Republic, and most recently parts of the Middle East, though sharp ethnic and religious fractures are less prevalent in Cuba. Distressing examples that Havana does not want to emulate are Panama City and Yangon, Myanmar—scenes of ugly urban chaos, lagging infrastructure, and half-empty luxury high-rise condominiums purchased by "hot" international capital.

Former States of the Soviet Union

Post-Soviet Eastern Europe and Central Asia offer a wide variety of relevant experiences, some more felicitous than others. A vibrant civil society enabled the Czech Republic to quickly become a high-quality capitalist democracy. However, Romania was birthed as an illiberal democracy where electoral competitiveness is limited to successors from the Romanian Communist Party; corruption is widespread, the administrative capacity of the state remains weak, and social services are in perpetual crisis. Oil-rich Kazakhstan enjoyed impressive growth but failed to diversify, and its economy is now in a downward spiral; the country's post-Soviet trajectory has been dominated by Nursultan Nazarbayev, who won reelection in 2015 with an implausible 97 percent of the vote. In Georgia, President Eduard Shevardnadze (eventually deposed by the 2003 Rose Revolution) became a focal point for the emerging class of criminally connected businessmen who made huge profits from skewed privatization processes; a similar process occurred in Belarus under long-ruling president Alexander Lukashenko.

Some post-Soviet states have been trapped in a partial reform equilibrium, where the winners have taken advantage of their privileged positions to strip SOEs of valuable assets or purchase state firms at fire-sale prices and use their oligopolistic levers to reap huge profits. These winners benefit from protected markets, and from the distortions that arise between the reformed and unreformed economies; they oppose further change, sometimes in league with poorer "losers" who harken back to the full-employment stability and social safety net of the Soviet era, when there was less street crime and glaring inequality. Market-oriented reforms are often announced but just as often remain unrealized; these conservative predatory coalitions benefit more from sabotaging proposed economic reforms than from implementing them. Strong-armed rulers tolerate political opposition parties but maintain power in an unequal playing field.

Country conditions vary, however, and in some cases younger generations are pressing for further reforms to improve the quality of governance and the efficiency of their economies.

Central America

In the 1980s and early 1990s the Northern Triangle countries of Central America transitioned from military dictatorships to formal electoral democracies. While progress is evident in some areas—social indicators show some improvement—overall the outcomes have been disappointing. Enduring tensions between the private sector and its allied political parties on the one hand and more popular movements and leftist political parties on the other continue to impede coherent public policy and discourage investment. GDP growth is modest at best, hobbled by low public and private investment rates. Per capita incomes are reduced by high population growth in Honduras and especially Guatemala (one problem Cuba does not face). The legacy of bloody civil wars and high underemployment among youth contribute to debilitating gang violence and common street crime. Periodic revelations of wanton corruption in high places diminish faith in public policy and undercut hope in the future.

Scenario 3: The Soft Landing—Sunny 2030

In this most optimistic scenario, by 2030 Cuba will be well on the road toward becoming firmly integrated into the global economy. The hybrid economy is stable, with a dynamic balance among public, private, and international sectors, and with growth rapid enough to sustain universal, high-quality social services. Public institutions will be shifting from the centralized command model to a smart regulatory state that is more decentralized. Political life could be vibrant: several alternative political outcomes are consistent with this economic-institutional model, ranging from a soft authoritarianism to a pluralistic democracy. Performance indicators will show improvement across the board; in particular, there will be healthy growth in the private sector and most especially in foreign investment. Ambitious millennials will benefit the most from the expansion of opportunities, and their outmigration will slow. Indeed, Cuba could again become a recipient country for regional migratory flows from economies with higher population growth or unemployment, such as Haiti and the

Dominican Republic, and possibly from some of the smaller English-speaking islands.

Economic Reform

Under strong, visionary leadership, Cuba will definitely break with its past and embark on systemic economic reform. State-owned enterprises will have to demonstrate profitability, private enterprise will be unshackled, and outstanding property claims will be settled and private property protected. Practices for engaging foreign investors will conform to international standards: approval procedures will be dramatically accelerated, workers will be directly hired by firms (not government employment brokers), and 100 percent foreign ownership will be widely permitted in practice, not just in theory. The authorization of private enterprise will shift from a positive to a negative list, and the list of excluded activities will be brief, permitting professionals the freedom to sell their services on private markets. Most prices for industrial inputs and consumer goods and services will be set by supply and demand. Particularly important for the average Cuban, fiscal policy will shift from an internal accounting exercise to a tax-based revenue system: taxes can be used to level inequalities that inevitably emerge during a market-oriented transition. Progressive taxation—compatible with socialism—also lends legitimacy to a market-driven economy; and it can generate resources to ensure high-quality universal social services and a safety net for those who lose ground during a process of rapid change. The delivery of education and health care will remain a public responsibility and a high priority.

In this reform-oriented future, the state will not wither away. SOEs will continue to dominate important sectors, including public utilities, infrastructure, and finance. The PCC will not want to give up its economic power base or its capacity to give orientation to economic policy. But SOEs will face market disciplines. Seeking access to technology, markets, and finance, the more profit-oriented SOEs will build alliances with foreign capital and even with the larger home-grown private firms.

The opening to private capital will pave the way to welcoming investment by the Cuban émigré community, including the Cuban diaspora living in the United States as well as in Spain, Canada, and Latin America. Some diaspora entrepreneurs have access to large-scale investment capital and could integrate their Cuban operations into transnational value chains. Other diaspora investors can help to finance limited partnerships with relatives and friends on the island and in this way jump-start small and medium-sized enterprises. Taking advantage of Cuba's central location, these small and medium-sized enterprises can not only supply domestic demand but also sell into markets around the Caribbean basin and beyond.

Among the more dynamic sectors that emerge may be medical tourism, built upon Cuba's excess of trained medical personnel; joint ventures that market Cuba's biotech discoveries; and the export-driven boom in tobacco and alcohol manufacturing. With continued investment in higher education and in performance facilities, Cuba could well become a global mecca for the performing arts. But rapid growth throughout the economy will propel all sectors forward, including energy, infrastructure, and the production of agricultural and even some industrial products for the domestic market. An export-oriented economic policy, anchored in a competitive exchange rate, will open many new markets for a widening array of made-in-Cuba products. Less educated Cubans located in the poorer eastern provinces will be happy to raise their living standards by working in assembly plants that are linked into global supply chains, possibly including what was the old Guantánamo naval base.

Cuba will have advanced to stage 4 in the capital accumulation process (see chapter 6, pages 164–65). The Cuban government will have accommodated rising entrepreneurs by offering them a level playing field where they can compete fairly with SOEs, and by promoting active collaboration and strategic alliances between public and private entities, to mutual benefit.

Institutional Change

Transitioning from a command economy to a smart state based on price signals and rule-based regulations—the Cuban variant of market socialism—is among the most difficult tasks confronting the soft-landing scenario. Rules must be established, institutions rebuilt, experts trained, and public attitudes reset.

In the rebuilding of the badly depleted stock of Cuban housing and commercial space, a high standard of architectural design and city planning is achievable. Already, the remodeling of Habana Vieja creatively blends historical restoration with commercial viability. Smaller regional towns, each with its own colonial center, can draw from this success.

With smart urban planning, Havana could regain its place among the world's most beautiful and livable spaces. What an opportunity for creative architects! Far-sighted planners could design a city space of medium-sized structures, appropriate to a tropical climate but with modern materials, with plenty of green spaces and public use facilities. Cuba's long and beautiful coastlines—with their white-sand beaches and crystalline waters, protected cays and healthy coral reefs—could also be carefully developed following guidelines that ensure sustainability both for the environment and for the economies of local communities.

But this vision will not be realized spontaneously if developers are allowed to pursue their singular commercial goals. It will require clear vision, strong institutions, and political will, all reinforced by a collective, informed consciousness that keeps decisionmakers on course, in pursuit of consensus goals.

Diversification can become a core characteristic both on the island and in Cuba's outward orientation. Policies to promote a balanced regional development will, among other regulations, direct large cruise ships to less developed provinces. Stimulus packages will situate new manufacturing facilities in the east, where unemployment is highest. A well-orchestrated international investment promotion strategy could ensure a healthy diversification of investments from across the globe: certainly from the United States but—avoiding the excessive dependency of the early twentieth century—also from the European Union, Canada, Brazil, and Northeast and Southeast Asia. Cuba could once again become a crossroads of civilizations.

At sustained 5 percent annual growth, Cuban labor markets will tighten and wages will rise. Because of Cuba's extraordinarily low fertility rates, demand for labor will exceed local supply. Thus the demand for workers will require Cuba to once again become an importer of foreign labor. Cuba will become a hub not only for commodity trade but for workers from around the Caribbean basin.

This prospective model of market socialism is distinct from neoliberalism, which in the minds of many Cubans connotes an unbridled capitalism riddled with gross inequalities. In contrast, the inclusion option is anchored in a strong state endowed with strategic enterprises and robust regulatory powers. Cooperatives governed by an assembly of the workers electing an executive board are another important pillar. All larger firms—whether foreign or domestically owned, public or private—could be required to practice corporate social responsibility and to uphold labor standards, demonstrate environmental stewardship, and contribute to the social welfare of surrounding communities.

Consistent with the guiding principles of the Cuban Revolution, the government could fine-tune fiscal policies of revenues and taxes to pursue a more equitable distribution of income and social services. Indeed, a more productive economy will be required to sustain the government's historical commitment to universal access to high-quality health care and education. If growth can be accelerated, the Cuban middle classes, having emerged from the masses and educated to an egalitarian ethos, could well support affirmative distribution policies.

Political Change

It would be overly mechanistic to suggest that this economic model necessarily requires, or would give birth to, a predetermined political system. Greater economic pluralism, coupled with an opening to international travel and global telecommunications, suggests a more relaxed political discourse and more open civil society. But as the country precedents discussed below suggest, there are many political systems consistent with the soft-landing scenario. Feasible options range from the one-party state of Vietnam, to the semiauthoritarian public-private collaboration of Nicaragua, and to the familiar multiparty democracy of Costa Rica.

Performance Indicators

In the sunny scenario, a dynamic Cuban economy attains a steady 5 percent growth rate. This solid performance would be feasible given the low starting point and the capacity of the economy to rapidly absorb existing technologies and to import capital and even labor. By 2030 per capita income will have surpassed $15,000, giving most Cubans a new sense of hope and optimism for the future. In this scenario, the private sector really takes off and becomes a central pillar of economic dynamism, reaching 2 million employees, or some 40 percent of the active labor force. The flow of FDI gathers steam, as early movers are joined by a swarm of foreign investors. Large multinationals and smaller, diaspora-connected ventures inject $5 billion a year, thus raising investment rates closer to the 20 percent norm for Latin America.

This would be a Cuba with social mobility and relative social equality, where the differences between rich and poor are less glaring than elsewhere in the region. The Gini coefficient (a measure of inequality, where

1 is the most unequal) would be around 0.35–0.40, or roughly where it is today and considerably less than the 0.5 level found throughout much of the rest of Latin America and the Caribbean. Social indicators regain the ground they lost in the early twenty-first century.

Cuba becomes a labor-importing, not -exporting, nation. Most millennials, excited at the new opportunities, elect to stay in their homeland. The more relaxed security atmosphere permits a modest uptick in street crime, but crime statistics remain comfortable relative to regional performance and sufficiently low not to deter tourism.

U.S. Reactions

In reaction to such a decisive economic opening, the United States would almost certainly fully repeal its economic embargo, open its markets to Cuban commerce, and permit its citizens to return to the island as investors and tourists. From the perspective of the modest-sized Cuban market, the United States is a virtually limitless opportunity, so this market opening would constitute a powerful positive external stimulus to the Cuban economic system. Indeed, an ample U.S. economic opening would make this scenario more likely by empowering pro-reform factions, bolstering private business, and generally providing liquidity to reduce transition trade-offs.

Precedents from around the World for Scenario 3

In realizing this sunny scenario, Cuba can find inspiration in other countries' effective solution to common problems of transitions. Countries with generally successful transitions from more centralized systems are many and include Vietnam, Costa Rica, Berlin/East Germany, and Nicaragua. Each offers important lessons for Cuba 2030.

Vietnam

With its location in Southeast Asia, its population of 90 million, and its countryside rich with family-run rice paddies, Vietnam may seem too unlike Cuba to offer any useful comparisons. Certainly Cuba will not become just like Vietnam. But the two nations have shared some defining experiences. In the mid-twentieth century, both waged costly anti-imperialist struggles that depleted their economies. Both nations imposed a highly centralized system of economic planning largely delinked from the global economy. Then in the 1980s, the Vietnamese leadership began a process of "Doi Moi" (economic reform) to reopen to the global economy and to gradually decentralize economic decision making. Doi Moi was not a linear process; there were periods of indecision and even backsliding. But by the 1990s the reform process accelerated, per capita income doubled and doubled again, and Vietnam became one of the most dynamic economies in the world.

Today, Vietnam has a hybrid economic system, neatly balanced between a still powerful public sector, a vibrant and growing private sector, and a brilliant foreign investment sector. Leading global firms with investments or major sourcing contracts in Vietnam hail from around the world—from Japan, Singapore, Thailand, Taiwan, and South Korea, and from throughout Europe and the United States. The three productive sectors both complement and compete with each other.

Vietnam has its shortcomings; for example, its institutions are of mixed quality. The Vietnamese complain bitterly about corruption in both the public and private spheres, whose borderlines are blurred by the personal networks and Communist Party affiliations that transcend legal divides. Many business executives begin their careers within the state apparatus and then take advantage of their insider contacts to do exceedingly well in private business. The judiciary remains permeated by the Communist Party, its independence compromised. Some regulatory bodies do not have the resources, expertise, independence, or political clout to adequately carry out their duties, although some city planning agencies, notably in Hanoi and Da Nang, have overseen rapid urban growth within an orderly framework that preserves public spaces. As is quickly evident in daily conversations, the Vietnamese are dissatisfied with the quality of social services. The government has given priority to economic growth, to the detriment of public education and health services. The newly wealthy and corporate expatriate communities abandon the underresourced educational system for expensive private schools. And too many Vietnamese have sad stories to tell about tragedies that befell their friends and family due to failures in the health care system.

An obvious attraction to the PCC, the Vietnamese Communist Party retains its monopoly on political power. But the government in Hanoi tolerates an uncensored Internet—Facebook is ubiquitous—and the official press contains lively discussions on public policy. Most Vietnamese seem willing to forego a fully active participation in political life in exchange for economic opportunity. Only time will tell whether this current equilibrium is stable in the long run.

Costa Rica

In the 1980s Costa Rica decided to dismantle the economic model that so many Latin American and Caribbean countries had adopted earlier in the century, in the wake of the Great Depression. Governments had erected high barriers to international trade in order to encourage investment in industries selling to the domestic market (the so-called import substitution industrialization model, ISI). In some senses, the Cuban model of closed centralism was simply a more extreme version of ISI. In its heyday, ISI raised living standards and created jobs throughout the region, but by the 1960s its usefulness had clearly been exhausted. Growth rates had slowed, labor productivity lagged, and balance of payments periodically fell into crisis for lack of export dynamism. The great Latin American debt crisis of the 1980s signed the death knell of the ISI model.

In response, Costa Rica moved forward decisively to open its economy to the international marketplace, lowering trade barriers and welcoming foreign investment. The state privatized many SOEs, while retaining control of some key sectors, including banking and finance and public utilities. At the same time, the government poured resources into universal coverage for education and health, and the nation's very good social indicators are the result.

In the contemporary Latin American context, Costa Rica demonstrates conclusively that an open, mixed economy, in the context of a competitive, multiparty democracy, can meet the social needs of its citizens—and on a sustainable basis. Costa Rica is also a model of environmental sustainability, as demonstrated by its massive reforestation efforts, extensive national parks, and commitment to renewable energy. For Costa Rica, environmental tourism is a proud national brand and a major source of foreign exchange earnings.

Berlin/East Germany

At first glance, the post–Cold War experience of East Germany (including East Berlin) might seem far removed from Cuba. But there are some striking similarities. By the 1980s East Germany had fallen visibly behind the West, and East Berlin looked shabby and depressing in comparison to a rapidly modernizing West Berlin. Like the rest of Eastern Europe, the regime and its extensive security apparatus appeared impregnable. Yet all of a sudden the central squares of major cities overflowed with anti-regime protests. With remarkable speed and, in the case of East Germany, thankfully with little violence, governments collapsed and turned over power to caretaker administrations. Within a year, a transition government in East Germany agreed to reunification and adoption of West German laws and administrative procedures. The government created a national trust to privatize East German state-owned enterprises—purchased mostly by West German investors—and procedures were opened for victims of both the Nazis and the Communists to reclaim lost residences and businesses. Citizens of East Germany were brought under the umbrella of West Germany's generous welfare system, including unemployment benefits and retraining programs, retirement pensions, and universal public education and health care. Today, the boundaries between what were East and West Berlin have largely faded. Berlin's very strong municipal planning authorities have imposed their strict building guidelines, ensuring wide tree-lined avenues, low-rise construction, excellent public transportation, and the preservation of historical buildings and museums, now including very public memorials to the victims of the Holocaust.

Some lessons for Cuba from the German experience include the various ways to overcome previous social divisions and profitably incorporate the diaspora; to offer some protections for those adversely affected (although perhaps Cuba could do better than Germany did in helping citizens psychologically adjust to their altered realities); and to construct strong public institutions that, among other tasks, oversee a creative urban renewal that protects public interests and engenders civic pride. To be sure, the West German treasury had the funds—augmented by a special supplemental reunification income tax—to facilitate a smooth and rapid transition. Cuba has no such ready benefactor. But with an attractive international economic policy, Cuba could tap a number of funding sources. The cumulative assistance from friendly governments, multilateral agencies, private corporations, and the diaspora could add up handsomely.

Nicaragua

Nicaragua experienced a socialist revolution in the 1980s, inspired and materially assisted by the Cuban Revolution. But the Sandinistas lost the

1990 elections and negotiated a peaceful transition with the victorious conservatives who promptly engineered a return to market economies and private property relations. In 2006 the Sandinista Party regained the presidency and eventually control of the legislature. This time around, however, the Sandinistas did not seek to re-nationalize the economy. On the contrary, President Daniel Ortega established a working dialogue with business leaders. The result has been reasonably good economic growth— certainly better than the more conflictive Northern Triangle nations—and apparent medium-term political stability, if at the cost of some restrictions on democratic practices.

There are several lessons for Cuba. First, for the PCC, there can be life after transition, as an active opposition force and a collaborator on mutual interests. Second, for individuals from the ancien régime, there can be many opportunities in state-owned enterprises, public-private ventures, or private firms doing business with the public sector. A third lesson lies in post-2006 Sandinista international economic diplomacy: Ortega's sound macroeconomic policies earned him the support of the multilateral financial institutions, while his left-wing credentials appealed to Hugo Chávez, who showered Ortega with largesse. Ortega's astute balancing act bolstered Nicaragua's fiscal accounts and balance of payments, facilitating steady payments on the government bonds that Nicaragua had issued to compensate property owners for their losses during the upheavals of the 1980s.

Building the New Cuba

These four nations—Vietnam, East Germany, Costa Rica, Nicaragua— while vastly different, are all cases of reasonably successful transformations to more market-oriented, decentralized economies definitively integrated into global commerce. All four countries have experienced solid economic growth and rising per capita incomes (although Nicaragua lags far behind Costa Rica's social progress). They enjoy stable politics under varying degrees of political liberalism. In all four cases, post-transition governments benefited from clear mission statements, a strong sense of direction, and a focus on economic expansion and market efficiency, seasoned with a robust concern—if sometimes diluted in implementation—for an equitable distribution of the fruits of growth.

Reviewing the three imaginary futures, we can already see germs of each in the Cuba of today. Like the inert Cuba of the first scenario, contemporary

Cuba already displays a mix of modest, halting economic reform struggling against the pushback of powerful status quo tendencies within the governing apparatus. Some millennials have found niches within which to exercise their talents, but too many feel they must move off-island for sufficiently attractive professional opportunities and lifestyles. Some positive attributes of the second scenario of botched transition and decay can already be found in the enthusiasm of some entrepreneurs and cooperative ventures, in the occasional approvals of exciting new joint ventures, and in the lukewarm efforts to reform state-owned firms. But endemic pilfering from state firms and pervasive petty corruption are danger signals of what could become more glaring systemic abuses. The green shoots of the sunny soft landing, foreshadowed in sections of the 2011 reform guidelines, are also visible in today's Cuba: the expanding nonstate sectors, the opening of the Mariel Special Development Zone, the relaxation of tensions with the United States and the attendant surge in international visitors, and the atmospheric decompression that permits a more open and honest discussion of the nation's economic problems.

I believe that the sunny soft landing scenario offers the most benefits for the largest number of Cubans, as well as for inter-American relations. However, should Cubans follow the first scenario of inertia and continuity, this path could still lay the foundations for a healthier future. I could add that I believe the sunny scenario is the most probable outcome, but that might be confusing preferences for predictions. Better to conclude that history is not predetermined: if Cubans decide that this is their best outcome and they see it clearly, it is more likely to occur.

Ultimately, Cubans will determine their own destinies, which are not yet written. International actors, including the United States government, multinational businesses, and many smaller investors and nonprofits, can contribute their experiences and resources, and try to nudge events toward the direction of the sunny soft landing. But the survey of other nations' experiences should make clear that Cuba has much room for choice—and too much space for error. Cuba harbors many assets—more than many other nations undergoing transitions from their authoritarian heritage. But Cuba is also saddled with destructive liabilities that Cubans would do well to recognize and exorcise. Cuba watchers can only hope that wise leadership emerges and that Cuba has its fair share of good luck. In that case, the Mariel slogan "Open for Business" will become a vibrant reality, to the benefit of the Cuban people and their many international partners.

Cuba

Basic Facts

Geography

Largest island nation in the Caribbean, roughly the size of the state of
Pennsylvania
Mostly flat to rolling plains, with modest mountains in the southeast
Guantánamo Naval Base remains part of Cuba; termination of lease by the
United States by mutual agreement only

Population

11.2 million
Urban: 78 percent (Havana 2.1 million)
Labor force: 5.1 million
Population growth rate: −0.15
Projected population 2030: 10.8 million

Social indicators

Life expectancy: 79 years
Fertility: 1.6 children per woman (as compared to 1.9 in the United States)
Literacy: 99.8 percent
Education (expected years): 14

Economy (2014)

GDP: $81 billion
GDP per capita: $7,200

Merchandise exports: $5.1 billion
Merchandise imports: $13.1 billion
Housing construction
    Government built: 3,734 (43 percent)
    Homeowner built: 6,329 (57 percent)

Tourism (2015)

3.5 million visitors (including 1.3 million Canadians)
62,000 hotel bedrooms
19,000 B&B bedrooms

Connectivity (2015)

Mobile cellular service: 30 per 100 persons (estimated)
700 public access points, including 65 Wi-Fi hot spots; 80 more to be added
    in 2016

Youth engagement

Military service: 2-year compulsory, both sexes
Suffrage: 16 years of age

National politics

One legal party, the Cuban Communist Party (PCC), 670,000 members
Government ownership of mass media (TV, radio, newspapers)
National legislature: 5-year terms, votes typically are unanimous
End of Raúl Castro's second presidential term: early 2018

Sources: Oficina Nacional de Estadística e Información (ONEI); CIA, The
World Factbook, 2013, 2014 (https://www.cia.gov/library/publications/
the-world-factbook/). Data on connectivity public access points are from
Alfonso Chardy, "Year End Interview of the President of ETECSA," The
Internet in Cuba blog, January 4, 2016 (http://laredcubana.blogspot.com/).

Basic data requested

Name, age, place of birth, education, profession

Specific questions asked

Describe your current employment. What do you like and not like about it?

In your professional life, where do you hope to be in 10–15 years?

What are the main obstacles that you will need to overcome to realize your professional goals? Do you have the skills and social networks necessary to achieve your professional goals?

What would you like to see the Cuban economy look like in 10–15 years? What obstacles must be removed for that dream to come true?

What do you think the Cuban economy is in fact likely to look like in 10–15 years?

What reforms would you like to see in the Cuban government over the next 10–15 years?

How likely do you think it is that these reforms will occur?

Do you plan to have children? How many—and why? Are there additional obstacles facing women in Cuba today?

Are you committed to remaining in Cuba, or are you contemplating emigration? Do you have family overseas?

Are you pleased with the new relationship with the United States? How would you like Cuba's relationship with the United States to evolve over the next 10–15 years?

Acknowledgments

My passion for Cuba has multiple origins. As a graduate student in international economics at Stanford University in the mid-1970s, I had the good fortune to encounter the Hungarian economist Janos Kornai, among the top experts on the economic reform experiments then under way in Eastern Europe. The distinguished visiting professor was kind enough to provide me with letters of introduction to his colleagues in Budapest and Belgrade, who shared with me their experiential insights into the challenges of reforming a centralized economy—and I was hooked! Nothing seemed more interesting—technically or politically—than engineering such a treacherous passage while minimizing the costs to the inevitable "losers" whose welfare depended upon the socialist state.

A second origin was my long-standing passion for the Latin American and Caribbean region, ignited during my formative years with the Peace Corps in Chile. In my nearly three years in Santiago and traveling around South America, I was inspired by the leading roles that social scientists were playing in defining alternatives to the status quo and then in actually governing their nations; and I was equally outraged at the appalling behavior of Richard Nixon and Henry Kissinger in purposely destabilizing Chile's democratically elected government.

These experiences in Eastern Europe and South America propelled my study of economics and my desire to become a public policy entrepreneur, eventually allowing me to move with agility between foreign policy posts in government (the Treasury, the Department of State, the White House), Washington-based think tanks, and academia. During my tours in government, Cuba was necessarily of interest because of the profound challenges it posed to U.S. foreign policy.

With these interests and experiences—my study of the economics of transitions, decades of work in Latin America and other developing regions, and stints at senior levels of U.S. diplomacy—my engagement with Cuba became an absolute natural once Raúl Castro began, however tentatively, to unwind his island's tightly centralized socialism and launch Cuba on a complex journey toward an unknown destiny.

Cuban studies had been a robust academic field in the heady days of the revolution, but by 2010 the field had grown considerably thinner. Initial enthusiasm had dimmed, especially among intellectuals disenchanted with Fidel Castro's overbearing authoritarianism, while a younger generation of scholars took less interest in what seemed a torpid state. The Cuban authorities also made it very difficult to conduct academic work; reliable data were scarce and nearly impossible to collect on one's own. The U.S. government was equally uninformed: the U.S. Interests Section in Havana had few staff, and its activities were tightly circumscribed by Cuban authorities. And U.S. officials were more focused on human rights violations than on economic reforms. Those who noticed the reforms under way tended to cynically dismiss them, recalling earlier reforms during the Fidel Castro years that the Cuban government had eventually reversed. I asked myself, why not pick up my pen and fill the knowledge gap myself?

So beginning in 2010 I undertook research—as much as was possible on the ground in Cuba—recording and assessing the incipient economic reforms. My analyses were informed by my former studies of socialist transitions, as well as my recent research trips to Nicaragua and Vietnam, which offered two relevant transition experiences. I was immensely fortunate to have as my publisher the Brookings Institution, whose outreach capacities and authoritative imprint ensured that my work would reach the desks of government officials, as well as academics and media who in turn help to shape the political context in which government operates. I am proud of the contributions, however modest, that my research and publications made to better informing the policy world about the rapidly changing realities of contemporary Cuba.

Prior to the December 2014 announcement of the decision by Presidents Barack Obama and Raúl Castro to normalize diplomatic relations, analysts in the U.S. government tended to perceive Cuba as stagnant and stable—and to see the United States as standing on the sidelines, without much influence on Cuba's choices. Throughout my writings, I emphasized that the United States could become a player and advance U.S. interests, but first it would have to recognize that changes were already under way. It would also have to recognize that by embracing positive change, it could speed that change along. The Obama White House came to share this assessment, and acted accordingly.

My first Brookings monograph, "Reaching Out: Cuba's New Economy and the International Response" (2011), sought to call attention to a rarity in international economic policy: Cuba was the only nation on the planet other than North Korea that was not a member of the two premier global financial institutions, the International Monetary Fund and the World Bank. Cuba had withdrawn in the early 1960s, never to return. Yet this anomaly deprived Cuba of two highly relevant assets: access to official monies to help absorb some of the costs of change and access to the vast institutional databases related to economic transitions around the world, showing what has worked well and what costly errors could be avoided. My second monograph, "The New Cuban Economy: What Roles for Foreign Investment?" (2012), drew attention to the relatively light footprint of foreign direct investment in Cuba, despite the vital contributions that it was making to the progress of other developing economies worldwide. For Cuba's economic transition to succeed, international experience suggested, it would have to access both the international financial institutions and foreign direct investment. Today, Cuba is moving forward, however tentatively, to grasp both opportunities.

The third monograph was the most ambitious. "Soft Landing in Cuba? Emerging Entrepreneurs and Middle Classes" (2013) sought to draw attention to the new Cuba, a nation with a talented, educated population fighting to build new businesses in the spaces the government was now opening for private enterprise. For Washington, D.C., these fresh images uncovered fertile ground for policy innovation: these middle classes and entrepreneurs could be the backbone of a new, more open-minded Cuba that the United States could embrace.

This book includes updated revisions of these three earlier policy papers. But it begins with the backstory to December 17, 2014: why did Cuba and the United States, bitter antagonists for over half a century, finally decide to break decisively with sterile confrontation and write a new chapter to their intertwined histories? This book also includes entirely fresh materials that seek to peer into Cuba's future and answer the questions, where is Cuba going, and what might it look like in 2030? In December 2015 I spent two fascinating weeks in Havana conversing with Cuban millennials, illustrious examples of the educated middle classes, the grandchildren of the revolution, who generally respect the struggles and accomplishments of their elders but most definitely seek a new normal: one in which Cuba rejoins the world, and where their talents and ambitions are allowed full flight. A final chapter speculates on three scenarios for Cuba's future; it warns of potential pitfalls that tripped up other transitional nations and suggests paths forward that could lead to a twenty-first-century Cuban renaissance.

An undertaking of this magnitude inevitably incurs innumerable debts to many individuals and institutions. My previous Brookings monographs recognize many of them. I would like to draw special attention to Philip Brenner, who was instrumental in directing me to the new stirrings within Cuba. Ace journalist Marc Frank, author of the brilliant *Cuban Revelations: Behind the Scenes in Havana*, ensures that my visits to Havana will be as personally pleasurable as they are politically revealing. The quality of media coverage of Cuba has vastly improved thanks to the hard work and professionalism of Victoria Burnett, Nick Miroff, Michael Weissenstein, and Daniel Trotta. William LeoGrande generously provided rapid-fire feedback on various short publications as well as on an entire draft of this book; his magnum opus (with Peter Kornbluth), *Back Channel to Cuba: The Hidden History of Negotiations between Washington and Havana*, is must reading for students of American diplomatic history. At UC San Diego, my colleagues Jesse Driscoll, Stephan Haggard, and Barry Naughton are outstanding scholars of socialist transitions. My Del Mar buddies, Stu Schreiber and Bart Ziegler, encouraged this enterprise from the outset. Collin Laverty, president of Cuba Educational Travel, knows Havana as well as any living being. Eric Leenson and I have made a long journey together, from wandering the bohemian streets of Allende's Chile to advancing corporate responsibility in Cuba. Sadly, one cherished friend is no longer with us: Robert Pastor leaves a legacy of brilliant scholarship and policy innovation from which we all continue to benefit. In 2015 I also lost two memorable mentors: my undergraduate professor, Tom Gleason, who showed me what it meant to be a true gentleman intellectual; and Sandy Berger, who embodied a humanitarian decency amid the thrust-and-parry of D.C. bureaucratic politics.

Many of the Cubans I have been privileged to make the acquaintance of are cited throughout this book. Without their many studies and warm collegiality this book would be much poorer. Special notice is due to Juan

Triana Cordoví, Omar Everleny Pérez Villanueva, and Ricardo Torres of the Center for the Study of the Cuban Economy (CEEC), Soraya Castro for her annual conferences on U.S.-Cuban relations, Carlos Alzugaray for his deep understanding of Cuban diplomacy, and Rafael Hernández, director of *Temas* magazine. Eusebio Leal and Josefina Vidal were unfailingly hospitable during my many sojourns in their capital city.

My dear friend and colleague at Brookings, Ted Piccone, has been a constant companion in this book's journey from concept to publication. Without Ashley Miller's professional expertise, this book would still be at the storyboard stage. Michael Ramirez provided spot-on research assistance. At Brookings Institution Press, I am profoundly indebted to the top-notch team of Valentina Kalk and Bill Finan, Yelba Quinn and Carrie Engel, and Janet Walker and Anne Himmelfarb. Remaining errors are, of course, my own.

I dedicate this book to my children, Sonya and Aaron, their spouses and children, Nii Moi and Sofía, Sephira and Ronen, and to the Cuban millennials—may their futures be as bright as the bluest of Havana skies.

Notes

Chapter 1

1. Marc Frank, "Signs of political thaw lift hopes for U.S. contractor in Cuba jail," *Financial Times*, December 1, 2014 (www.ft.com/intl/cms/s/0/de74e682-7943-11e4-a57d-00144feabdc0.html#axzz3rmJh0aVk).

2. "Speech by Cuban President Raul Castro on Re-establishing U.S.-Cuba Relations," *Washington Post*, December 17, 2014 (www.washingtonpost.com/world/full-text-speech-by-cuban-president-raul-castro-on-re-establishing-us-cuba-relations/2014/12/17/45bc2f88-8616-11e4-b9b7-b8632ae73d25_story.html).

3. Chapters 2 and 3 are updated revisions of "Reaching Out: Cuba's New Economy and the International Response" (Brookings, Latin America Initiative, November 2011), chapters 4 and 5 of "The New Cuban Economy: What Roles for Foreign Investment?" (December 2012), and chapter 6 of "Soft Landing in Cuba?: Emerging Entrepreneurs and Middle Classes" (November 2013).

4. Barack Obama, "Remarks by the President at the Summit of the Americas Opening Ceremony," Port of Spain, Trinidad and Tobago, April 17, 2009 (www.whitehouse.gov/the-press-office/remarks-president-summit-americas-opening-ceremony).

5. Hugh Gladwin and Guillermo J. Grenier, *2014 FIU Cuba Poll: How Cuban Americans in Miami View U.S. Policies toward Cuba* (Miami: Cuban Research Institute, 2014) (https://cri.fiu.edu/research/cuba-poll/2014-fiu-cuba-poll.pdf).

6. Atlantic Council, *U.S.-Cuba: A New Public Survey Supports Policy Change* (Washington, D.C., 2014) (www.atlanticcouncil.org/images/publications/2014cubapoll/US-CubaPoll.pdf).

7. However, Cuban American Republicans continued to favor a harder line toward Havana, which explained why candidates in the 2016 Republican Party primaries, including Floridians Jeb Bush and Marco Rubio, were highly critical of Obama's Cuba initiatives.

8. Pew Research Center, "Growing Public Support for U.S. Ties with Cuba—And an End to the Trade Embargo," July 21, 2015 (www.people-press.org/2015/07/21/growing-public-support-for-u-s-ties-with-cuba-and-an-end-to-the-trade-embargo/).

9. U.S. Department of the Treasury, "Cuba Sanctions," November 4, 2015 (www.treasury.gov/resource-center/sanctions/Programs/pages/cuba.aspx).

10. Leigh Thomas, "Cuba Open for Business, Ministers Tell French Executives," Reuters, February 3, 2016.

11. U.S. Treasury Department, Office of Public Affairs, "Treasury and Commerce Announce Further Amendment to the Cuba Sanctions" (www.treasury.gov/resource-center/sanctions/Programs/Documents/fact_sheet_01262016.pdf).

12. International Monetary Fund, "Direction of Trade Statistics" (www.imf.org/external/pubs/cat/longres.aspx?sk=19305.0).

Chapter 2

Unless otherwise noted, statistics on the Cuban economy used in the section "The Revolution's Neglect" are from the website of the Cuban Office of National Statistics and Information (Oficina Nacional de Estadística y Información, ONEI), specifically from *Anuario Estadístico de Cuba* and *Panorama Económica y Social* (www.one.cu/Catalogo Publicaciones.html).

1. United Nations Development Program, "Human Development Reports: Cuba" (http://hdr.undp.org/en/countries/profiles/CUB); World Bank, "Data: Fertility Rate" (http://data.worldbank.org/indicator/SP.DYN.TFRT.IN).

2. United Nations Development Program, "Human Development Reports: Dominican Republic" (http://hdr.undp.org/en/countries/profiles/DOM). Data on Cuba's social indicators are summarized in appendix A, along with basic facts about its economy, population, and so on.

3. A report on the Cuban economy prepared for the United States Agency for International Development (USAID) by Nathan Associates made this comment on data quality and format: "In general, data on Cuba present problems of availability, reliability, timeliness, and transparency. . . . Many gaps exist, and the definitions of the official statistics and the methodology used in deriving the indicators are not always clear. Furthermore, the absence of support to Cuba from the IMF and World Bank make international comparisons difficult . . . Thus, the data and our interpretation of the data should be interpreted with caution." Nathan Associates, *Cuba: Economic Performance Assessment* (USAID, October 2009) (http://pdf.usaid.gov/pdf_docs/Pnadq895.pdf). On data problems, also see Carmelo Mesa-Lago, "Social and Economic Problems in Cuba during the Crisis and Subsequent Recovery," *CEPAL Review* 86, no. 1 (2005), 177–99 (www.cepal.org/en/publications/11099-social-and-economic-problems-cuba-during-crisis-and-subsequent-recovery); Gabriel Di Bella and Andy Wolfe, "Cuba: Economic Growth and International Linkages—Challenges for Measurement and Vulnerabilities in a Bimonetary Economy," paper prepared for the 19th annual meeting of the Association for the Study of the Cuban Economy, Miami, July 30–August 1, 2009 (www.ascecuba.org/c/wp-content/uploads/2014/09/v19-dibellawolfe.pdf); Rafael Romeu, "Inferring Quarterly Real Gross Domestic Product Growth in Cuba During the Global Financial Crisis," in *The Cuban Economy: Recent Trends*, edited by José Raúl Perales (Washington, D.C.: Woodrow Wilson International Center for Scholars, 2011), 7–29 (www.cubastudygroup.org/index.cfm/cuba-s-economic-reforms).

4. Figures are for 2014. World Bank, "GDP Per Capita" (http://data.worldbank.org/indicator/NY.GDP.PCAP.CD).

5. Youth who neither work nor study have also become a commonplace problem in Latin America. See Mauricio Cardenas, Rafael de Hoyos, and Miguel Székely, "Idle Youth in Latin America: A Persistent Problem in a Decade of Prosperity" (Brookings, Latin America Initiative, August 2011) (www.brookings.edu/~/media/research/files/papers/2011/9/07-idle-youth-cardenas/idle-youth-in-latin-america_final.pdf).

6. Ernesto Hernandez-Cata, "The Fall and Recovery of the Cuban Economy in the 1990s: Mirage or Reality?" Working Paper WP/01/48 (Washington, D.C.: International Monetary Fund, December 2000) (www.imf.org/external/pubs/ft/wp/2001/wp0148.pdf).

7. On the reforms of the 1990s, see UN Economic Commission for Latin America and the Caribbean, *The Cuban Economy: Structural Reforms and Economic Performance in the 1990s* (Mexico City: ECLAC, 2001) (www.cepal.org/en/publications/25529-cuban-economy-structural-reforms-and-economic-performance-1990s); Jorge Dominguez, Omar Everleny Pérez Villanueva, and Lorena Barberia, eds., *The Cuban Economy at the Start of the Twenty-First Century* (Harvard University Press, 2004); and Hernandez-Cata, "Fall and Recovery of the Cuban Economy." An active participant in the reforms, Jose Luis Rodriguez, published an account of his experiences in *Notas Sobre La Economía Cuba* (Havana: Instituto Cubano de Investigación Cultural Juan Marinello, 2011).

8. Omar Everleny Perez Villanueva, *The External Sector of the Cuban Economy* (Washington, D.C.: Woodrow Wilson International Center for Scholars, 2010), 3 (www.wilsoncenter.org/sites/default/files/LAP_Everleny_nl1.pdf). See also Emily Morris, "Cuba's New Relationship with Foreign Capital: Economic Policy-Making Since 1990," *Journal of Latin American Studies* 40, no. 4 (2008), 769–92 (http://journals.cambridge.org/abstract_S0022216X08004756).

9. Jorge Dominguez, "Cuba's Economic Transition: Successes, Deficiencies, and Challenges," in *The Cuban Economy at the Start of the Twenty-First Century*, edited by Dominguez, Pérez Villanueva, and Barberia, 30–37.

10. Sixth Congress of the Communist Party of Cuba, "Resolution on the Guidelines of the Economic and Social Policy of the Party and the Revolution," April 18, 2011 (www.cuba.cu/gobierno/documentos/2011/ing/l160711i.html).

11. UN Economic Commission for Latin America and the Caribbean, *Cuba: Evolución Económica Durante 2010* (Mexico City: CEPAL, 2011), 37–38 (www.cepal.org/publicaciones/xml/5/42055/2011-011-Nota_Cuba-L985-Rev1.pdf).

12. ONEI, *Panorama Económica y Social*, 2011, table 35; 2014, table 33 (www.onei.cu/CatalogoPublicaciones.html).

13. For an informed critique of the government's agricultural policies, see Armando Nova Gonzalez, "Valoración del impacto de las medidas más recientes en los resultados de la agricultura en Cuba. El Sector Agropecuario y los Lineamientos de la Política Económica Social," Center for the Study of the Cuban Economy, Havana, June 2011, unpublished paper (www.nodo50.org/cubasigloXXI/economia/nova_311211.pdf). See also Armando Nova Gonzalez, "Agricultura," in *Miradas a la Economía Cubana II* (Havana: Editorial Caminos, 2010), 39–85; and Armando Nova Gonzalez, "Reforma en la agricultura: lineamientos y resultados recientes," in *Miradas a la Economía Cubana: El proceso de actualización*, edited by Pavel Vidal Alejandro and Omar Everleny Pérez Villanueva (Havana: Editorial Caminos, 2012), 53–72.

14. In early 2016 the government reported that 21 percent of the guidelines had been implemented and that 71 percent were in progress. See "Plenum of the Party Central Committee Evaluates Documents to Be Discussed at the 7th Party Congress," *Granma*, January 15, 2016 (http://en.granma.cu/cuba/2016-01-15/plenum-of-the-party-central-committee-evaluates-documents-to-be-discussed-at-the-7th-party-congress).

15. This section draws from Richard F. Feinberg and Ted Piccone, eds., *Cuba's Economic Change in Comparative Perspective* (Brookings, Latin America Initiative, November 2014) (www.brookings.edu/~/media/research/files/papers/2014/11/cuba-economic-change-comparative-perspective/cubas-economic-change--english--web.pdf); Carmelo Mesa-Lago and Jorge Pérez-López, *Cuba Under Raúl Castro: Assessing the Reforms* (Boulder, Colo.: Lynne Rienner, 2013); Colectivo de Autores, *Economía Cubana: Transformación y Desafíos* (Havana: Ciencias Sociales, 2014); Gonzalez, "Reforma en la agricultura: lineamientos y resultados recientes"; and Omar Everleny Pérez Villanueva and Ricardo Torres Pérez, "Cuba: una vision de la economía global y sus territorios," in *Miradas a la Economía Cubana: Desde una perspectiva territorial* (Havana: Editorial Caminos, 2014), 25–26.

16. José Luis Perelló Cabrera, "El sector no estatal y su papel en el desarrollo del turismo cubano en un escenario de relaciones con los Estados Unidos," in *Miradas a la Economía*

Cubana: Análisis del sector no estatal, edited by Omar Everleny Pérez Villanueva and Ricardo Torres Pérez (Havana: Editorial Caminos, 2015), 87; and Pérez Villanueva and Torres, "Cuba: una vision de la economía global y sus territories."

17. Gabino Manguela, "Ejercen más de 496,400 cuentapropistas en todo el país," *Trabajadores,* January 10, 2016 (www.trabajadores.cu/20160110/ejercen-mas-de-496-mil-400-cuentapropistas-en-todo-el-pais/). This number represents a slight dip from the mid-2015 figure of 505,000 reported in Yuniel Labacena Romero, "Superado el medio millón de trabajadores por cuenta propia," *Juventud Rebelde,* June 12, 2015 (www.juventudre belde.cu/cuba/2015-06-12/superado-el-medio-millon-de-trabajadores-por-cuenta-propia).

18. Luciana Chamorro, who studied at the University of Havana, argues that by legalizing self-employment, the Cuban regime not only increases tax revenues but also co-opts potentially dissident voices. See "The Re-Emergence of Self-Employment in Cuba: The Incorporation of New Practices into the Planned Economy," Princeton University, 2011, undergraduate paper.

19. "Con el corazón puesto en la tierra," *Juventud Rebelde,* November 10, 2012 (www. juventudrebelde.cu/cuba/2012-11-10/con-el-corazon-puesto-en-la-tierra). See also Gonzalez, "Valoración del impacto." On April 16, 2016, addressing the 7th Congress of the PCC, Minister Marino Murillo offered this update: since 2008, 1.8 million hectares had been distributed to 214,000 individuals.

20. Camila Pineiro Harnecker, "Cooperativas no agropecuarias en la Habana: Diagnóstico Preliminar," in *Economía Cubana: Transformación y Desafíos,* 291–334; and Rafael Betancourt, presentation at the Brookings Institution, June 2, 2015.

21. Ileana Diáz Fernandez, "Nuevas Medidas a Empresas Estatales: Retos para el Crecimiento," in *Economía Cubana: Transformación y Desafíos,* 410. For a discussion among senior government officials, see "Nueva Mirada a la empresa estatal cubana," *Mesa Redonda,* Televisión Cubana, March 8, 2016 (www.cubadebate.cu/noticias/2016/03/08/nueva-mirada-a-la-empresa-estatal-cubana-fotos-video-e-infografia/#.Vv87L00UWt9).

22. Feinberg and Piccone, *Cuba's Economic Change,* 61.

23. Juan Triana Cordoví, "2016 Will Be a Tense Year for the Cuban Economy," *oncubamagazine.com,* January 11, 2016 (http://oncubamagazine.com/economy-business/2016-will-be-a-tense-year-for-the-cuban-economy/).

24. ONEI, *Anuario Estadístico de Cuba,* 2014, table 11.1 (www.onei.cu/aec2014.htm).

25. Economist Intelligence Unit, *Country Report: Cuba* (London: The Economist Group, 2011), 14 (http://country.eiu.com/cuba#).

26. ONEI, *Anuario Estadístico de Cuba,* 2014, "Sector Externo," table 8.12 (www.onei. cu/aec2014.htm).

27. Di Bella and Wolfe, "Economic Growth."

28. Omar Everleny Perez Villanueva, "La actualización del modelo económico Cubano," in *Political Economy of Change in Cuba,* edited by Mauricio Font (New York: Bildner Center for Western Hemisphere Studies, 2011), figure 1-5.

29. ONEI, *Anuario Estadístico de Cuba,* 2014, "Sector Externo," table 8.3 (http://www. onei.cu/aec2014/08%20Sector%20Externo.pdf).

30. World Bank, "Exports of Goods and Services (% of GDP)" (http://data.worldbank. org/indicator/NE.EXP.GNFS.ZS).

31. Sergio Diaz-Briquet, "Major Problems, Few Solutions: Cuba's Demographic Outlook," *Cuban Studies* 43, no. 1 (2015), 3–18 (https://muse.jhu.edu/journals/cuban_studies/v043/43.diaz-briquets.html).

32. "Moody's: Paris Club Agreement First Step in Account for Cuba's Total Debt," *Moody's,* June 18, 2015 (www.moodys.com/research/Moodys-Paris-Club-agreement-first-step-in-accounting-for-Cubas--PR_328305?WT.mc_id=AM~RmluYW56ZW4ubmV0X1J TQl9SYXRpbmdzX05ld3NfTm9fVHJhbnNsYXRpb25z~20150618_PR_328305).

33. Marc Frank, "Cuba Inches toward Transparency," Reuters, December 24, 2014 (http://thecubaneconomy.com/articles/tag/external-debt/).

34. European Commission, *Cuba Country Strategy Paper and National Indicative Programme for the Period 2011–2013* (Brussels: European Commission, 2010), 84–85 (https://ec.europa.eu/europeaid/country-strategy-paper-and-national-indicative-programme-period-2011-2013-cuba_en).

35. Marc Frank, "Cuba's Debt Deal: Easy Terms, but Severe Penalties if Late Again," Reuters, December 15, 2015.

36. "Moody's Changes Cuba's Outlook to Positive from Stable; Caa2 Rating Affirmed," *Moody's*, December 10, 2015 (https://www.moodys.com/research/Moodys-changes-Cubas-outlook-to-positive-from-stable-Caa2-rating--PR_339779). The other two major credit rating agencies, Standard and Poor's and Fitch, do not rate Cuban paper.

37. Economist Intelligence Unit, *Country Report: Cuba*, January 2016, 9.

38. For a more thorough discussion of policy prescriptions for the long-term, see Feinberg and Piccone, *Cuba's Economic Change.*

Chapter 3

The section "Brazil and Its Near Abroad" draws heavily from a memorandum generously provided by the Brazilian embassy in Washington, "Relações Bilaterais Brasil-Cuba," June 2011, and from interviews with Brazilian diplomats and business executives stationed in Havana, 2011–15.

1. Omar Everleny Perez Villannueva, *The External Sector of the Cuban Economy* (Washington, D.C.: Woodrow Wilson International Center for Scholars, 2010), 3 (www.wilsoncenter.org/sites/default/files/LAP_Everleny_nl1.pdf).

2. Author interviews conducted in Cuba with Cuban officials and economists and with diplomats, foreign journalists, and international lawyers, June 2011.

3. "Export Development Canada's Economic and Political Review of Cuba," *Havana Journal*, November 22, 2011 (http://havanajournal.com/business/entry/export-development-canadas-economic-and-political-review-of-cuba).

4. Carlos Alzugaray, "La actualización de la política exterior cubana," *Política Exterior* 161, no. 1 (2014), 77 (www.academia.edu/11406145/La_actualización_de_la_pol%C3%ADtica_exterior_cubana).

5. See Andres Serbin, *Chávez, Venezuela y la Reconfiguracion Politica de America Latina y El Caribe* (Buenos Aires, Argentina: Siglo XXI, 2011) (www.academia.edu/928535/Chávez_Venezuela_y_la_reconfiguración_de_América_Latina_y_cl_Caribe).

6. See Ted Piccone and Harold Trinkunas, "The Cuba-Venezuela Alliance: The Beginning of the End?," policy brief (Brookings, Latin American Initiative, June 2014) (www.brookings.edu/~/media/research/files/papers/2014/06/16-cuba-venezuela-alliance-piccone-trinkunas/cubavenezuela-alliance-piccone-trinkunas.pdf).

7. John M. Kirk, *Healthcare without Borders: Understanding Cuban Medical Internationalism* (Gainesville: University Press of Florida, 2015), table C.1, 274.

8. Jose Raúl Perales, ed., "The United States and Cuba: Implications of an Economic Relationship" (Washington, D.C.: Woodrow Wilson International Center for Scholars, Latin American Program, 2010) (www.wilsoncenter.org/sites/default/files/LAP_Cuba_Implications.pdf); and Jorge R. Pinon and Jonathan Benjamin-Alvarado, "Extracting Cuba's Oil and Gas: Challenges and Opportunities," in *Cuba's Energy Future: Strategic Approaches to Cooperation*, edited by J. Benjamin-Alvarado (Brookings, 2010), 221–47 (www.brookings.edu/research/books/2010/cubasenergyfuture).

9. The $2 billion–$3 billion estimate is from the Center for Democracy in the Americas, *As Cuba Plans to Drill in the Gulf of Mexico, U.S. Policy Poses Needless Risks to Our National Interest* (Washington, D.C., 2011), 13 (http://democracyinamericas.org/pdfs/Cuba_Drilling_and_US_Policy.pdf).

10. The estimate of $1.2 billion is from Pavel Vidal, *Economic Trend Report Q2 2015* (Miami: Cuba Standard, 2015); the estimate of $1.9 billion is from Francisco Toro, "Cuba Is Hoping to Replace Venezuelan Oil with American Tourists," *FiveThirtyEight Economics*, January 16, 2015 (http://fivethirtyeight.com/features/cuba-is-hoping-to-replace-venezuelan-oil-with-american-tourists/).

11. Omar Everleny Pérez Villanueva, "La Inversion Extranjera Directa: Experiencias para Cuba," paper prepared for the annual conference of the Center for the Study of the Cuban Economy (CEEC), Havana, June 2011. Pérez Villanueva directs the prestigious CEEC, University of Havana.

12. Author interviews with Chinese diplomats, Havana, 2011, 2014. Also see Mao Xianglin, "China and Cuba: Past, Present, and Future," in *China Engages Latin America: Tracing the Trajectory*, edited by Adrian H. Hearn and Jose Luis Leon-Manriquez (Boulder, Colo.: Lynne Rienner, 2011), 187–201.

13. Alzugaray, "La actualización de la politica exterior cubana," 77.

14. China typically does not release precise numbers on its development assistance. See Carol Lancaster, *The Chinese Aid System* (Washington, D.C.: Center for Global Development, 2007) (www.cgdev.org/sites/default/files/13953_file_Chinese_aid.pdf); Thomas Lum and others, *China's Foreign Aid Activities in Africa, Latin America, and Southeast Asia* (Washington, D.C.: Congressional Research Service, 2009) (www.fas.org/sgp/crs/row/R40361.pdf); and Ken Miller, "Coping with China's Financial Power," *Foreign Affairs* 89, no. 4 (2010), 96–109 (www.foreignaffairs.com/articles/china/2010-07-01/coping-chinas-financial-power).

15. Pin Zuo, "A Survey of the Relationship Between Cuba and China: A Chinese Perspective," paper prepared for the 20th annual meeting of the Association for the Study of the Cuban Economy, Miami, July 29–31, 2010 (www.ascecuba.org/c/wp-content/uploads/2014/09/v20-pinzuo.pdf); and Miriam Leiva, "Cuba's International Relations," in *Cuba: Latin America in Focus*, edited by Ted A. Henken, Miriam Celaya, and Dimas Castellanos (Santa Barbara, Calif.: ABC-CLIO, 2013), 443–49.

16. Richard L. Bernal, "The Dragon in the Caribbean: China-CARICOM Economic Relations," *Round Table: The Commonwealth Journal of International Affairs* 99, no. 408 (2010), 281–302 (www.tandfonline.com/doi/abs/10.1080/00358533.2010.484144). See also Richard Feinberg, "China, Latin America, and the United States: Congruent Interests or Tectonic Turbulence?," *Latin American Research Review* 46, no. 2 (2011), 215–24 (http://muse.jhu.edu/login?auth=0&type=summary&url=/journals/latin_american_research_review/v046/46.2.feinberg.pdf).

17. Marc Frank, "China Restructures Cuban Debt, Backs Reform," Reuters, December 23, 2010, (www.reuters.com/article/2010/12/23/cuba-china-debt-idUSN2313446920101223#RqG3pATdyBmV4yH5.97).

18. Author interview with senior Chinese diplomat, Havana, December, 2014.

19. Economist Intelligence Unit, "Brazil Extends Contracts for 11,500 Cuban Doctors," September 3, 2014 (http://country.eiu.com/article.aspx?articleid=1782243562&Country=Cuba&topic=Politics&subtopic=Forecast&subsubtopic=Political+stability&u=1&pid=1553677939&oid=1553677939&uid=1).

20. I am indebted to Professor Ana Covarrubias, El Colegio de Mexico, for this felicitous phrase. Interview in Mexico City, July 29, 2011.

21. Ana Covarrubias, "Mexico and Cuba: The End of a Convenient Partnership," in *The United States and Cuba: Intimate Enemies*, edited by Marifeli Perez-Stable (New York: Routledge, 2011), 147–64.

22. These observations are based on author interviews, conducted in Washington, D.C., and Mexico City in 2011, with informed Mexican business experts, diplomats, academics, and journalists who preferred to remain anonymous. See also Demetria Tsoutouras and Julia Sabebien, "Mexico-Cuba Commercial Relations in the 1990s," paper

prepared for the eighth annual meeting of the Association for the Study of the Cuban Economy, Miami, August 6–8, 1998 (www.ascecuba.org/c/wp-content/uploads/2014/09/v08-24tsoutouras.pdf).

23. ZED Mariel, "Open to the World," November 2015, slide presentation prepared by Conas and EY, 15. See also "Ocho inversionistas aprobados en la Zona Especial de Desarrollo Mariel," *Juventud Rebelde* (www.juventudrebelde.cu/cuba/2015-11-06/ocho-inversionistas-aprobados-en-la-zona-especial-de-desarrollo-mariel-/); and Arline Alberty Loforte, "Mariel: en el vórtice del desarrollo económico cubano," *Granma*, January 14, 2016.

24. Centro de Investigaciones y Docencia Economicas, *The Americas and the World* (Mexico City, 2009), 64 (http://mexicoyelmundo.cide.edu/Informacion/Imgs/ENcomparado final.pdf).

25. On the Merida meeting, see William LeoGrande, "U.S.-Cuba Normalization Allows Mexico and Cuba to Repair Old Times," *World Politics Review*, November 30, 2015.

26. "Russia Leases Planes to Cuba, Writes off Soviet Debt," Reuters, February 21, 2013.

Chapter 4

The section "Open for Business: 246 Opportunities for Foreign Investment" is an updated version of Richard Feinberg, "Cuba's Foreign Investment Invitation: Insights into Internal Struggles," Brookings Up Front Blog, November 21, 2014 (www.brookings.edu/blogs/up-front/posts/2014/11/21-cuba-foreign-investment-feinberg).

1. UNCTADStat, "FDI Direct Investment: Inward and Outward Flows and Stock, Annual, 1980–2014" (http://unctadstat.unctad.org/wds/TableViewer/tableView.aspx?ReportId=96740).

2. Foreign direct investment is defined as "an investment involving a long-term relationship and reflecting a lasting interest and control by a resident entity in one economy in an enterprise that is resident in an economy other than that of the foreign direct investor. It comprises equity investment, reinvested earnings, and intra-company loans." World Bank Group and Multilateral Investment Guarantee Agency, *World Investment and Political Risk 2010* (Washington, D.C., 2011), 26, note 1.

3. Oficina Nacional de Estadística e Información (ONEI), *Anuario Estadístico de Cuba*, 2014, "Cuentas Nacionales," table 5.2. The figure is for 2014.

4. Richard E. Feinberg, "Reaching Out: Cuba's New Economy and the International Response" (Brookings, Latin America Initiative, November 2011) (www.brookings.edu/research/papers/2011/11/18-cuba-feinberg).

5. For a good survey of the academic literature, see Theodore H. Moran, *Foreign Direct Investment and Development: Launching a Second Generation of Policy Research* (Washington, D.C.: Peterson Institute for International Economics, 2011). Other notable sources include Eduardo R. Borensztein, Jose de Gregorio, and Jong-Wha Lee, "How Does Foreign Direct Investment Affect Economic Growth?," *Journal of International Economics* 45 (1998), 115–35; Sanjaya Lall and Rajneesh Narula, "Foreign Direct Investment and Its Role in Economic Development: Do We Need a New Agenda?," *European Journal of Development Research* 16, no. 3, (August 2004), 447–64; Robert E. Lipsey, "Home- and Host-Country Effects of Foreign Direct Investment," in *Challenges to Globalization: Analyzing the Economics*, edited by Robert E. Baldwin and L. Alan Winters (Chicago: University of Chicago Press and the National Bureau of Economic Research, 2004); and Xiaoying Li and Xiaming Liu, "Foreign Direct Investment and Economic Growth: An Increasingly Endogenous Relationship," *World Development* 33, no. 3 (2005), 393–407. For a critical Cuban perspective, see Martha Zaldivar Puig, "Trasnacionales, pymes, microcrédito, su papel en

el desarrollo en los macros de la globalización," in *Globalización y Problemas del Desarrollo*, edited by Oneida Álvarez (Havana: Asociación de Economistas de América Latina y el Caribe, 2009), 413–36.

6. Moran, *Foreign Direct Investment and Development,* 1. One could add agriculture, and also call for further disaggregation within these sectors: for example, exploring for petroleum and gas is very different from mining gold and silver, and within the manufacturing sector textiles and apparel are radically different from microprocessors and telecommunications.

7. On the potential equity impacts in Cuba of further economic openness and pro-market reforms, see Mayra Espina Prieto, "Retos y cambios en la política social," in *Miradas a la Economía Cubana: El proceso de actualización*, edited by Pavel Vidal Alejandro and Omar Everleny Pérez Villanueva (Havana: Editorial Caminos, 2012), 157–75.

8. For a critical discussion of performance requirements, see Moran, *Foreign Direct Investment and Development*.

9. Richard E. Feinberg, "Reconciling U.S. Property Claims in Cuba: From Trauma to Opportunity" (Brookings, Latin America Initiative, December 2015) (www.brookings.edu/research/papers/2015/12/01-reconciling-us-property-claims-cuba-feinberg).

10. As described in Embassy of Brazil in Havana, *La industria de la cana de azucar en Cuba*, sector report, 2012.

11. Sixth Congress of the Communist Party of Cuba, "Resolution on the Guidelines of the Economic and Social Policy of the Party and the Revolution," April 18, 2011 (www.cuba.cu/gobierno/documentos/2011/ing/l160711i.html).

12. "Texto de la Ley No. 118 de la Inversión Extranjera," *Granma*, April 16, 2014 (www.granma.cu/cuba/2014-04-16/asamblea-nacional-del-poder-popular).

13. Law 50 of 1982 had established a ceiling of 49 percent for the participation of foreign capital in joint ventures. Law 77 opened the door to joint ventures with either majority or minority foreign ownership shares, as well as to wholly foreign-owned ventures. Formally, Law 77 of 1995 allows for FDI to take one of several forms: 1) a joint venture in which one or more foreign investors participate with one or more national investors to form a Cuban commercial company that adopts the form of a nominal share corporation; 2) an international economic association contract, in which the national and foreign investors cooperate without the establishment of a legal entity distinct from each of the parties; and 3) a totally foreign capital company, without the involvement of any national investor. An "international economic association" includes the first two forms, namely JVs and international economic association contracts. Further, regulation 5290 (2004) allows for production cooperation agreements and for administrative contracts for both goods and services, as well as for hotel administration contracts.

14. For a full discussion by a renowned Cuban expert and arbiter, see Rodolfo Dávalos Fernandez, "Arbitraje Comercial Internacional en Cuba," in *El Arbitraje Comercial Internacional en iberoamerica: Marco Legal y Jurisprudencial*, edited by Antonio Hierro Hernández-Mora and Cristian Conejero Roos (La Ley, 2009).

15. Among the more influential personalities reportedly are Vice President Ricardo Cabrisas, MINCEX minister Rodrigo Malmierca, and the minister of economy and planning, Marino Murillo.

16. Center for the Study of the Cuban Economy, *La Inversión Extranjera y de la Unión Europea en Cuba* (European Union, 2012), 5 (eeas.europa.eu/delegations/cuba/documents/press_corner/estudio_de_inversion_extranjera_en.pdf).

17. In the one international arbitration award that has been made public, the arbitral tribunal found in favor of the Cuban government in 2008, albeit with a dissenting opinion from the Italian arbitrator, who rejected the claims advanced by the government of Italy under the bilateral investment treaty on behalf of a number of smaller Italian investors. Investment Treaty Arbitration, *Italian Republic v. Republic of Cuba*, ad hoc state-state arbitration (www.italaw.com/cases/documents/582).

18. Cuba has two currencies: the Cuba convertible peso (CUC) and the Cuba peso (CUP), the latter generally referred to as the national currency in which wages are paid. The official exchange rates are US$1 to CUC 1, and US$1 to CUP 24. The Cuban government has said it is planning a monetary reform to create a single currency, but has not announced a precise timetable.

19. Pavel Vidal Alejandro and Omar Everleny Pérez Villanueva, "Apertura al cuentapropismo y la microempresa, una pieza clave del ajuste estructural," in *Miradas a la Economía Cubana El proceso de actualización*, edited by Vidal Alejandro and Pérez Villanueva (Havana: Editorial Caminos, 2012), 51.

20. Speaking to National Public Radio following her October 2015 visit to Cuba, U.S. secretary of commerce Penny Pritzker referred to the problematic Cuban labor system: "I come from the business community; if Cuba wants more foreign investment, those issues (including the inability to directly hire workers, regulations that are not predictable, the confusing dual currency system) are impediments to their achieving their goals." Scott Horsley, "U.S. Regulators Visit Cuba to Explore Boundaries of New Trade Opportunities," NPR, October 13, 2015 (www.npr.org/2015/10/08/446980214/u-s-regulators-visit-cuba-to-explore-boundaries-of-new-trade-opportunities).

21. World Bank Group and International Finance Corporation, *Investing Across Borders* (Washington, D.C., 2010), 11.

22. Ibid.

23. The countries are Argentina, Bolivia, Brazil, Chile, Colombia, Costa Rica, Ecuador, Guatemala, Haiti, Honduras, Mexico, Nicaragua, Peru, and Venezuela.

24. Decree-Law No. 165. Duty-free Zones and Industrial Parks (1996) (www.cubaindustria.cu/Juridica/Decreto%20165.htm); translated by Cuba Transition Project, Institute for Cuban and Cuban-American Studies, University of Miami (http://ctp.iccas.miami.edu/LawDocs/ldl00136.pdf).

25. CubaFirst, "Free Zones and Industrial Parks" (www.commerceincuba.com/english/zonas.asp).

26. Emily Morris, "Cuba's New Relationship with Foreign Capital: Economic Policy-Making since 1990," *Journal of Latin American Studies* 40 (2008), 784.

27. Larry Willmore, "Export Processing Zones in Cuba," DESA Discussion Paper 12 (United Nations Department of Economic and Social Affairs, 2000) (www.un.org/esa/desa/papers/2000/esa00dp12.pdf).

28. Author interview with Cuban lawyer specializing in foreign investment, Havana, December 2015.

29. Author interview with senior official from ZED Mariel, Havana, December 2015.

30. ONEI, *Anuario Estadístico de Cuba*, 2014, "Sector Externo, Notas Metodológicas" (http://www.one.cu/aec2014/08%20Sector%20Externo.pdf).

31. Omar Everleny Pérez Villanueva and Pavel Vidal Alejandro, "La Inversión Extranjera Directa y la Actualización del Modelo Económico Cubano," paper prepared for the annual conference of the Center for the Study of the Cuban Economy (CEEC), Havana, June 20, 2012.

32. Interestingly, the number of reported Venezuelan joint ventures declined from 31 in 2009 to 11 in 2011, apparently because project commitments failed to materialize. Omar Everleny Pérez Villanueva, *The External Sector of the Cuban Economy* (Washington, D.C.: Woodrow Wilson International Center for Scholars, 2010); and MINCEX, as cited in Pérez Villanueva and Vidal Alejandro, "La Inversión Extranjera Directa."

33. UNCTAD, "Web Table 34. Number of Parent Corporations and Foreign Affiliates, by Region and Economy, 2010" (http://goo.gl/F6Gt1). These country numbers should be treated as rough orders of magnitude, as country reporting methodologies are not uniform and may understate quantities.

34. Center for the Study of the Cuban Economy, *La Inversión Extranjera y de la Unión Europea en Cuba*; see also Morris, "Cuba's New Relationship with Foreign Capital"; and

Paolo Spadoni, "Foreign Investment in Cuba: Recent Developments and Role in the Economy," in *Cuba in Transition: Volume 12* (Miami: Association for the Study of the Cuban Economy, 2002).

35. U.S.-Cuba Trade and Economic Council, "Foreign Investment Policy Change," *Economic Eye on Cuba*, February 16–22, 1998 (http://www.cubatrade.org/eyeonr.html#4); see also Economist Intelligence Unit, "Foreign Investment Focuses on Large Projects," *Cuba Country Briefing*, February 12, 2001.

36. Mayra Espina Prieto and Viviana Togores Gonzalez, "Structural Change and Routes of Social Mobility in Today's Cuba: Patterns, Profiles, and Subjectivities," in *Cuban Economic and Social Development: Policy Reforms and Challenges in the 21st Century*, edited by Jorge I. Dominguez and others (Cambridge: Harvard University Press, 2012), 267, table 8.2. A 2014 government-informed article put the number of JV workers at "more than 40,000." See "Workers of Foreign Investment: New Wage Regulations," *OnCuba*, November 20, 2015 (http://oncubamagazine.com/society/workers-of-foreign-investment-new-wage-regulations/).

37. Myra Espina Prieto, e-mail communication with the author, June 2012.

38. Pérez Villanueva, *The External Sector of the Cuban Economy*. See also Omar Everleny Pérez Villanueva, "Foreign Direct Investment in China, Vietnam, and Cuba: Pertinent Experiences for Cuba," in *Cuban Economic and Social Development*, edited by Dominguez and others, 193–225. In 2009 mining exports were $839 million, sugar industry exports (for example, rum) were $226 million, and tobacco exports (cigars and cigarettes) were $212 million. In each sector, brand name JVs were dominant. ONEI, *Anuario Estadístico de Cuba*, 2010, "Sector Externo," table 8.7 (http://www.one.cu/aec2010/esp/08_tabla_cuadro.htm).

39. Communications, however, has since been fully nationalized, as has Rio Zaza. The contribution of Sherritt to exports will vary with the market prices for nickel and cobalt. The tourism exports attributed to foreign investment would capture joint ventures but not hotels managed by service contracts with international hotel operators.

40. Also excluded in practice have been domestic and international commerce and legal consultancy. See Rolando Anillo, "Cuban Reforms and Foreign Investment Legislation: Knowing Your Neighbor and Future Partner," *Cuba Law Update*, no date (www.frfirm.com/files/Cuban_Foreign_Investment_-_Knowing_your_Neighbor.pdf).

41. Marc Frank, "Britain's Havana Energy Sets Cuban Bioenergy Venture," Reuters, November 12, 2012.

42. On joint ventures in China, see Julio A. Diaz Vazquez, *China-Cuba: relaciones economicas 1960–2010* (Mexico City: Universidad Nacional Autonoma de Mexico, Cuadernos de Trabajo del CECHIMEX, 2011), 7, table 2.

43. ONEI, *Anuario Estadístico de Cuba*, 2014, "Sector Externo," table 8.11 (http://www.one.cu/aec2014/08%20Sector%20Externo.pdf).

44. Kelvin Lee, "Pioneering U.S.-Cuban Cooperation to Prevent and Treat Cancer," paper prepared for the 14th Annual Conference on Cuba in the Foreign Policy of the United States, ISRI, Havana, December 14–16, 2015.

45. MINCEX, "Portfolio of Opportunities for Foreign Investment," 2014 (www.caribbean-council.org/wp-content/uploads/2014/11/Cuba-foreign-investment-projects-Nov-2014-official.pdf).

46. Ibid., 2.

47. "Cuba Presents $8.7 Billion Investment Wish List," *Cuba Standard*, November 8, 2014 (www.cubastandard.com/?p=11911).

48. Lilliam Riera, "Kempinski Looking to Havana," *Granma*, June 18, 2014 (www.granma.cu/idiomas/ingles/cuba-i/18jun-Kempinski%20looking.html).

49. See the project website at www.zedmariel.com. For Mariel's one-stop shop (offices in Havana Vieja located at Desamparados No. 166, between Havana and Compostela) see ventanillaunica@zedmariel.com.cu.

50. In October 2015 a visiting U.S. government delegation headed by U.S. secretary of commerce Penny Pritzker was told that eight investments had been approved for Mariel. As announced by ZED Mariel, these eight were Container Terminal of Mariel (Cuban, managed by PSA International), Logistical Services Mariel (logistics, Cuban), BDC Log (logistics, Belgium), BDC Tec (electronics, Belgium), Richmeat of Cuba (food processing, Mexican), Profood Services (food processing, Spanish), DeVox Caribe (paint, Mexican), and Brascuba (cigarettes, Cuban-Brazilian JV). One academic insider, Omar Everleny, reported 300 proposals for Mariel as of mid-2015. Omar Everleny, "Relaunching Foreign Indirect Investment in Cuba," *On Cuba*, August 7, 2015 (http://oncubamagazine. com/economy-business/relaunching-direct-foreign-investment-in-cuba/). For an interview with the executive director of ZED Mariel, Ana Teresa Igarza Martínez, see Arline Alberty Loforte, "Mariel: en el vórtice del desarrollo económico cubano," *Granma*, January 14, 2016.

51. Author interview with senior official from ZED Mariel, Havana, December 2015.

52. Antonio R. Zamora, "The Impact of Cuba's New Real Estate Laws on the Island and the Diaspora," paper prepared for the 22nd annual meeting of the Association for the Study of the Cuban Economy, Miami, August 2–4, 2012.

53. One knowledgeable observer estimated the value of remittances entering Cuba at $2.2 billion and of merchandise entering as packages at $2.0 billion–$2.5 billion in 2011. Emilio Morales, "What's Behind the New Cuban Tariffs," *Havana Consulting Group*, July 9, 2012 (http://thehavanaconsultinggroups.com/index.php?option=com_content& view=article&id=329%3Awhats-behind-the-new-cuban-tariffs&catid=47%3Aeconomy& lang=en). A former executive with the SOE CIMEX, Morales attributed the new taxes in part to pressure from state-owned firms suffering from the competition. See also Marc Frank, "Reforms and Informal Market Hit Cuban State's Retail Sales," Reuters, September 14, 2012.

54. Jessica León Mundul and David J. Pajón Espina, "Política crediticia en Cuba: evolución reciente y efectos sobre el sector no estatal," in *Miradas a la Economía Cubana: Análisis del sector no estatal*, edited by Omar Everleny Pérez Villanueva and Ricardo Torres Pérez (Havana: Editorial Caminos, 2015), 105–13.

55. For a discussion of settlement options, see Feinberg, "Reconciling U.S. Property Claims in Cuba."

Chapter 5

Unless otherwise noted, sources for case study 1 are Sherritt International Corporation, *Annual Report*, 2010, 2011, 2013; and the Sherritt website (www.Sherritt.com). Figures are in Canadian dollars unless otherwise indicated.

Unless otherwise noted, sources for case study 2 are the Habanos website (www.habanos. com); Imperial Tobacco, *Annual Report*, 2011; and author interviews.

Sources for case study 3 include Meliá Hotels International, *Annual Report and CSR*, 2014; Melia.com, "Hotels in Cuba" (www.melia.com/en/hotels/cuba/home.htm); Havanatur, "Catalogue" (no date); *Hosteltur*, January 2012; Omar Everleny Pérez Villanueva, "FDI in China, Vietnam, and Cuba," in *Cuban Economic and Social Development: Policy Reforms and Challenges in the 21st Century*, edited by Jorge Dominguez and others (Harvard University Press, 2012); and author interviews.

Unless otherwise indicated, sources for case study 4 include Nestlé, *Annual Report*, 2011, 2014; Coralsa website (www.cubagob.cu/ingles/des_eco/minal/coralsa/coralsa.html); and author interviews.

Sources for case study 6 include Unilever, *Annual Report and Accounts*, 2011, 2014; Suchel Camacho website (www.suchelcamacho.cu); and author interviews.

1. In the comprehensive International Monetary Fund database on FDI, the Coordinated Direct Investment Survey, Venezuela does not participate and China does not release information on outward investment. China's reported inward investment from Cuba was $53 million (2010). The most publicized Venezuelan investment has been the Cienfuegos oil refinery, a 49/51 joint venture between the Venezuelan SOE PDVSA and its Cuban counterpart CUPET. An initial modest investment by PDVSA reopened the mothballed Soviet-era plant. An additional investment (variously estimated at between $2 billion and $4.5 billion), financed by Chinese loans guaranteed by PDVSA oil sales, was planned to double capacity to 150,000 barrels per day by 2015. In 2012 the author observed some Chinese construction equipment on site even as the Cubans balked at Chinese proposals to import large numbers of Chinese construction workers. There was also talk of an associated petrochemical complex, including a fertilizer plant (but with 100 percent Cuban ownership). With the deepening problems in the Venezuelan economy and then the collapse of energy prices, the expansion projects appear to have been put on hold.

2. Figures are in Canadian dollars unless otherwise indicated.

3. The early history of Ian Delaney and Sherritt recounted here is based on Rachel Pulfer, "Castro's Favorite Capitalist," *The Walrus*, December 2009 (http://walrusmagazine.com/articles/2009.12-business-castros-favourite-capitalist/5/).

4. Archibald R. M. Ritter, "Canada's Economic Relations with Cuba, 1990 to 2010 and Beyond," *Canadian Foreign Policy* 16, no. 1 (Spring 2010), 119–40. Intrigued by the unusual deal, rumors circulated among Havana's chattering classes that the Castro brothers themselves had a stake in Sherritt's Alberta refinery.

5. Marc Frank, "Cuba to Cut Nickel Output for Major Overhaul," Reuters, February 3, 2014.

6. Oficina Nacional de Estadística e Información (ONEI), *Anuario Estadístico de Cuba*, various years, "Sector Externo," tables 8.7, 8.11.

7. Sherritt International Corporation, *Annual Report*, 2013, 14–15.

8. Archibald Ritter, "Does Sherritt International Have a Future in Cuba?," Cuban Economy Blog, October 20, 2010 (http://thecubaneconomy.com/articles/2010/10/does-sherritt-international-have-a-future-in-cuba/).

9. Sherritt International Corporation, *Annual Information Form*, 2009.

10. Sherritt International Corporation, *Annual Report*, 2003, 30.

11. Paolo Spadoni, *Failed Sanctions: Why the U.S. Embargo against Cuba Could Never Work* (University Press of Florida, 2010), 65–66.

12. Sherritt International Corporation, *Annual Information Form*, 2011.

13. Accounting for nearly half of national nickel production capacity of 75,000 tons, Sherritt shares the rich Holguín nickel fields with two SOEs, Che Guevara and Rene Ramos Latour. A new Cuban-Venezuelan joint venture, Cuba Quality S.A., has announced plans for a US$700 million investment in a ferro-nickel plant, even as markets express heightened uncertainty about Venezuelan investment capacities.

14. For an account of the Venezuelan firm Polar and how its extensive CSR program helped sustain it during the reign of Hugo Chávez, see Richard E. Feinberg and Carlued Leon, "Workers of Polar Unite . . . In Defense of Capitalism!," *Americas Quarterly* (Fall 2012) (www.americasquarterly.org/Workers-of-Polar-Unite-in-Defense-of-Capitalism-0).

15. Among certified U.S. property claimants, Moa Bay Mining is the third highest, at $88 million. See Richard E. Feinberg, "Reconciling U.S. Property Claims in Cuba: From Trauma to Opportunity" (Brookings, Latin America Initiative, 2015) (www.brookings.edu/research/papers/2015/12/01-reconciling-us-property-claims-cuba-feinberg), 42.

16. Sherritt International Corporation, *Annual Report*, 2011, 59–60.

17. As quoted in Pulfer, "Castro's Favorite Capitalist."

18. Apparently, before switching to the proportional consolidation accounting method, Habanos reported $428 million in revenues for 2015. "Habanos SA compensa las malas

cosechas de tabaco con mejores semillas," *Diario de Cuba*, March 1, 2016 (http://www. diariodecuba.com/cuba/1456858346_20603.html).

19. According to one informed source, 90 percent of Habanos sales are accounted for by exports. Emilio Morales and Joseph Scarpaci, *Marketing without Advertising: Brand Preference and Consumer Choice in Cuba* (New York: Routledge, 2012), chapters 5–6.

20. Imperial Tobacco Group, *Annual Report,* 2013, 11.

21. "Cuba's Cigar Industry: Smoked Out," *The Economist*, April 28, 2011 (www.economist. com/node/18621276).

22. ONEI, "Turismo. Llegada de Visitantes Internacionales," December 2015 (www.one. cu/publicaciones/06turismoycomercio/llegadadevisitantes/mensual/3.pdf).

23. ONEI, *Anuario Estadistico de Cuba*, 2014, table 15.11. This figure, however, is gross revenues, and hence does not reflect the imports consumed by the tourism industry.

24. Julio Cervino and Jose Maria Cubillo, "Hotel and Tourism Development in Cuba: Opportunities, Management Challenges, and Future Trends," *Cornell Hotel and Restaurant Administration Quarterly* 26 (2005), 17.

25. A mid-2000s study reported monthly salaries for hotels at $300–$1,500 per month. Ibid., 19.

26. Venus Carrillo, "Destino Cuba, listo para la ola?," *Cubahora*, August 26, 2015 (www. cubahora.cu/economia/destino-cuba-listo-para-la-ola). Another source puts the number of private sector rooms for rent at 18,000, making these B&Bs the second-largest "hotel chain" in the country, only exceeded by Gaviota, the state tourism enterprise. Pavel Vidal, *Economic Trend Report Q2 2015* (Miami: Cuba Standard, 2015). For the higher estimate of 19,000, see José Luis Perelló Cabrera, "El sector no estatal y su papel en el desarrollo del turismo cubano en un escenario de relaciones con los Estados Unidos," in *Miradas a la Economía Cubana: Análisis del sector no estatal*, edited by Omar Everleny Pérez Villanueva and Ricardo Torres Pérez (Havana: Editorial Caminos, 2015), 85–91.

27. Pérez Villanueva, "FDI in China, Vietnam, and Cuba," 220–21.

28. Arne Sorenson, "Marriott's CEO on Why Now Is the Moment to Embrace Business in Cuba," *Skift*, July 22, 2015 (http://skift.com/2015/07/22/marriotts-ceo-on-why-now-is-the-moment-to-embrace-business-in-cuba/).

29. *Hosteltur*, January 2012, 9.

30. Coppelia has had to reduce its offerings of flavors because of high production costs and negative earnings. Morales and Scarpaci, *Marketing without Advertising*, chapter 6.

31. Ibid., table 3.3.

32. Julio Cervino and Jaime Bonache, "Cuban Retailing: From a Centrally Planned to a Mixed Dual System," *International Journal of Retail and Distribution* 33, no. 1 (2005), 79–94.

33. Morales and Scarpaci, *Marketing without Advertising*, chapter 6.

34. A questionnaire survey of Cuban business executives, some working for JVs, confirmed that JVs focus more attention on marketing than Cuban firms. Julio Cervino, Joan Llonch, and Josep Rialp, "Market Orientation and Business Performance in Cuban Firms: A Comparative Analysis of State-Owned versus Joint Venture Cuban Firms," paper prepared for the 22nd annual meeting of the Association for the Study of the Cuban Economy, Miami, August 2–4, 2012.

35. A study of the tourism industry similarly found that "because there is little opportunity for financial gain, general managers find it difficult to motivate staff to take on additional responsibility or do jobs to the best of their ability." Cervino and Cubillo, "Hotel and Tourism Development in Cuba," 20.

36. Souza Cruz is BAT's largest subsidiary. BAT, Imperial Tobacco, Philip Morris, and Japan Tobacco are the four biggest tobacco companies. See "Interview of BAT CEO Nicandro Durante: The Running Man of Big Tobacco," *Financial Times*, October 1, 2012, 14. BAT's CEO Durante is Brazilian.

37. According to one source, Brascuba began in the following manner: In 1995, with an initial investment of $7 million, Brascuba renovated an existing cigarette factory in Havana and started producing and selling several brands of cigarettes for both the foreign market and—in competition with SOEs—the domestic market. Then, in 1999, Brascuba negotiated a new agreement with the Cuban government that practically gave Brascuba the monopoly on cigarettes in the domestic hard-currency and export markets. In return Brascuba helped finance an SOE-owned cigarette factory in Holguín producing for the local currency domestic market. Paolo Spadoni, "Foreign Investment in Cuba: Recent Developments and Role in the Economy," in *Cuba in Transition: Volume 12* (Miami: Association for the Study of the Cuban Economy, 2002), 167, note 36, citing an interview with a news correspondent stationed in Havana.

38. Morales and Scarpaci, *Marketing without Advertising*, chapter 6. Of course, economic success in the tobacco industry affects public health, especially in developing countries; see Cheng Li, "The Political Mapping of China's Tobacco Industry and Anti-Smoking Campaign," China Center Monograph (Brookings, 2012) (www.brookings.edu/research/papers/2012/10/25-china-tobacco-li).

39. "Resolución 17: de la letra a la empresa," *Cubahora*, July 4, 2015 (www.cubahora.cu/economia/resolucion-17-de-la-letra-a-la-empresa).

40. Radio Rebelde, "Brascuba: 20 años en la produccion y la eficiencia," based on an interview with Jorge Abraham Maloff, Brascuba Cuban co-president, April 17, 2015.

41. Arline Alberty Loforte, "Mariel: en el vórtice del desarrollo económico cubano," *Granma*, January 14, 2016.

42. Author interview with Brascuba executive, Havana, December 2015.

43. Unilever, *Annual Report and Accounts*, 2011, 109.

44. This point is made by a Unilever executive; see Cervino and Bonache, "Cuban Retailing." The two U.S. giants in consumer products both held claims against their properties nationalized in the early days of the revolution. See Feinberg, "Reconciling U.S. Property Claims in Cuba."

45. A study of the hotel industry found that "employee theft is rampant due to workers' subsistence wages. Thefts typically involve all the employees in a department: to make sure no one rats out the culprits, all employees share in the proceeds, even managers and those on vacation." Cervino and Cubillo, "Hotel and Tourism Development in Cuba," 20.

46. Quoted in Marc Frank, "Cuba Drags Feet on Foreign Investment," Reuters, May 15, 2012.

47. Richard Feinberg, "Unilever and British American Tobacco Invest: A New Realism in Cuba," Opinion, January 14, 2016, Brookings (originally published in *Cuba Standard*) (www.brookings.edu/research/opinions/2016/01/14-unilever-british-american-tobacco-cuba-feinberg).

48. Cristobal Pena, "La fortuna y el poder que Max Marambio construyo a expensas de Cuba," CIPER Chile, March 11, 2010 (http://ciperchile.cl/2010/11/03/la-fortuna-y-el-poder-que-max-marambio-construyo-a-expensas-de-cuba/).

49. Marambio's memoir, *Las Armas de Ayer* (Santiago: La Tercera/Debate, 2007), recounts his early years.

50. "Cohecho, Actos en Perjuicio de la Actividad Economica y de la Contratacion, Malversacion, Falsificacion de Documentos Bancarios y de Comercio y Estafa," *Gaceta Oficial de la Republica de Cuba*, no. 21 (August 3, 2010), 135.

51. Paul Haven, "Cuba Goes after Corruption," Associated Press, November 21, 2011 (http://theadvocate.com/news/business/1370905-123/cuba-goes-after-corruption.html); Marc Frank, "Foreign Executives Arrested in Cuba in 2011 Await Charges," Reuters, October 9, 2012.

52. Cervino, Llonch, and Rialp, "Market Orientation and Business Performance in Cuban Firms."

53. Morales and Scarpaci, *Marketing without Advertising*, chapter 6. Before emigrating to the United States in 2006, Morales served as director of strategic marketing in CIMEX's Planning Department.

54. Center for the Study of the Cuban Economy, *La Inversión Extranjera y de la Unión Europea en Cuba*, (Havana: European Union, 2012) (eeas.europa.eu/delegations/cuba/documents/press_corner/estudio_de_inversion_extranjera_en.pdf).

Chapter 6

The section "Historical Background" draws on a number of earlier studies on the stormy history of the private sector under Cuban socialism, including Jorge Pérez-López, *Cuba's Second Economy: From Behind the Scenes to Center Stage* (New Brunswick, N.J.: Transaction Books, 1995); Phillip Peters and Joseph Scarpaci, *Five Years of Small-Scale Capitalism in Cuba* (Alexandria, Va.: Lexington Institute, 1998); Archibald Ritter, "Entrepreneurship, Microenterprise, and Public Policy in Cuba: Promotion, Containment, or Asphyxiation?," *Journal of Interamerican Studies and World Affairs* 40, no. 2 (Summer 1998), 63–94; Carmelo Mesa-Lago, *Market, Socialist, and Mixed Economies: Comparative Policy and Performance in Chile, Cuba and Costa Rica* (Johns Hopkins University Press, 2000); Ted Henken, "Condemned to Informality: Cuba's Experiments with Self-Employment during the Special Period," Ph.D. dissertation, Tulane University, 2002; Archibald Ritter, *Economic Illegalities and the Underground Economy in Cuba* (Ottawa, Ont.: FOCAL, 2006); and Ileana Díaz Fernández, Héctor Pastori, and Camila Piñeiro Harnecker, "El trabajo por cuenta propia en Cuba: lecciones de la experiencia Uruguaya," *Boletín Cuatrimestral*, Centro de Estudios de la Economía Cubana (CEEC), April 2012.

1. For data in this paragraph, see Oficina Nacional de Estadísticas e Información (ONEI), *Anuario Estadístico de Cuba*, 2014, "Empleo y Salarios," table 7.1 (http://www.onei.cu/aec2014.htm); "Number of Self-employed in Cuba Exceeds Half a Million," *14yMedio*, June 13, 2015 (www.14ymedio.com/englishedition/Number-Self-employed-Exceeds-Half-Million_0_1798020197.html); and sources cited for table 6-1.

2. The plural "middle classes" is intended to suggest the heterogeneity of middle-class occupations in both the private and public sectors, as well as the spread of income levels and spatial locations.

3. ONEI, *Anuario Estadístico de Cuba*, 2014, "Empleo y Salarios," table 7.4 (http://www.onei.cu/aec2014.htm). In a speech to the National Assembly in December 2015, as reported by government media, Minister of the Economy and Planning Marino Murillo stated that the average wage that year had risen to CUP 640. Ismael Francisco and Rafael Arzuaga, "Ratifica Asamblea Nacional que economía cubana crece un 4 por ciento este 2015," *Cubadebate* (www.cubadebate.cu/noticias/2015/12/29/ratifica-asamblea-nacional-que-economia-cubana-crece-un-4-por-ciento-este-2015/#.VrLZSE0UUqR). In April 2016, ONEI reported an average monthly wage of 688 CUP for 2015.

4. Marc Frank, *Cuban Revelations: Behind the Scenes* (University Press of Florida, 2013).

5. For an earlier listing of informal activities, see Ritter, *Economic Illegalities and the Underground Economy in Cuba*.

6. For official numbers on "private sector employment," defined to include TCPs, service and credit cooperatives, and private farmers, see ONEI, *Anuario Estadístico de Cuba*, 2014, "Empleo y Salarios," table 7.2. Properly excluded are the Unidades Básicas de Producción Cooperativa (UBPC) and Cooperativas de Producción Agropecuaria (CPA), which have characteristics of state-owned firms.

7. ONEI, *Anuario Estadístico de Cuba*, "Empleo y Salarios," table 7.1. Lack of data inhibits more formal estimation of the informal sector, for example as undertaken in Guillermo Vuletin, "Measuring the Informal Economy in Latin America and the Caribbean," Working Paper WP/08/102 (Washington, D.C.: International Monetary Fund, 2008).

8. Ritter, *Economic Illegalities and the Underground Economy in Cuba*, 7, 16.

9. In an International Republican Institute poll with a sample size of 688, 15 percent of Cuban adults over 18 placed themselves in the "informal economy—illicit/black market" category, which translates to 1,343,000 persons, up from 6 percent just a year earlier. The survey's findings support the notion that many Cubans continue to work privately without official authorization. Moreover, the survey lacked a category to capture those who both work in the public sector and hold a second, private sector occupation (GESPI). International Republican Institute, "Cuban Public Opinion Survey, January 20–February 20, 2013" (www.iri.org/sites/default/files/2013%20May%2024%20Survey%20of%20Cuban%20 Public%20Opinion,%20January%2020-February%2020,%202013%20--%20English%20 version.pdf).

10. "Aprueban en Cuba constitución de cooperativas en sectores no agropecuarios," *Cubadebate*, December 11, 2012 (http://www.cubadebate.cu/noticias/2012/12/11/en-vigor-nuevo-decreto-ley-que-establece-constitucion-experimental-de-cooperativas-en-sectores-no-agropecuarios/#.VobV1U1gkqR).

11. Camila Piñeiro Harnecker, "Cuban Cooperatives: Current Situation and Prospects," paper prepared for the 31st Congress of the Latin American Studies Association, Washington, D.C., May 29–June 1, 2013; and "Nuevas cooperativas cubanas: logros y dificultades," in *Miradas a la Economía Cubana: Análisis del sector no estatal*, edited by Omar Everleny Pérez Villanueva and Ricardo Torres Pérez (Havana: Editorial Caminos, 2015), 53–61. See also Marc Frank, "Cuba's Non-Farm Co-Ops Debut This Week amid Move toward Markets," *Reuters*, June 30, 2013; "Continúa avanzando actualización del modelo económico cubano," *Granma*, September 24, 2013; ZED Mariel, "Open to the World," 2014, 15; and Pavel Vidal, *Economic Trend Report Q2 2015* (Miami: Cuba Standard, 2015). *Granma* is the official publication of the PCC.

12. Piñeiro Harnecker, "Cuban Cooperatives: Current Situation and Prospects." See also Camila Piñeiro Harnecker, ed., *Cooperatives and Socialism: The View from Cuba* (New York: Palgrave Macmillan, 2013), especially her introduction, 1–45.

13. *Gaceta Oficial*, no. 3, Special Edition, Resolution 21/2013 (January 29, 2013). The expanded list of authorized activities appears in *Gaceta Oficial*, no. 027, Special Edition (September 26, 2013).

14. Archibald R. M. Ritter and Ted A. Henken, *Entrepreneurial Cuba: The Changing Policy Landscape* (Boulder, Colo.: First Forum Press, 2015); Pérez Villanueva and Torres Pérez eds., *Miradas a la Economía Cubana*; and "Over 430,000 Cubans Work in Private Sector, Official Report Says," *Latin American Herald Tribune*, August 17, 2013, citing figures from the Ministry of Labor and Social Security.

15. *Gaceta Oficial*, no. 12, Special Edition (October 8, 2010). See also *Gaceta Oficial*, no. 029, Special Edition, Resolution 298/2011 (September 2011); *Gaceta Oficial*, no. 053, Law 113 (November 2012); *Gaceta Oficial*, no. 3, Special Edition, Resolution 21/2013 (January, 2013); Pavel Vidal Alejandro and Omar Everleny Pérez Villanueva, "Apertura al cuentapropismo, una pieza clave del ajuste estructural," in *Miradas a la economía cubana: El proceso de actualización*, edited by Alejandro and Pérez Villanueva (Havana: Editorial Caminos, 2012), 41–52; and Juan Triana Cordoví, *From the Submerged Economy to Micro-Enterprise: Are There Any Guarantees for the Future?* (Miami: Cuba Study Group, 2012) (www.cubastudygroup.org/index.cfm/files/serve? File_id=b8f37ffd-575b-4d7f-a0df-1de11eb7b229).

16. Díaz Fernández, Pastori, and Piñeiro Harnecker, "El trabajo por cuenta propia en Cuba."

17. A survey of 850 small neighborhood convenience stores found initial start-up costs to be under $100 for nearly half of Nicaraguan stores and a quarter of El Salvadoran stores. Michael J. Pisani, "A Study of Small Neighborhood *Tienditas* in Central America," *Latin American Research Review* 47, Special Issue (2012), 116–38.

18. For a review of some of the best *paladares*, see Victoria Burnett, "In Havana, Family-Run Dining Goes Upscale," *New York Times*, March 16, 2012. Increasingly, Cuban restaurants appear on TripAdvisor and other travel websites. For a Cuban website directory of *paladares*, see www.alamesacuba.com.

19. In a follow-up interview in December 2015, Ms. Hernandez reported proudly that "Big Bang has achieved its goals of offering fast food, breakfast, and snacks in a clean, warm environment with good-quality cuisine."

20. Vidal, *Economic Trend Report Q2 2015*; and Jose Luis Perelló Cabrera, "El sector no estatal y su papel en el desarrollo del turismo Cubano en un escenario de relaciones con los Estados Unidos," in *Miradas a la Economía Cubana*, edited by Pérez Villanueva and Torres Peréz, 85–91. Since some B&B owners with multiple rooms underreport the number of rooms they are renting out to avoid taxes, the total number of B&B offerings no doubt exceeds the official figure.

21. For details, see Sarah Kessler, "Airbnb's Secret to Scaling in Cuba," July 8, 2015 (www.fastcompany.com/3048272/innovation-agents/airbnbs-secret-to-scaling-in-cuba).

22. For TCPs with annual revenues over CUP 100,000 ($4,000), tax laws explicitly require conformance with the accounting system as established by the Ministry of Finance and Prices. *Gaceta Oficial*, no. 053, Law 113, Article 58 (November 21, 2012).

23. By 2015 the first authorized cooperative of accountants, Havana-based Scenius, was offering services to both TCPs and state entities. Over 50 professionals were participating in Scenius's network of subcontractors. See Yisell Rodríguez Milán, "Scenius: la cooperativa que pone las cuentas claras," *OnCuba*, December 23, 2015 (http://oncubamagazine.com/economia-negocios/scenius-la-cooperativa-que-pone-las-cuentas-claras/).

24. On women entrepreneurs, see Ileana Diáz Fernández and Dayma Echevarría León, "Mujeres emprendedoras en Cuba: análisis imprescindible," in *Miradas a la Economía Cubana*, edited by Pérez Villanueva and Torres Peréz, 147–57.

25. Richard Feinberg, "Cuba's Emerging Entrepreneurs: Update One Year On," Brookings Up Front blog, April 15, 2014 (www.brookings.edu/blogs/up-front/posts/2014/04/15-cuba-emerging-entrepreneurs-update-feinberg).

26. The findings here are generally aligned with those in Joseph L. Scarpaci, "Fifteen Years of Entrepreneurship in Cuba: Challenges and Opportunities," *Cuba in Transition* (Association for the Study of the Cuban Economy, 2009). In a nonrandomized survey of 154 *cuentapropistas* in Havana conducted in 2008, interviewees prioritized these challenges: supplies (costs and availability), taxes and licensing fees, and inspections and regulations. The Scarpaci survey used a "snowballing technique" to locate interviewees and focused on the very small-scale micro-entrepreneurs typical of the period. In contrast, I held purposive conversations with entrepreneurs independent of each other in an effort to yield a more varied sample of TCPs and identify future-oriented businesses with growth potential. Whereas less than 5 percent of the Scarpaci sample cited "weak demand" as a principal challenge, the individuals I interviewed focused on impediments to future expansion, such as weak consumer demand, credit scarcity, and the uncertain business climate.

27. See Jessica León Mundul and David J. Pajón Espina, "Política crediticia en Cuba: evolución reciente y efectos sobre el sector no estatal," in *Miradas a la Economía Cubana*, edited by Pérez Villanueva and Torres Peréz, 105–13.

28. Oficinas del Historiador, *Luces y Simientes: Territorio y Gestión en Cinco Centros Históricos Cubanos* (Ediciones Boloña, 2012), 113–14 (for Havana), 401 (for Cienfuegos).

29. *Juventud Rebelde* reported approval of rental space to 1,183 food establishments (April 16, 2013). Earlier, Cuban state television had mentioned that 5,000 private businesses were renting space from state entities.

30. A 2008 survey of 154 TCPs found their net income to be 386 percent of the average Cuban salary. Scarpaci, "Fifteen Years of Entrepreneurship in Cuba: Challenges and Opportunities," table 1, 351. A more recent study asserts that in Havana private cafeterias

pay their employees about CUC 2 daily, 2.6 times the province's average salary. Carlos Garcimartín, Omar Everleny Pérez, and Saira Pons, "Reforma Tributaria y Emprendimiento," in *Quo Vadis, Cuba?*, edited by José Antonio Alonso and Pavel Vidal (Madrid: La Catarata, 2013), 181–82. However, these findings of average salary do not by themselves negate the possibility of TCP owners mistreating their employees, especially if they are not legally registered ("informal").

31. I am indebted to Saira Pons Pérez of the Center for the Study of the Cuban Economy for assistance in understanding the evolving Cuban tax regime. See her excellent chapter (with Carlos Garcimartín and Omar Everleny Pérez) "Reforma Tributaria y Emprendimiento," in *Quo Vadis, Cuba?*, edited by Alonso and Vidal, 148–88. See also Saira Pons Pérez, "Emprendimiento y Reforma Tributaria en Cuba," slide presentation prepared for the 31st Congress of the Latin American Studies Association, Washington, D.C., June 1, 2013; and Ritter and Henken, *Entrepreneurial Cuba: The Changing Policy Landscape*, 150–57.

32. Earlier studies of TCPs also found widespread underreporting. See Henken, "Condemned to Informality," a 2002 study based on 64 in-depth interviews of TCPs; and Ritter, "Entrepreneurship, Microenterprise, and Public Policy in Cuba," and *Economic Illegalities and the Underground Economy in Cuba*; and Ritter and Henken, *Entrepreneurial Cuba: The Changing Policy Landscape*.

33. *Gaceta Oficial*, no. 053, Law 113, Article 26 (November 21, 2012).

34. *Gaceta Oficial*, no. 029, Special Edition, Resolution 298/2011, Articles 26–27 (September 7, 2011).

35. Law 113, Articles 132–39.

36. Law 113, Articles 234–37.

37. Law 113, Articles 336–58.

38. International Finance Corporation, *Doing Business 2012* (Washington, D.C., 2012). Cuba is not included in this study.

39. In his survey of 850 micro-businesses in Central America, Michael J. Pisani found a similar range of possible outcomes, from "subsistence to prosperity." "A Study of Small Neighborhood *Tienditas* in Central America," 127.

40. Abhijit Banerjee and Esther Duflo, "What Is Middle Class about the Middle Class?," *Journal of Economic Perspectives* 22, no. 2 (2008), 3–28.

41. United Nations Development Program, "Human Development Reports" (http://hdr.undp.org/en/countries/profiles/CUB). See also ONEI, *Anuario Estadístico de Cuba*, 2014, "Cuentas Nacionales," table 5.12. The GNI data are internationally standardized on a purchasing power parity basis. The Cuban data, however, are not without controversy: results could be altered in the event of a major devaluation of the CUC; and the reported per capita income and consumption, which well exceed the average wage rates as paid in Cuban pesos, include government-provided services such as health care, education, and culture, as explained in ONEI, *Anuario Estadístico de Cuba*, "Notas Metodológicas."

42. Francisco H. G. Ferreira and others, *Economic Mobility and the Rise of the Latin American Middle Class* (Washington, D.C.: World Bank, 2013). The study fixed the outer bound for the middle class at $50 per capita per day, only some 2 percent of the population achieving this upper-income ranking. For further elaboration, see the feature section "Meet the Real Middle Class" in *Americas Quarterly* 6, no. 4 (Fall 2012), 50–91.

43. Ferreira and others, *Economic Mobility and the Rise of the Latin American Middle Class*, 147, table 5.2; and Nancy Birdsall, "A Note on the Middle Class in Latin America," Working Paper 303 (Washington, D.C.: Center for Global Development, August 2012), table 1.

44. William Easterly, "The Middle Class Consensus and Economic Development," *Journal of Economic Growth* 6, no. 4 (2001), 317–35; and Andres Solimano, "The Middle Class and the Development Process," *Serie Macroeconomía del Desarrollo* 65 (Santiago: UN Economic Commission for Latin America and the Caribbean), 2008.

45. Nancy Birdsall, Carol Graham, and Stefano Pettinato, "Stuck in the Tunnel: Is Globalization Muddling the Middle Class?," Working Paper 14 (Brookings, 2000). In their minds, the middle class is "the large group of households that are neither wealthy nor poor, but that form the backbone of both the market economy and of democracy in most advanced societies" (1).

46. Mayra Espina Prieto and Viviana Togores González, "Structural Change and Routes of Social Mobility in Today's Cuba: Patterns, Profiles, and Subjectivities," in *Cuban Economic and Social Development: Policy Reforms and Challenges in the 21st Century*, edited by Jorge Dominguez and others (Harvard University Press, 2012), 270. The Gini coefficient ranges from 1 to 0; the higher the number, the greater the degree of inequality.

47. International Monetary Fund, *Western Hemisphere Regional Economic Outlook* (Washington, D.C., 2013), 24, table 2.3, based on data from the Socio-Economic Database for Latin America and the Caribbean (SEDLAC).

48. ONEI, *Anuario Estadística de Cuba*, 2014, "Empleo y Salarios," table 7.8. Admittedly, some workers classified as "clerical" or "manual" might fall below the middle-class threshold by some definitions, while some workers classified as "services" might well rank as middle class. This measurement is further complicated in the Cuban case by workers holding more than one job, as for example the GESPI population, and by the countries' "inverted pyramid," whereby taxi drivers and bellhops with access to convertible pesos can earn more than physicians and university professors paid in national currency.

49. Birdsall, "A Note on the Middle Class in Latin America," table 6.

50. United Nations Development Program, "Human Development Index," 2012. In the UNDP's education index (2012), Cuba ranked the highest for Latin America (http://hdr.undp.org/en/content/education-index).

51. ONEI, *Anuario Estadístico de Cuba*, 2011, "Cuentas Nacionales," table 7.20.

52. ONEI, *Encuesta Nacional de Fecundidad*, 2009 (www.one.cu/enf.htm); World Bank, "Fertility Rate," 2013 (www.data.worldbank.org/indicator/SP.DYN.TFRT.IN).

53. Cuba has "the most generous" pension system in Latin America, according to Carmelo Mesa-Lago, *Cuba en la era de Raúl Castro: Reformas económico-sociales y sus efectos* (Madrid: Editorial Colibrí, 2012), 200. At 50 percent of public sector wages, average pensions are about CUP 250 ($10 at the 24:1 exchange rate) per month. However, unregistered informal workers without public sector jobs would fall outside of the social security system.

54. Maurico Cárdenas, Homi Kharas, and Camila Henao, "Latin America's Global Middle Class" (Brookings, April 26, 2011), 3.

55. ITU, "Cuba–ICT Statistics" (www.itu.int/ITU-D/icteye/DisplayCountry.aspx?countryId=63).

56. Quoted in Nick Caistor, *Fidel Castro* (London: Reaktion Books, 2013), 140.

57. Emilio Morales and Joseph Scarpaci, *Marketing without Advertising: Brand Preference and Consumer Choice in Cuba* (New York: Routledge, 2012).

58. Espina Prieto and Togores González, "Structural Change and Routes of Social Mobility in Today's Cuba," 280.

59. National Intelligence Council, *Global Trends 2030: Alternative Worlds* (www.dni.gov/files/documents/GlobalTrends_2030.pdf), 10. For evidence that fear of high levels of street crime can also be used to justify an authoritarian response, see Kevin Casas-Zamora, *The Besieged Polis: Citizen Insecurity and Democracy in Latin America* (Brookings, 2013), 38–52.

Chapter 7

1. The poll was conducted for Univision Noticias and Fusion, in collaboration with the *Washington Post*, and consisted of 1,200 in-person interviews. Among households

where interviews were attempted, 39 percent completed the survey. See "Cubans Welcome Warmer Relations with the U.S.," *Washington Post*, April 8, 2015 (www.washingtonpost. com/graphics/world/cuba-poll-2015/).

Chapter 8

For the subtitle of this chapter, thanks to Cristina Garcia, *Dreaming in Cuban* (New York: Alfred A. Knopf, 1992).

The section on Vietnam is largely based on Richard E. Feinberg, "Principles and Power: The Treatment of Property Claims by Socialist Vietnam," *Problems of Post-Communism* 63, No. 2 (2016), and Richard E. Feinberg, "Could Cuba Be Vietnam in the Caribbean?," *Financial Times*, January 15, 2015.

The section on Costa Rica is drawn from Alberto Trejos, "Economic Growth and Restructuring through Trade and FDI: Costa Rican Experiences of Interest to Cuba," in *The Cuban Economy in Comparative Perspective*, edited by Richard E. Feinberg and Ted Piccone (Brookings, 2014) (www.brookings.edu/research/papers/2014/11/cuba-economic-change-comparative-perspective).

1. Fidel Castro, "Speech to Intellectuals" (Havana, June 30, 1961).

2. Pico Iyer, *Cuba and the Night* (New York: Vintage Contemporaries Edition, 1996), 132.

3. Thomas Picketty, comment during the Helen Edison Lecture, University of California–San Diego, October 22, 2015.

4. Rachel Price, *Planet/Cuba: Art, Culture, and the Future of the Island* (New York: Verso Books, 2015), 10. Price also writes of "the depth of contemporary weariness with Cuban exceptionalism" (11).

5. See also Richard E. Feinberg, "Ten Lessons We Can Learn from Cuba," Huffington Post, January 6, 2015 (www.huffingtonpost.com/richard-e-feinberg/10-takeaways-from-cuba_b_6424470.html).

6. Phillippe Diederich, *Sofrito* (El Paso, Tex.: Cinco Puntos Press, 2015), 168.

Index

Boxes, figures, and tables are indicated by "b," "f," and "t" following page numbers.